500
GREAT
·
FILMS

500

GREAT
·
FILMS

Exeter Books

NEW YORK

A Bison Book

First published in U.S.A. in 1987
by Exeter Books
Distributed by Bookthrift
Exeter is a trademark of Bookthrift Marketing, Inc.
Bookthrift is a registered trademark of Bookthrift Marketing, Inc.
New York, New York

ISBN 0-671-08931-5

Printed in Hong Kong

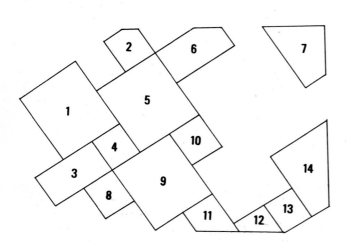

1 *My Fairy Lady* – 1964 (Bison Picture Library)
2 *Funny Girl* – 1968 (Bison Picture Library)
3 *Butch Cassidy and the Sundance Kid* – 1969 (Bison Picture Library)
4 *Richard III* – 1956 (Phototeque)
5 *Gone With the Wind* – 1939 (Bison Picture Library)
6 *Jaws* – 1975 (National Film Archive, London)
7 *Snow White and the Seven Dwarfs* – 1937 (Phototeque)
8 *Raiders of the Lost Ark* – 1981 (National Film Archive, London)
9 *Cabaret* – 1972 (Bison Picture Library)
10 *Terms of Endearment* – 1983 (Bison Picture Library)
11 & 13 *All the President's Men* – 1976 (Bison Picture Library)
12 *Beverly Hills Cop* – 1984 (Phototeque)
14 *The Wizard of Oz* – 1939 (Bison Picture Library)

Contents

Introduction 9
A Nous La Liberté 10
Adam's Rib 10
The Adventures Of Robin Hood 10
The African Queen 11
Alexander Nevsky 11
Alexander's Ragtime Band 12
Alfie 12
All About Eve 13
All Quiet On The Western Front 13
All That Money Can Buy 13
All The King's Men 14
All The President's Men 14
Amadeus 14
American Graffiti 14
An American In Paris 17
And Then There Were None 17
Angels With Dirty Faces 18
Animal Crackers 18
Anna Christie 19
Annie Hall 19
Aparajito 19
The Apartment 20
Arise My Love 20
Around The World In Eighty Days 20
Arsenic And Old Lace 21
Ashes And Diamonds 21
The Asphalt Jungle 22
L'Atalante 22
Atlantic City 22
Babes In Arms 23
The Bad And The Beautiful 23
Bad Day At Black Rock 23
Ballad Of A Soldier 24
Bambi 24
The Band Wagon 25
The Bank Dick 25
Beat The Devil 25
Beau Geste 26
Bedazzled 26
La Belle Et La Bete 27
Ben Hur 27
The Best Years Of Our Lives 28
Beverly Hills Cop 28
Bicycle Thieves 29
The Big Chill 29
The Big Parade 30
The Big Sleep 30
A Bill Of Divorcement 30
Billy Liar 32
The Birds 32
The Birth Of A Nation 33
Black Narcissus 34
Black Orpheus 34
Blade Runner 35
Blithe Spirit 35
The Blue Angel 35
The Blue Lamp 36
The Body Snatcher 36
Bonnie And Clyde 36
Born Yesterday 36
Breaker Morant 37
The Bride Of Frankenstein 37
The Bridge On The River Kwai 38
Brief Encounter 38
Bringing Up Baby 39
Broken Blossoms 39
Bullitt 39
Butch Cassidy And The Sundance Kid 40

Cabaret 41
Cabin In The Sky 42
The Cabinet Of Dr Caligari 42
Camille 42
Captain Blood 42
Captains Courageous 43
Un Carnet De Bal 43
Casablanca 44
Le Casque D'Or 44
The Cat And The Canary 44
Cat On A Hot Tin Roof 46
The Champ 46
Chariots Of Fire 46
Un Chien Andalou 47
Chinatown 47
Citizen Kane 49
City Lights 50
Civilization 50
A Clockwork Orange 50
Close Encounters Of The Third Kind 51
Coal Miner's Daughter 51
The Colditz Story 52
The Covered Wagon 52
The Crowd 52
The Cruel Sea 52
Dames 53
The Damned 53
Dark Victory 54
Darling 54
David Copperfield 54
The Dawn Patrol (1930) 55
The Dawn Patrol (1938) 55
A Day At The Races 55
Day For Night 55
Day Of Wrath 56
Days Of Wine And Roses 56
Dead End 56
Dead Of Night 57
Death Of A Salesman 57
The Deer Hunter 58
The Defiant Ones 58
The Desert Fox 59
Destry Rides Again 59
La Diable Au Corps 59
Dinner At Eight 60
The Discreet Charm Of The Bourgeoisie 61
Divorce Italian Style 61
Dr Jekyll And Mr Hyde 61
Doctor No 62
Dr Strangelove 62
Doctor Zhivago 62
La Dolce Vita 63
Double Indemnity 63
Down To The Sea In Ships 64
Dracula 64
Die Dreigroschenoper 64
Duck Soup 65
Dumbo 65
E.T. 66
Earth 66
East Of Eden 66
Easter Parade 68
Easy Rider 68
Eight And A Half 68
Les Enfants Du Paradis 69
The Exorcist 69
The Face 70
Fanny And Alexander 70
Fantasia 70

Farewell My Lovely 70
Le Femme Du Boulanger 70
The First Of The Few 72
Five Graves To Cairo 72
Flying Down To Rio 72
Foolish Wives 73
Footlight Parade 73
Forty-Ninth Parallel 73
Forty-Second Street 74
The Four Feathers 74
The Four Horsemen Of The Apocalypse 75
Frankenstein 77
Freaks 77
The French Connection 77
From Here To Eternity 78
The Front Page 78
Funny Girl 78
Gallipoli 80
Gandhi 80
The Garden Of Allah 81
Gaslight 81
Gate Of Hell 81
The Gay Divorcee 82
The General 82
Il Generale Della Rovere 83
Ghostbusters 83
The Ghost Goes West 83
Gigi 84
Gilda 84
The Godfather 84
The Godfather, Part II 84
Going My Way 84
Gold Diggers Of 1933 86
The Gold Rush 86
Der Golem 87
Gone With The Wind 88
Goodbye Mr Chips 90
The Gospel According To St Matthew 90
The Graduate 91
Grand Hotel 91
La Grande Illusion 92
The Grapes Of Wrath 92
The Great Dictator 92
The Great Escape 92
Great Expectations 93
The Great Train Robbery 94
Greed 94
Gunfight At The OK Corral 95
Gunga Din 95
Hail The Conquering Hero 96
Hamlet 96
Hannah And Her Sisters 96
A Hard Day's Night 96
Harvey 97
Heaven Can Wait 97
The Heiress 97
Hell's Angels 98
Henry V 98
Here Comes Mr Jordan 99
High Noon 99
High Sierra 100
Holiday 100
Horse Feathers 100
The Hound Of The Baskervilles 101
The House On 92nd Street 101
How Green Was My Valley 101
Hud 102
The Hunchback Of Notre Dame 102
I Am A Fugitive From A Chain Gang 104
I Married A Witch 104
I Was A Male War Bride 104

If 105
I'm No Angel 105
The Importance Of Being Ernest 106
In Which We Serve 106
The Informer 106
Inherit The Wind 107
The Innocents 107
Intermezzo 108
Intolerance 108
Intruder In The Dust 108
Invasion Of The Body Snatchers 108
The Invisible Man 108
The Iron Horse 110
It Happened One Night 110
It's A Wonderful Life 110
Ivan The Terrible (Parts I and II) 111
Jane Eyre 112
Jaws 112
The Jazz Singer 113
Les Jeux Interdits 113
Jew Süss 114
Jezebel 114
Johnny Belinda 115
The Jolson Story 115
Le Jour Se Leve 115
Jules Et Jim 116
Julia 116
Julius Caesar 118
Kameradschaft 118
La Kermesse Heroique 119
Key Largo 121
Kind Hearts And Coronets 121
The King And I 122
King Kong 122
King Of Hearts 123
King Solomon's Mines 123
Kiss Me Kate 123
Klute 124
The Knack 124
Knife In The Water 124
Kramers Vs Kramer 124
The Lady Eve 125
The Lady Vanishes 125
The Ladykillers 125
Lassie Come Home 126
The Last Laugh 127
The Last Picture Show 127
The Last Wave 127
Laura 127
The Lavender Hill Mob 128
Lawrence Of Arabia 129
The League Of Gentlemen 129
The Letter 130
The Life And Death Of Colonel Blimp 131
The Life Of Emile Zola 131
Lilies Of The Field 131
The Lion In Winter 132
Little Caesar 132
The Little Colonel 133
Little Women 134
Lives Of A Bengal Lancer 134
Local Hero 134
Lost Horizon 135
The Lost Weekend 135
Love Me Tonight 135
M 136
Mad Max 136
Maedchen In Uniform 136
The Magnificent Ambersons 136
Major Barbara 137
The Maltese Falcon 137

A Man For All Seasons	138
The Man In The White Suit	138
The Man Who Came To Dinner	139
The Man Who Knew Too Much	139
Marty	140
M★A★S★H	140
The Mask Of Dimitrios	140
A Matter Of Life And Death	140
Meet Me In St Louis	142
Metropolis	143
Midnight Cowboy	143
Mildred Pierce	144
Le Million	144
The Miracle Of Morgan's Creek	144
Miracle On 34th Street	144
Mr Blandings Builds His Dream House	144
Mr Deeds Goes To Town	145
Mister Roberts	145
Mr Smith Goes To Washington	145
Mrs Miniver	146
Modern Times	146
Monsieur Hulot's Holiday	146
Monty Python And The Holy Grail	147
Morocco	147
The Music Man	147
Mutiny On The Bounty	148
My Fair Lady	148
My Little Chickadee	149
My Man Godfrey	149
Mystery Of The Wax Museum	149
The Naked City	150
Nanook Of The North	150
Napoleon	150
National Lampoon's Animal House	150
National Velvet	151
Network	151
The Niebelungen	152
A Night At The Opera	152
Night Of The Hunter	153
Ninotchka	153
Norma Rae	153
North By Northwest	155
Nosferatu	155
Nothing Sacred	155
Now, Voyager	155
Occupe-Toi D'Amelie	156
Odd Man Out	156
Oh Mr Porter	156
Oliver!	156
Oliver Twist	157
Los Olvidados	158
Olympische Spiele	158
On Golden Pond	159
On The Town	160
On The Waterfront	160
One Flew Over The Cuckoo's Nest	161
Open City	161
Ordinary People	162
Orphans Of The Storm	162
Orphée	163
The Ox-Bow Incident	163
Paisan	164
The Palm Beach Story	164
Pandora's Box	164
Les Parapluies De Cherbourg	165
Pather Panchali	165
Paths Of Glory	165
Patton	166
The Petrified Forest	166
The Phantom Of The Opera	167
The Philadelphia Story	168
Picnic At Hanging Rock	168
The Pink Panther	169
Pinocchio	169
The Plainsman	170
Les Portes De La Nuit	170
Portrait Of Jennie	170
The Postman Always Rings Twice	171
Potemkin	172
Pride And Prejudice	172
The Pride Of The Yankees	173
The Prisoner Of Zenda	173
The Private Life Of Henry VIII	174
Psycho	174
Public Enemy	177
Pygmalion	177
Les Quatre Cents Coups	178
Queen Christina	178
The Quiet Man	178
Raiders Of The Lost Ark	181
Rashomon	181
Rear Window	182
Rebecca	182
The Red Badge Of Courage	183
Red Dust	183
The Red Shoes	184
Richard III	184
Rififi	184
Risky Business	186
The Road To Singapore	186
Rocky	186
Roman Holiday	188
La Ronde	188
Safety Last	189
San Francisco	190
Le Sang D'Un Poete	190
Saturday Night And Sunday Morning	190
Saturday Night Fever	191
The Scarlet Pimpernel	191
The Searchers	191
Sergeant York	192
The Servant	192
Seven Brides For Seven Brothers	193
Seven Samurai	193
The Seven Year Itch	194
The Seventh Seal	194
Shane	194
Shanghai Express	195
She Done Him Wrong	196
She Wore A Yellow Ribbon	196
Shoeshine	197
Showboat	197
Singin' In The Rain	199
Smiles Of A Summer Night	199
The Snake Pit	199
Snow White And The Seven Dwarfs	200
Some Like It Hot	201
Sons Of The Desert	201
Sophie's Choice	202
The Sorrow And The Pity	202
Sorry Wrong Number	202
The Sound Of Music	203
Sous Les Toits De Paris	204
The Southerner	204
Spellbound	204
Stagecoach	205
A Star Is Born	205
Star Wars	206
The Stars Look Down	206
The Sting	207
The Story Of Gösta Berling	207
La Strada	207

Strangers On A Train	208	
A Streetcar Named Desire	208	
Strike	209	
Die Student Von Prag	209	
Sullivan's Travels	209	
Sunset Boulevard	209	
Superman	210	
Suspicion	210	
Sweet Smell Of Success	210	
Swing Time	212	
La Symphonie Pastorale	212	
A Tale Of Two Cities	213	
Tarzan, The Ape Man	214	
Terms Of Endearment	215	
The Testament Of Dr Mabuse	215	
The Thin Man	215	
Things To Come	216	
The Third Man	218	
The 39 Steps	219	
This Happy Breed	219	
Throne Of Blood	219	
Thunder Rock	220	
Tiger Bay	220	
To Be Or Not To Be	220	
To Catch A Thief	221	
To Kill A Mockingbird	221	
Tom Jones	222	
Tootsie	223	
Top Hat	225	
Topper	225	
The Treasure Of The Sierra Madre	226	
Triumph Of The Will	226	
Trouble In Paradise	226	
The True Glory	226	
True Grit	228	
Tunes Of Glory	228	
Twelve Angry Men	228	
Twelve O'Clock High	228	
Twentieth Century	229	
2001: A Space Odyssey	229	

Two Women	229
Ugetsu	230
Umberto D	230
The Uninvited	230
Union Pacific	231
The Virgin Spring	231
Les Visiteurs Du Soir	231
Wages Of Fear	232
A Walk In The Sun	232
Walkabout	233
War And Peace	233
Way Down East	233
The Way We Were	234
West Side Story	234
Whiskey Galore	235
White Heat	235
Who's Afraid Of Virginia Woolf	236
Why We Fight	236
The Wild One	236
Wild Strawberries	238
The Wind	238
Wings	239
The Winslow Boy	239
Witness For The Prosecution	239
The Wizard Of Oz	240
The Wolf Man	240
Woman Of The Year	242
The Women	242
Woodstock	243
The World Of Apu	244
The Wrong Box	244
Wuthering Heights	245
Yankee Doodle Dandy	247
The Year Of Living Dangerously	247
You Can't Take It With You	248
Young Frankenstein	248
Z	250
Zero Du Conduite	250
Zulu	251

Introduction

At one time a book like this would have been primarily of historical interest. Except for the revival of an occasional classic like *Gone With The Wind*, or the regular returns of Disney features, movie theaters showed only current films. Television was better, but not much better. The *Wizard of Oz* was run annually, and classic films like *Casablanca* turned up often. But usually the film you wanted to see was on at two in the morning or some other impossible time. Films were routinely mutilated for television, and commercial breaks killed any chance of really appreciating what you were watching. There were film societies and film festivals, but they were few and far between. So your chances of catching a particular great old film was slim.

The videocassette has changed all of that. Most of the films covered in this book are available on videocassette somewhere, and more are being made available all the time. If, while looking over this book, you find a film you had missed and now want to see, or if you are reminded of a great film you saw years ago, and want to see again, the chances are good that you can.

A few words about how this particular list of 500 great films was arrived at is necessary. There are some films, *Citizen Kane*, *Psycho*, *The Red Shoes*, that everyone will agree are great. But there is no precise definition of what constitutes a 'great' film. You may think that some of the films included here are not 'great' or even 'good.' You may wonder how the authors could have been so blind and stupid to have left off this or that favorite of yours. Deciding what films to leave out was the hardest part of the job. But even if we had been able to cover 1000 great films, we would still feel some had been omitted, and you probably would too.

Though the list is largely a personal one, that is films we have liked, we did try to be objective as well. We didn't include all the films of Alfred Hitchcock or Stanley Kubrick just because they happen to be favorites of ours. We tried to pick representative films from different eras, different countries, different genres, the serious and the frivolous. But in the end the list is still a personal one. We don't expect you to agree with all of our choices, but we do hope that this book will not only be an exercise in nostalgia, but that it will tell you about some fine films that you'll want to see.

Daniel and Susan Cohen

A Nous La Liberté (1931) FRANCE, DIRECTOR – RENÉ CLAIR

This enchanting operetta-style satirical comedy, starring Raymond Cordy, Henri Marchand, Rolla France, and Paul Olivier, tells the story of a factory owner who when blackmailed about his past receives help from an old prison chum and the two take up a vagabond life. *A Nous la Liberté* heavily influenced actor/director Charles Chaplin as can be seen in Chaplin's *Modern Times*. *A Nous la Liberté* was written as well as directed by the great René Clair who has been compared to Rouben Mamoulian and Ernst Lubitsch. But Clair's comic flair, technical skill, and impeccable taste place him in a class of his own.

Adam's Rib (1949) USA, DIRECTOR – GEORGE CUKOR

In their sixth film together Spencer Tracy and Katharine Hepburn play married lawyers who are on opposite sides of a courtroom case. Tracy's the prosecutor and Hepburn's the defense. Judy Holliday co-stars as the wife on trial for shooting her roving husband Tom Ewell. Beautifully written by Garson Kanin and his wife Ruth Gordon the movie portrays the battle of the sexes with wit and style as Tracy and Hepburn carry their courtroom fight into the bedroom. David Wayne plays a songwriter who's in love with Hepburn. His song 'Farewell, Amanda' was really written by Cole Porter at Hepburn's request.

Counsel for the defense Katharine Hepburn confronts her husband, the prosecutor Spencer Tracy in *Adam's Rib* (49).

The Adventures Of Robin Hood (1938) USA, DIRECTORS – MICHAEL CURTIZ, WILLIAM KEIGHLEY

A vehicle for one of Hollywood's most handsome, most charming, and roguish heroes, Errol Flynn, this movie combined romance and swashbuckling adventure in vivid technicolor with triumphant skill receiving an Oscar nomination for Best Picture. Flynn stars as the outlaw who bests the wicked Sheriff of Nottingham played with sinister grace by Basil Rathbone and wins the love and hand of Maid Marian played with wide-eyed appeal by Olivia de Havilland. The usurping Prince John is played by Claude Rains, and Ian Hunter plays King Richard. Robin's band of Merry Men includes Alan Hale as Little John, Eugene Pallette as Friar Tuck and Patric Knowles as Will Scarlett. Erich Wolfgang wrote the stirring score which did win an Academy Award. The final duel between Rathbone and Flynn, two of Hollywood's best swordsmen, is one of the reasons for the film's continuing popularity.

The African Queen   (1951) USA; DIRECTOR – JOHN HUSTON

Set in German East Africa at the beginning of World War I this magnificent comedy tells the tale of an unlikely romance between a hard-drinking middle-aged mailboat skipper and a priggish spinster missionary. The movie, filled with adventure, has the pair bringing the old mailboat down a river infested with leeches, reeds and rapids to pursue a German gunboat. The movie won Humphrey Bogart as skipper Charlie Allnut the Oscar for Best Actor over Marlon Brando in *A Streetcar Named Desire*. The picture brought Katharine Hepburn a fifth Oscar nomination for her role as Rose Sayre. Nominations went to director John Huston, and screen writer James Agee who adapted CS Forester's novel.

Bogart and Hepburn, *The African Queen* in tow, wade through the last of their journey to sink a German gunboat (51).

Alexander Nevsky   (1938) USSR, DIRECTOR – SERGEI M EISENSTEIN

One of the great masterpieces of cinema, the sweep and splendor of the film's pagentry can only be described as operatic in scale, made more magnificent still by an original score composed by Sergei Prokofiev. A historical epic set in 1242 the movie depicts the campaign led by the heroic Prince Alexander Nevsky (Nicolai Cherkasov) against an invading army of Teutonic Knights on ice-coated Lake Peipus. Eisenstein was virtually the inventor of montage and the battle sequence is one of his most significant artistic triumphs. The movie which represented a stylistic and theoretical departure for Eisenstein proved immensely popular in the USSR and abroad when it first appeared. The film was withdrawn from circulation in the USSR after the signing of the German – Soviet Pact of 1939.

Nicolai Cherkasov, the victorious prince in *Alexander Nevsky* (38).

Alexander's Ragtime Band   (1938) USA, DIRECTOR – HENRY KING

In an era of warbling sopranos Alice Faye's nice contralto was a boon to movie musicals and the pretty blonde was at her best in *Alexander's Ragtime Band*. Set in the years 1911 to 1939 the movie's central plot device is the rivalry between two songwriters in love with a musical comedy performer on her way up. A superior cast including Don Ameche, Tyrone Power, Ethel Merman and Jack Haley added to Faye's lustre and the film's panache. The movie which boasts no less than twenty six songs by Irving Berlin received an Oscar nomination for Best Picture as well as an Oscar nomination in the musical category. Alfred Newman won an Oscar for his musical direction of the film.

Alfie   (1966) GREAT BRITAIN, DIRECTOR – LEWIS GILBERT

This film was a major winner for British actor Michael Caine who was superb in the title role. Paramount made the movie on a shoestring budget expecting little from it and wound up with a potential Oscar-winner. The movie received a nomination for Best Picture and Caine was nominated for Best Actor. Also nominated were actress Vivien Merchant and Bill Naughton who wrote both the screenplay and the original stage play. Even the title song received a nomination. *Alfie* is about a Cockney womanizer, immoral and proud of it until a near-tragedy helps him mature. Frank for its time, this sexual comedy not only won critical success but was a smash at the box office.

Michael Caine received an Oscar nomination for his moving portrayal of a rogue womanizer in *Alfie* (66).

All About Eve (1950) USA, DIRECTOR – JOSEPH L MANKIEWICZ

Witty and sharp, this brilliantly written movie won six Academy Awards including Best Picture, Director, and Screenplay. Bette Davis was at the peak of her powers as the stage actress, Margo Channing, betrayed by her protégé, the seemingly innocent but in reality crafty and ambitious Eve Harrington, played by Anne Baxter. Gary Merrill co-starred as the husband who stays loyal to Margo. Hugh Marlowe played the playwright taken in by Eve and Celeste Holm was wonderful as the playwright's forgiving wife who is Margo's best friend. Thelma Ritter is perfect as Margo's acid-tongued dresser. So is George Sanders as Addison Dewitt, the elegant critic who outsmarts the calculating Eve. With lines like Margo's 'Fasten your seatbelts – it's going to be a bumpy night', this Hollywood movie made the Broadway theater sound great off stage as well as on.

Bette Davis (right) as stage actress Margo Channing suspects the motives of her protegé, Eve Harrington (Anne Baxter), in *All About Eve* (50).

All Quiet On The Western Front

(1930) USA, DIRECTOR – LEWIS MILESTONE

Based on Erich Maria Remarque's novel of the same name *All Quiet On The Western Front* is a great pacifist film which illuminates the lunacy and futility of war. Seven patriotic German students volunteer for military service in 1914 at the onset of World War I. Total disillusionment follows for all and none survive. Outstanding in the cast are Lew Ayres as a young soldier, in his first starring role and Louis Wolheim as an old soldier, in one of his final performances. The scenes of trench warfare are brilliantly and painfully depicted. The film which won Oscars for Best Picture and Best Director so affected actor Ayres that he became a conscientious objector during World War II, serving bravely in the Medical Corps. The film's sequel, *The Road Back* (1937), was directed by James Whale.

Lew Ayres starred as the young German volunteer who loses his innocence and life in the trenches of World War I in *All Quiet on the Western Front* (30).

All That Money Can Buy

(1941) USA, DIRECTOR – WILLIAM DIETERLE

Based on Steven Vincent Benet's short story, *The Devil and Daniel Webster*, this variation of the original *Faust* legend is set in nineteenth-century New Hampshire where a farmer with a bushel's worth of troubles makes a pact with the Devil. But the farmer is saved from the fate awaiting him by Daniel Webster, the great lawyer beautifully played by Edward Arnold, who comes to the farmer's defense at a supernatural trial. The movie relies on all kinds of clever cinematic gimmicks including comedy asides to dazzle the audience but the real reason for the film's magic is actor Walter Huston who is simply fantastic as the Devil, Mr Scratch. Huston received an Academy Award nomination for his performance which still works like a charm.

All The King's Men   (1949) USA, DIRECTOR – ROBERT ROSSEN

This Academy Award winning film about the rise and fall of a corrupt demogogue is based on Robert Penn Warren's novel of the same name. Broderick Crawford played the populist demogogue, Willie Stark, a thinly disguised version of Huey Long, former governor of Louisiana. Crawford won an Oscar for his performance as the reformer who starts out an honest man, is seduced by power, and is finally assassinated. Mercedes McCambridge also received an Oscar for her brilliant performance as Stark's confidante. The movie has great cinematic style and its use of flashbacks is reminiscent of *Citizen Kane*. Director Rossen received an Oscar nomination but soon after was black-listed.

Mercedes McCambridge, John Ireland and Broderick Crawford in *All the King's Men* (49).

All The President's Men   (1976) USA, DIRECTOR – ALAN J PAKULA

Robert Redford played Bob Woodward and Dustin Hoffman Carl Bernstein in this film adaptation of the book in which Washington *Post* reporters Woodward and Bernstein detailed how they uncovered evidence linking President Richard Nixon to the break-in at Democratic National Headquarters. The movie does an excellent job of dramatizing the Watergate Scandal as the break-in and the events leading up to Nixon's resignation are recalled. The movie received a Best Picture nomination and a nomination also went to supporting actress Jane Alexander. Jason Robards won an Oscar for his portrayal of *Post* editor Ben Bradlee.

Amadeus   (1984) USA, DIRECTOR – MILOS FORMAN

One of the most entertaining movies to emerge from Hollywood in the 1980s, *Amadeus* has beautiful music, colorful costumes, a terrific script based on the original stage play, both written by Peter Shaffer, superb acting performances and a stirring and exciting story. Tom Hulce starred as the immortal Wolfgang Mozart, genius and buffoon and F Murray Abraham his embittered rival, the jealous court composer Antonio Salieri who, it is suggested, drove Mozart to his death through overwork. The film culminates in a brilliant scene in which Salieri helps the dying Mozart to write the *Requiem*, and begins to understand, briefly, how he composed. The movie won seven Oscars including Best Picture, writing, direction and for Abraham the Best Actor Award.

Tom Hulce as the young composer Mozart in *Amadeus* (84).

American Graffiti   (1973) USA, DIRECTOR – GEORGE LUCAS

Francis Ford Coppola financed future movie mogul Lucas's production for less than a million dollars. It turned out to be one of the top grossing films of all time and received several Oscar nominations including Best Picture. Based on Lucas's memories of his own teen years in Modesto, California, *American Graffiti* is a pop tribute to the innocent adolescence joys of driving around, picking up girls, eating hamburgers and listening to the radio as a high school class celebrates the last night before they break up. Despite its innocence the movie isn't simple minded. Most of the kids are en route to a banal adulthood and the audience knows full well that the turbulent Vietnam War years loom just ahead. The period of the early 1960s is brilliantly captured by the sound track which includes such popular hits as 'Louie, Louie,' 'Barbara Anne', 'Chantilly Lace', 'Teen Angel' and 'Sixteen Candles.' The cast includes several performers who went on to make names for themselves, Richard Dreyfuss, Ron Howard, Harrison Ford and Cindy Williams.

An American In Paris

(1951) USA, DIRECTOR – VINCENTE MINNELLI

This delightful Hollywood fantasy with its romantic vision of Paris was shot almost entirely on the MGM studio lot. Gene Kelly plays ex-GI Jerry Mulligan who's studying painting in Paris when he falls in love with the adorable Lise (Leslie Caron). The selection of songs by George and Ira Gershwin make the movie memorable. Oscar Levant costars as a concert pianist who becomes a whole orchestra of Oscar Levants in the film's 'Ego Fantasy' sequence. Best of all is the dancing which won choreographer Gene Kelly a special Oscar. Few scenes in musicals match the eighteen-minute ballet, set to the Gershwin tone poem that brings this enchanting movie to a close. The film won the Academy Award for Best Picture in 1952.

Gene Kelly and Leslie Caron in the ballet finale of *An American in Paris* (51).

And Then There Were None

(1945) USA, DIRECTOR – RENÉ CLAIR

Dudley Nichols wrote the screenplay for this gem of a movie based on Agatha Christie's mystery novel. An unknown host invites ten guests to a mansion on an island. All are presumed by their shadowy host to have committed crimes and one by one they are murdered. The cast includes Walter Huston, Judith Anderson, Barry Fitzgerald, Louis Hayward, Roland Young, C Aubrey Smith, Mischa Auer and Richard Haydn. All are marvelous. The hauntingly beautiful black and white cinematography of Lucien Andriot and Mario Castelnuovo-Tedesco's memorable score add to the picture's charms but it is René Clair's masterful direction that makes *And Then There Were None*, also known as *Ten Little Indians* arguably the best whodunnit on film.

Six of the suspects in *And Then There Were None* (45).

Angels With Dirty Faces   (1938) USA, DIRECTOR – MICHAEL CURTIZ

This classic gangster melodrama established James Cagney as a sympathetic crook and Humphrey Bogart as an unsympathetic one. It also did a lot for the careers of Pat O'Brien, who plays a priest, and female lead Ann Sheridan. The picture has a moral twist as the brave Cagney pretends to be a coward when he goes to the electric chair just so the Dead End Kids won't look upon him as a hero. Apparently the kids got the message for they soon began appearing in comedies as the Bowery Boys.

Animal Crackers   (1930) USA, DIRECTOR – VICTOR HEERMAN

Shot at Paramount's Astoria studios in New York and originally a Broadway musical-comedy by George S Kaufman, Bert Kalmar, Morris Ryskind and Harry Ruby, this great comic film has proved to be one of the most durably popular movies the Marx Brothers ever made. Groucho plays Captain Geoffrey Spaulding, a guest of Mrs Rittenhouse, an upper-crust matron (Margaret Dumont who appears with the Marx Brothers in seven of their thirteen films). Zeppo plays Groucho's secretary. Chico and Harpo happen to be there too. Together the brothers puncture the pretenses of high society, especially those of Louis Sorin, the art critic who used to be a fish peddler. Lillian Roth and Hal Thompson play the engaged couple enmeshed in the theft of the Beauregarde painting. Groucho's theme song 'Hooray for Captain Spaulding' was introduced in *Animal Crackers*.

Harpo takes a swing at Chico in socialite Margaret Dumont's living room as brother Groucho looks on in *Animal Crackers* (30).

Anna Christie   (1930) USA, DIRECTOR – CLARENCE BROWN

Based on the play by Eugene O'Neill, MGM selected this film project with care so its legendary star Greta Garbo could make her talking picture debut as a character who could conceivably have a Swedish accent. As Anna, Garbo portrays a prostitute whose sordid career is revealed to her family and the young seaman (Charles Farrell) who is in love with her. While MGM top brass trembled, Garbo's husky uttering of these immortal words, 'Gimme a visky.

Chincher ale on the side. And don't be stingee, baybee' proved to audiences she could talk. Garbo received an Academy Award nomination for *Anna Christie* and the picture was a hit. The German language version filmed at the same time was one of Garbo's personal favorites.

Greta Garbo as *Anna Christie* (30) with her father (George F Marion).

Annie Hall   (1977) USA, DIRECTOR – WOODY ALLEN

Based on the real life romance of director Allen and the movie's star Diane (nickname Annie) Keaton (real last name Hall) which had ended by the time the movie was made, *Annie Hall* the movie went a long way towards establishing Allen in the front ranks of serious directors. The film features director Woody Allen in his basic identity as a neurotic Jewish New Yorker who is funny, sad, self-centered, basically decent, alienated and a hypochondriac all at the same time. Heavy on biography and psychoanalysis the movie develops via flashbacks, monologues, and blackout sketches. Keaton plays the All-American midwestern girl gone a little goofy and chaotic, and won the Academy Award for Best Actress. Allen won the Award for Best Director, and the film for Best Picture.

Walter Bernstein and Diane Keaton meet Woody Allen and Sigourney Weaver (in her first movie role) in *Annie Hall* (77).

Aparajito   (1956) INDIA, DIRECTOR – SATYAJIT RAY

After his father's death a poor boy in rural India is encouraged by his mother to continue his education. Written as well as directed by Ray, with music by the noted sitar player Ravi Shankar, this film should not be viewed as an isolated entity for with *Pather Panchali* and *Apu Sansar/The World of Apu* it is part of one of the most brilliant film series ever made. Ray's films are timeless

documents of life, scrupulously authentic, universal in meaning, remorseless yet magically beautiful in their simplicity. *Aparajito* (The Unvanquished), made in the Bengali language, is the second film in Ray's prize-winning Apu Trilogy which introduced serious Indian cinema to the West.

The Apartment   (1960) USA, DIRECTOR – BILLY WILDER

Jack Lemmon stars as the ambitious but lonely underling courting favor with the office bigwigs by letting them use his apartment for their romantic assignations. Lemmon is attracted to Shirley MacLaine the office elevator operator. Unknown to Lemmon, MacLaine is involved with the brutal head of personnel played by Fred MacMurray. A controversial comedy when it was made, *The Apartment* is also brightly funny and deliciously cynical. Partly because it relies on a suicide attempt to make its point about how human beings should be treated it's also poignant. The film won the Oscar for Best Picture, and Wilder won Oscars for writing and direction. Both Lemmon and MacLaine received nominations.

Jack Lemmon strains spaghetti in *The Apartment* (60).

Arise My Love   (1940) USA, DIRECTOR – MITCHELL LEISEN

A historically important film, *Arise My Love* was one of Hollywood's earliest attempts to awaken the American people to the reality of World War II and the film ends with a warning against isolationism. Despite its theme the movie isn't somber but is a highly entertaining sophisticated comedy and drama starring two delightful stars in top form, Claudette Colbert and Ray Milland, who play American reporters in love in Europe. The Spanish Civil War, a tough editor played by Walter Abel, and the sinking of the passenger liner, the *Athenia*, at the start of World War II can't do Colbert and Milland in. The movie received several Oscar nominations and won an Award in the writing category.

Around The World In Eighty Days   (1956) USA, DIRECTORS - MICHAEL ANDERSON, KEVIN McCLORY

The word that best describes this film is 'big'. A creation of impresario Mike Todd, best known for his marriage to Elizabeth Taylor, the movie filmed in Todd-AO filled the wide screen with big name celebrities in cameo roles. Based roughly on Jules Verne's adventure novel *Around The World In Eighty Days* the film is essentially a travelogue which takes a Victorian gentleman and his valet on a race around the globe. Though slow and dull in spots the movie somehow managed to dazzle the Academy of Motion Picture Arts and Sciences into giving it the Best Picture Award as well as the writing and music awards. The star-spangled cast is headed by David Niven, Cantinflas and Shirley MacLaine.

David Niven charms Shirley MacLaine, the Indian princess he has rescued, in *Around the World in Eighty Days* (56).

Arsenic And Old Lace   (1944) USA, DIRECTOR – FRANK CAPRA

Based on a Broadway stage play by Joseph Kesselring but in no way inferior to it this is a gem of a comedy. Two charming elderly ladies (Josephine Hull and Jean Adair) invite poor lonely old men into their house in Brooklyn, then poison them with elderberry wine to put them out of their misery. The bodies are buried in the cellar by their crazy brother (John Alexander) who thinks he's Teddy Roosevelt. Raymond Massey plays a homicidal nephew who looks like Boris Karloff thanks to the handiwork of a crooked plastic surgeon played by Peter Lorre. Capra wanted Karloff for the role of homicidal nephew, and Karloff had played the part on stage, but contractual complications got in the way. Cary Grant is splendid as the one sane member of the family, and his performance alone is worth the price of admission.

Jean Adair, Josephine Hull and Cary Grant starred in *Arsenic and Old Lace* (44).

Zbigniew Cybulski (c) played a Polish partisan in *Ashes and Diamonds* (58).

Ashes And Diamonds   (1958) POLAND, DIRECTOR – ANDRZEJ WAJDA

A Generation, (1954), *Kanal*, (1957), and *Popiol y diament/Ashes and Diamonds* form a powerful film trilogy in which director Wadja questions the tradition of glorifying heroism in combat and sensitively examines the plight of individuals who find themselves in the midst of events they cannot control. The chief character is a Polish partisan who is unable to understand why the killing must continue after World War II is over. The film is the clearest expression of Wadja's fascination with the bitter aftermath of war and the intellectual contradictions war creates. *Ashes and Diamonds* starred Zbigniew Cybulski whose accidental death in 1967 deprived cinema of a gifted actor.

The Asphalt Jungle   (1950) USA, DIRECTOR – JOHN HUSTON

Thanks to its emphasis on character and its insider's view of a robbery this *film noir* about an old crook (Sam Jaffe) fresh out of jail who brings a gang of criminals together for one last crime spawned a host of imitations including Jules Dassin's *Rififi* (1954). Louis Calhern starred as the crooked lawyer who double crosses the gang and Sterling Hayden played the prototypical criminal loner to perfection. Outstanding performances were also given by Jean Hagen and Jaffe while starlet Marilyn Monroe was notably sexy in a bit role as Calhern's mistress. Harold Rosson received an Oscar nomination for his cinematography. John Huston was nominated not only for direction but for the clever screenplay which he wrote with Ben Maddow.

Sam Jaffe (left) explains his plan to Sterling Hayden, Brad Dexter, James Whitmore in *The Asphalt Jungle* (50).

L'Atalante   (1934) FRANCE, DIRECTOR – JEAN VIGO

Jean Daste, Dita Parlo, Michel Simon, and Giles Margarites appear in this film classic about the captain of a barge and his bride travelling down river. The work is the masterpiece of the great French director Jean Vigo whose tragic death of leukemia at the age of twenty-nine proved a severe loss to French cinema. Both *L'Atalante* and *Zero de Conduite* (1933) combine lyricism with realism and surrealism and reflect Vigo's cynical anarchistic view of life. The highly experimental and innovative *L'Atalante* was savagely mutilated by its producers who feared that the filmgoing public would not accept a movie so blatantly and critically anti-bourgeois.

Atlantic City   (1981) USA, DIRECTOR - LOUIS MALLE

An understated elegy set in the run-down seaside resort of Atlantic City, New Jersey, this compassionate, humanistic movie stars Burt Lancaster in his finest screen performance. Lancaster plays a shabby gangster well past his prime, hustling to survive, a symbol of the city itself. The movie is really about life's illusions and small time losers' dreams of making it big. Costars Susan Sarandon and Kate Reid are both good but it's director Malle's picture and his use of the locale, including the boardwalk, is intriguing. The well-written screenplay by John Guare received an Oscar nomination as did Malle, Lancaster, Sarandon and the picture itself.

Susan Sarandon and Burt Lancaster starred in *Atlantic City* (81).

La Belle Et La Bête (1946) FRANCE, DIRECTOR – JEAN COCTEAU

Visually rich and lyrically expressive this film adaptation of the fairy tale *Beauty and The Beast* is a masterpiece, filled with haunting imagery. Beauty offers herself to the Beast who has kidnapped her father and through the magic of love the Beast becomes a handsome prince. Jean Marais, who appears in practically all of Cocteau's films stars as the Beast. The rest of the cast includes Josette Day as Beauty, Mila Parély, Marcel André, and Michael Auclair. The multi-talented Cocteau wrote as well as directed the picture and the glorious art direction is by Christian Bérard. Cocteau kept a diary during the production, outlining his search for locations, the difficulties of shooting and the physical hardships involved in making a film in a country after four years of Nazi occupation. Published as *Diary of a Film*, it also describes some of the methods used by Cocteau to create his fantasies.

Josette Day joins the beast (Jean Marais) for dinner in *La Belle et la Bête* (46).

Messala (Stephen Boyd) and Ben Hur (Charlton Heston) in the chariot races in *Ben Hur* (59).

Ben Hur (1959) USA, DIRECTOR – WILLIAM WYLER

This vast fifteen-million dollar epic set in the Roman Empire's province of Judea, starred Charlton Heston as the Jewish prince, Judah Ben Hur, whose childhood friendship with the Roman tribune Messala (Stephen Boyd) turns to enmity when Messala destroys the Hur family for the sake of his career. Sentenced to the galleys, Ben Hur rescues a Roman admiral (Jack Hawkins) during a sea battle and is adopted by him. Making his way back to Jerusalem, he defeats Messala in a climactic chariot race and rescues his mother and sister who have become lepers. They are cured by Christ at the moment of the Crucifixion. The bare bones of the plot do not begin to reveal the pomp and pageantry of this film which was lucky enough also to have an extremely literate script, written with assistance from Christopher Fry, Gore Vidal, and S N Berman, although screen credit was given to Karl Tunberg. The chariot race was directed by Andrew Marton and Yakima Canutt. The picture won eleven Oscars, including Best Picture, Best Actor (Heston), Best Director and Best Supporting Actor (Hugh Griffith as the Bedouin sheik Ilderim who provides Ben Hur with his team for the race).

The Best Years Of Our Lives   (1946) USA, DIRECTOR – WILLIAM WYLER

A vintage postwar film about three GIs returning home after World War II and the difficulties they encounter in adapting to peacetime, *The Best Years of Our Lives* touched a deep chord in the American film-going public. Fredric March starred as the banker, married to Myrna Loy, for whom the war was a brief interlude. Theresa Wright played their daughter who falls in love with another of the veterans, Dana Andrews, the ex-bomber pilot, for whom the war was the high point of his life. Virginia Mayo costarred as his unfaithful wife. Harold Russell, a real World War II amputee gave a standout performance as the veteran struggling to cope with his handicap. Cathy O'Donnell played his understanding girlfriend. It was Russell's acting debut, and he was not seen on screen again until *Inside Moves* (1980). Nominated for eight Academy Awards, the film won seven including a special award for Russell (who also won in the Best Supporting Actor category) and Best Picture.

Beverly Hills Cop   (1985) USA, DIRECTOR – MARTIN BREST

A wonderful vehicle for gifted comedian actor Eddie Murphy this movie takes a black streetwise detective to Beverly Hills ostensibly to investigate the murder of a friend but really to give Murphy a chance to go on a rollicking series of adventures which includes putting an end to a drug smuggling operation. Murphy's cop is an anti-establishment con artist who has the audience rooting for him as he breaks every rule in the book, creating havoc in fancy restaurants and glitzy art galleries, triumphing over just about everybody he meets. Judge Reinhold, John Ashton, and Lisa Eilbacher costar.

Eddie Murphy stakes out a house in Beverly Hills with style in the closing scenes of *Beverly Hills Cop* (85).

Bicycle Thieves   (1947) ITALY, DIRECTOR – VITTORIO DE SICA

The collaboration of director de Sica and screenwriter Cesare Zavattini resulted in two postwar Italian neorealistic films, the 1946 *Shoeshine/Sciusciá* and *Bicycle Thieves/Ladri di Biciclette*. Both films explore the urban chaos of Rome in the aftermath of World War II and both films draw superb performances from nonprofessional actors. Against the backdrop of stark city streets *Bicycle Thieves* tells the story of an unemployed Italian worker whose bicycle is stolen. Without a bicycle he cannot look for work and he and his small son search Rome for the precious conveyance. Father and son have a tender relationship and the movie is suffused with humanity. Truly a work of art it won a special Academy Award for Best Foreign Film released in 1949.

Lamberto Maggiorani and Enzo Staiola played the father and son in *Bicycle Thieves* (47).

The Big Chill   (1983) USA, DIRECTOR – LAWRENCE KASDAN

Fine ensemble acting makes this aptly titled movie about college radicals co-opted by the establishment a memorable film. The cast includes Kevin Kline, Glenn Close, Tom Berenger, Mary Kay Place, Jeff Goldblum, JoBeth Williams, William Hurt and Meg Tilly. A group of mostly affluent old college activists meet once again at the funeral of a friend who's committed suicide. Achievements real and imagined, self-deceptions, frustrations, and the passage of time dominate the reunion and a steady stream of songs from the 1960s contributes to the nostalgia for days gone by. The movie was heavily influenced by director John Sayles's *The Return Of The Secaucus Seven* (1981).

Glenn Close and William Hurt played old college friends in *The Big Chill* (83).

The Big Parade

(1925) USA, DIRECTOR – KING VIDOR

Dubbed 'the epic of the American doughboy' this extraordinary silent film about a young American during World War I is one of noted director Vidor's outstanding triumphs. John Gilbert gave his best performance as the doughboy, Jimmy Apperson, and Renée Adorée costarred as the French peasant girl, Melisande. The screenplay was by Lawrence Stallings, who also wrote *What Price Glory?* The film is both massive spectacle and sentimental drama yet manages to achieve moments of genuine sensitivity. Following *The Big Parade* Vidor created a second silent masterpiece, *The Crowd*, about the anonymity of urban life. Today Vidor's silent films are still impressive though sometimes it is the camera mobility of individual scenes and the powerful statement such scenes make rather than the entire movie which captivates because by modern standards the movies tend to be maudlin.

Karl Dane looks on as Melisande (Renée Adorée) bids farewell to Jimmy Apperson (John Gilbert) in *The Big Parade* (25).

The Big Sleep

(1946) USA, DIRECTOR - HOWARD HAWKS

The story is a hodgepodge of nymphomania, pornography, drug addiction and insanity, merely hinted at in the film thanks to the puritanical Hollywood Production Code in force in the 1940s. To this day no one can figure out the plot but it may help if you remember that each murder is committed by a different killer who in turn is bumped off. Lauren Bacall and her new husband Humphrey Bogart teamed up to make this compelling hard-boiled thriller which features Bogart as Philip Marlowe, novelist Raymond Chandler's fictional detective. Adding to the film's virtues is a terrific performance by Elisha Cook Jr. Credit for the complex screenplay goes to three writers including, believe it or not, William Faulkner. An unsuccessful remake starring Robert Mitchum was released in 1977.

A Bill Of Divorcement

(1932) USA, DIRECTOR – GEORGE CUKOR

Katharine Hepburn made her screen debut in this film opposite John Barrymore. Based on Clemence Dane's stage play the movie concerns a deranged middle-aged man, the father of a strong assertive daughter. He is released from a mental hospital and returns home to find his wife has fallen in love with another man. His daughter breaks off her engagement when she finds that the disease is hereditary. Though the film is dated it still works as a vehicle for two compelling stars and the acting alone makes it well worth seeing. The movie was remade in 1940 with Adolphe Menjou and Maureen O'Hara.

Billy Liar   (1963) GREAT BRITAIN, DIRECTOR JOHN SCHLESINGER

One of actor Tom Courtenay's earliest films it was a smash hit of almost mythic proportions, marred only by being filmed in Cinemascope which didn't suit it. In a dreary North Country town in Britain an undertaker's clerk escapes reality by creating a world of fantasy. Keith Waterhouse and Willis Hall wrote the screenplay, based on their play which was adapted from Waterhouse's novel. The movie was later redone as a television series and was also made into a popular live musical for the stage. The cast of this brilliant and perceptive comedy includes Julie Christie, Wilfred Pickles, Mona Washbourne, Ethel Griffies and Leonard Rossiter.

The Birds   (1963) USA, DIRECTOR – ALFRED HITCHCOCK

Daphne du Maurier wrote the short story which forms the basis of this terrifying thriller crafted by the master of the suspense genre, Alfred Hitchcock. Beautiful blond Tippi Hedren buys lovebirds for lawyer Rod Taylor and follows him to his family place in Bodega Bay, California. There, for no apparent reason, flocks of birds turn on the human species including Tippi. The special effects are fantastic and the lack of a musical score leaves the birds to make the noise that raises the tension. Following du Maurier's lead, Hitchcock offers no explanation for this revolution among the class *aves*, thus making the movie more mysterious.

Rod Taylor escorts a frightened and shocked Tippi Hedren home after the first attack in *The Birds* (63).

Henry B Walthall starred as the Little Colonel in the controversial film, *The Birth of a Nation* (15).

The Birth Of A Nation   (1915) USA, DIRECTOR – D W GRIFFITH

David Wark Griffith was the master of the silent movie and *Birth of a Nation* confirmed his position as one of the all-time towering giants of cinema. The movie was the first major epic in the history of film, a technical tour de force, which originally ran for three hours and starred Lillian Gish, Mae Marsh, Henry B Walthall and Wallace Ried. It is an elaborate and complex depiction of Northern and Southern families caught up in the whirlwind of the American Civil War. Originally titled *The Clansman* and

based on the novel of the same name by Thomas Dixon, Jr, the movie's greatness is marred by its subject matter, the glorification of the Ku Klux Klan. Blacks and liberal whites attacked the film but the movie was an immense success at the box office even though tickets were an incredibly high two dollars apiece. In 1930, the film was reissued with music, sound effects and a prologue of conversation between Griffith and actor Walter Huston.

Black Narcissus (1946) GREAT BRITAIN, DIRECTORS — MICHAEL POWELL, EMERIC PRESSBURGER

This visually beautiful technicolor film based on a novel by Rumer Godden still packs an emotional wallop. It centers on the lives of a group of Anglo-Catholic nuns in the Himalayas trying to cope with the climate, spiritual needs, and each other. Cinematographer Jack Cardiff won an Oscar for his work. Deborah Kerr's portrayal of a nun was so persuasive she caught the attention of the powers-that-be in Hollywood and was brought to California to launch an American film career. The cast includes David Farrar, Sabu, Jean Simmons, Flora Robson, Kathleen Byron, Esmond Knight, Jenny Laird, May Hallatt, and Judith Furse.

David Farrar, Deborah Kerr and May Hallatt as the kneeling Indian woman visit a saddhu in *Black Narcissus* (46).

The Samba School prepares to go down the mountain for Carnéval in *Black Orpheus* (58).

✗ *Black Orpheus* (1958) FRANCE/ITALY/BRAZIL, DIRECTOR — MARCEL CAMUS

Orfeu Negro/Black Orpheus is one of the most visually stunning movies ever filmed. Shot in vividly colored cinemascope in Brazil and featuring an all black cast the movie is based on the legend of Orpheus and Euridyce. During carnival in Rio a tram driver named Orpheus accidentally kills his beloved, who has been fleeing from the image of Death, then kills himself to be with her.

Cinematography, dancing, samba music, carnival costumes, and most of all, the actors are gorgeous. Breno Mello, Marpessa Dawn, Ademar de Silva and Lourdes de Oliviera star. The movie took first prize at both the Cannes and Venice film festivals and won the 1959 Academy Award for Best Foreign Film.

Blade Runner (1982) USA, DIRECTOR – RIDLEY SCOTT

It's hardly surprising that this is one of the finest science fiction movies ever made since its director was also responsible for the superb horror film *Alien*. Harrison Ford plays a cop whose job it is to kill rebellious robots called replicants. The robots in this film are not metal monsters, but strikingly human and Ford falls in love with one. The movie raises a number of interesting questions about blind prejudice and cruelty. Based on Philip K Dick's novel *Do Androids Dream of Electric Sheep?* the movie, set in a sleazy rainy Los Angeles in AD 2019, is also a good thriller, a kind of futuristic *film noir*. Besides Ford the universally fine cast includes Rutger Hauer, Sean Young, Edward James Olmos, M Emmet Walsh and Daryl Hannah.

Blithe Spirit (1945) GREAT BRITAIN, DIRECTOR – DAVID LEAN

A classic from the moment it first appeared on the screen, this witty urbane comedy, written by Noel Coward and based on his play of the same name, is very nearly perfect. Rex Harrison plays the mystery writer who invites an eccentric medium to conduct a seance so he can get material for a book. She manages to raise the sexy and playful ghost of his first wife, Elvira. The problem is his efficient down-to-earth second wife Ruth is very much alive, at least temporarily. Margaret Rutherford costars as the medium and marvelous performances, too, are given by Kay Hammond and Constance Cummings, as the two wives.

The Blue Angel (1930) GERMANY, DIRECTOR – JOSEF VON STERNBERG

Emil Jannings's much touted first talkie turned out to be the vehicle which catapulted a beautiful young blonde named Marlene Dietrich to stardom. The legendary Dietrich first sang two of her most famous songs 'Falling In Love Again' and 'They Call Me Naughty Lola' in this film. A tale of social decadence and sexual obsession the movie stars Jannings as a stuffy puritanical professor who becomes fascinated with Lola Lola, a tawdry vamp who sadistically humiliates him. The movie is a work of art, powerful and disturbing, even nightmarish. Shot in English as well as German the movie was a huge international success. A 1959 remake with Curt Jurgens and May Britt was merely a pale imitation.

'They call me naughty Lola' – Marlene Dietrich starred as the nightclub singer in *The Blue Angel* (30).

The Blue Lamp   (1949) GREAT BRITAIN, DIRECTOR – BASIL DEARDEN

This well-paced popular crime thriller started a trend for documentary-style fictional films. A young policeman is trained by an older policeman played by British character actor Jack Warner. The older policeman is eventually killed in a shootout but the killer, Dirk Bogarde, is caught. Not only audiences but police, too, liked the movie which presents a positive image of the police force. But as far as *The Blue Lamp* is concerned the movie was only the beginning. The film spawned a twenty-year BBC television series called *Dixon of Dock Green*. The murdered policeman was brought back to life for the series and Warner portrayed the character on TV.

Dirk Bogarde played the vengeful cop killer in *The Blue Lamp* (49).

The Body Snatcher   (1945) USA, DIRECTOR – ROBERT WISE

The gifted Val Lewton using the pseudonym Carlos Keith wrote the script for this stunning horror film which is considered one of the finest examples of the genre. Lewton turned to a story by Robert Louis Stevenson for inspiration. The characters in *The Body Snatcher* derive from the nineteenth-century grave robbers Burke and Hare who plied their unseemly trade in Edinburgh, Scotland. The movie stars Boris Karloff as Gray, the murderous cab driver who acquired corpses for a physician played by Henry Daniell. Bela Lugosi costars as the doctor's simple-minded assistant, a role created specifically for him. For once Lugosi is a victim. The film is literate, atmospheric, even poetic and scary as anything.

Bonnie And Clyde   (1967) USA, DIRECTOR – ARTHUR PENN

Warren Beatty produced this massive box office hit known for its extraordinary violence which ushered in a whole era of ultra-brutal films. During the Depression of the 1930s, Beatty plays small-time crook Clyde Barrow and Faye Dunaway costars as Bonnie Parker, a duo who see themselves as Robin Hood, i.e. they steal from banks (the rich) but take pride in their reputation as robbers who would never steal from the down and out. Their adventures provide a perverse glamour in a gray world and they become glorified myths larger than life, but poignant and doomed lovers as well. The movie received numerous Oscar nominations and Estelle Parsons as Clyde's sister-in-law won the Best Supporting Actress Award for her performance. Outstanding, too, in the cast were Gene Hackman and Michael J Pollard.

Faye Dunaway played Bonnie Parker and Warren Beatty Clyde Barrow in the box office hit *Bonnie and Clyde* (67).

Born Yesterday   (1950) USA, DIRECTOR - GEORGE CUKOR

Judy Holliday stars in this political comedy set in Washington, DC. Based on Garson Kanin's play the movie tells the story of an ex-chorus girl whose rich and crooked lover played by Broderick Crawford decides she needs to improve her English. She gets a course in English and in ethics, which is more than Crawford bargained for, from teacher William Holden, a newspaperman. Naturally Holliday falls in love with Holden, and learns a lot about good government in the process. For her role as Billy Dawn the archetypal dumb blonde who is not so dumb Holliday won the Best Actress Oscar over such competition as Bette Davis in *All About Eve* and Gloria Swanson in *Sunset Boulevard*.

Breaker Morant   (1980), AUSTRALIA, DIRECTOR — BRUCE BERESFORD

This fine film with Edward Woodward, Bryan Brown, Jack Thompson, Lewis Fitz-Gerald, Charles Tingwell, Terence Donovan and Vincent Ball is proof enough that some of the best movies made these days come from Australia. Based on an actual historic incident the film follows the case of three Australian officers courtmartialled and executed by British authorities on the charge of murdering prisoners during the Boer War. Not only does *Breaker Morant* work on a dramatic level but it is a whopping good adventure film. The script received an Oscar nomination.

The Bride Of Frankenstein   (1935) USA, DIRECTOR — JAMES WHALE

Director Whale followed his brilliant original *Frankenstein* with a sequel again starring Boris Karloff as the monster with a tortured soul. Elsa Lanchester costarred as his designated but highly resistant mate. The script was good, the movie well-paced, and Franz Waxman's score added to the whole. Ernest Thesinger played the macabre Dr Pretorius who blackmails Baron Frankenstein, played again by Colin Clive, into reviving the monster and crafting a mate for him. Lanchester also played author Mary Shelley in the prologue. *The Bride*, (1985) a tedious remake of the original, starred Jennifer Beals in the title role and Sting as the doctor.

Lanchester and Karloff in *The Bride of Frankenstein* (35).

The Bridge On The River Kwai   (1957) GREAT BRITAIN, DIRECTOR – DAVID LEAN

This exceptional war movie, photographed by Jack Hilyard, is known for its great visual beauty. Set in a Japanese Prisoner of War camp in Burma the movie presents plenty of adventure but is most interesting when it deals with the inner conflicts of the characters. Alec Guinness won an Oscar for his magnificent performance as the brave British colonel who cannot be tortured into submission but who eventually comes to identify with his captors when he is put in charge of building a bridge, work that fulfills his need for order and discipline. The cast also includes Jack Hawkins, William Holden, James Donald and Sessue Hayakawa, who received an Oscar nomination for his portrayal of the Japanese commandant. Lean won an Oscar for the direction and the film won the Award for Best Picture.

James Donald congratulates British colonel Alec Guinness on completion of the bridge in *The Bridge on the River Kwai* (57).

Brief Encounter   (1945) GREAT BRITAIN, DIRECTOR – DAVID LEAN

Noel Coward wrote the script for this highly polished yet touching love story indelibly linked to trains and railroad stations. One of the first great postwar films to emerge from Britain *Brief Encounter* depicts the unfulfilled romance between a middle-aged suburban housewife and a quiet middle-aged doctor, both of whom are married. Celia Johnson and Trevor Howard are superb in the lead roles and Stanley Holloway, Joyce Carey, and Cyril Raymond also give fine performances. An inferior version of the movie was made for television in 1975, starring Richard Burton and Sophia Loren. *Falling In Love* (1984) with Robert DeNiro and Meryl Streep also owes a debt to *Brief Encounter*.

Bringing Up Baby   (1938) USA, DIRECTOR – HOWARD HAWKS

The 'baby' in *Bringing Up Baby*, is a leopard. The dog that buries dinosaur bones is the famed Asta of *The Thin Man*. The flustered paleontologist is Cary Grant who modeled his characterization of the long-suffering professor on comic Harold Lloyd. As for the cause of much of the suffering, a fetching and lovable zany, she is Katharine Hepburn, in her first comedy role. This just may be the best screwball comedy Hollywood produced in that golden age of comedies, the thirties. Chaos abounds and the action never ceases. *Bringing Up Baby* provided the inspiration for Peter Bogdanovich's 1971 *What's Up, Doc?* starring Barbra Streisand and Ryan O'Neal.

Katharine Hepburn and Cary Grant in *Bringing Up Baby* (38).

Broken Blossoms   (1919) USA, DIRECTOR – D W GRIFFITH

Some critics consider this intimate silent melodrama a violent yet tender tragedy. Others consider it overtly Victorian in style and hopelessly sentimental. Either way the movie is visually beautiful and highly atmospheric, all fogs and shadows. Based on Thomas Burke's story with the rather startling title *The Chink And The Child* the film is set in the Limehouse section of London. A young Chinese man falls in love with a girl. When the innocent waif is murdered by her monstrous father, the young Chinese man kills the father and then commits suicide. Richard Barthelmess and Lillian Gish star. A parody, *Broken Bottles*, was filmed in 1920 and a 1936 British remake written by Emlyn Williams succeeded artistically but bombed at the box office.

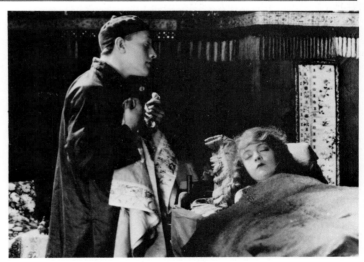

Richard Barthelmess and Lillian Gish in *Broken Blossoms* (19).

Bullitt   (1968) USA, DIRECTOR – PETER YATES

One of the most popular stars of the 1960s and 1970s was Steve McQueen who is at his charismatic best in this stylish film about a California cop who keeps secret the murder of an underground witness he was supposed to protect and who then pursues the killers himself. Jacqueline Bisset, Robert Vaughn, Don Gordon, Robert Duvall, and Simon Oakland round out the cast. The movie boasts one of the best car chases on film but most of all it is McQueen, full of contradictions, who makes the film work. He's the anti-hero who's a hero, the loner with charm, and an introvert loaded with energy. The movie is based on the novel *Mute Witness* by Robert L Pike.

Butch Cassidy And The Sundance Kid (1969) USA, DIRECTOR – GEORGE ROY HILL

Paul Newman and Robert Redford starred as the fallible lovable heroes who bungle bank robberies and manage to stay one step ahead of the law until they are tracked down in, of all places, Bolivia. The movie, a warm friendly comic western, is a refreshing change from the usual deadpan violent tale of the old west. Katharine Ross gave her best performance as Etta Place the schoolmarm who went with them but the film's real appeal lies with Newman and Redford. Burt Bacharach wrote the Academy Award winning song 'Raindrops Keep Falling On My Head' and also won an Oscar for the film's score.

Paul Newman, Katharine Ross and Robert Redford in *Butch Cassidy and the Sundance Kid* (69).

Liza Minnelli and Joel Grey sing about the joys of 'Money' in pre-war Berlin – *Cabaret* (72).

Cabaret   (1972) USA, DIRECTOR – BOB FOSSE

Writer Christopher Isherwood's quasi-autobiographical novel, *Goodbye To Berlin* has appeared in various theatrical guises since its publication in 1939. The film version follows John Van Druten's play *I Am A Camera* rather than the Broadway musical which featured a stronger role for the decadent master of ceremonies arrestingly portrayed by Joel Grey. The movie, set in Berlin in the early thirties during the rise of Nazi power, stars Liza Minnelli as the frenzied yet touching girl, Sally Bowles, who has become a nightclub entertainer. Michael York plays the lover she shares with a bisexual baron, Helmut Griem. Marisa Berenson costars as their Jewish friend Natalia. Minnelli, Grey and Fosse all won Oscars.

Cabin In The Sky (1943) USA, DIRECTOR – VINCENTE MINNELLI

Eddie 'Rochester' Anderson, Ethel Waters, Lena Horne, Cab Calloway, Louis Armstrong and John W Bubbles all appear in this all black musical based on the Broadway show. The film features Waters in her only film musical starring role, as Petunia, the wife of gambler Little Joe. He is stabbed and a battle ensues for his soul with Lena Horne as Lucifer's tempting bait. Unlike the stage musical it all turns out to be a dream. Harold Arlen and E Y Harburg's song 'Happiness Is Just A Thing Called Joe' received an Oscar nomination. Though by modern standards the movie is racist, in its day it represented an advance in Hollywood film characterizations of blacks.

Ethel Waters and Kenneth Spencer in *Cabin in the Sky* (43).

The Cabinet Of Dr Caligari (1919) GERMANY, DIRECTOR – ROBERT WIENE

Dr Caligari (Werner Krauss) sends a somnambulist (Conrad Veidt) out to commit murders, or does he? *Das Kabinett des Dr Caligari* could be only a madman's dream. Written by Austrian-born Carl Mayer and Czech poet Hans Janowitz this visually fascinating totally paranoid silent horror film known for its expressionist sets, bizarre acting style, and original camera angles was to influence movie-making in Germany for an entire decade. The cast includes Lil Dagover, Friedrich Feher and Hans von Twadowski. The gifted cinematographer is Willi Hameister. The movie still has the power to disturb and surprise audiences but such originality and the strange mood is nowhere visible in the poor American remake of 1962.

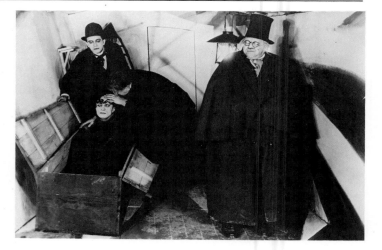

Conrad Veidt and Werner Krauss: *The Cabinet of Dr Caligari* (19).

Camille (1936) USA, DIRECTOR – GEORGE CUKOR

In 1948 Alexandre Dumas *fils* wrote a novel about a courtesan dying of consumption who falls madly in love with an innocent aristocrat who adores her. His father disapproves, they separate, and he returns just in time for poor Camille to die in his arms. Theda Bara, Nazimova, Pola Negri and Norma Talmadge played Camille on screen, but none of them have had the impact of Greta Garbo who is superb in this elegant MGM production. Some of the credit belongs to director Cukor, who was known for his ability to obtain the best performance from famous actresses. The cast includes Robert Taylor as the young lover Armand and Lionel Barrymore as his father. Garbo received an Oscar nomination for her performance.

Captain Blood (1935) USA, DIRECTOR – MICHAEL CURTIZ

This Oscar-nominated swashbuckling romantic adventure film, based on the novel by Rafael Sabatini, propelled Errol Flynn to stardom, and marked his first screen pairing with Olivia de Havilland. Flynn played Captain Peter Blood, an English surgeon who is forced to become a Caribbean pirate following his exile after Monmouth's Rebellion. He is pardoned on the accession of William and Mary but first come sea battles, love scenes, a wonderful Errol Flynn-Basil Rathbone duel and some rather nasty villainy on the part of Lionel Atwill. In 1963 Flynn's son Sean appeared in *Son of Captain Blood*.

Errol Flynn leads his men on board a pirate ship in *Captain Blood* (35).

Spencer Tracy and Freddie Bartholomew starred in *Captains Courageous* (37).

Captains Courageous (1937) USA, DIRECTOR – VICTOR FLEMING

Freddie Bartholomew starred as Harvey Cheyne the spoiled brat who falls off a cruise liner, and Spencer Tracy as Manuel, the Portugese fisherman who rescues him. Living with fishermen forces Freddie to learn to care about people and he develops character. This classic film, based on Rudyard Kipling's adventure tale, brought Spencer Tracy his first Academy Award. Enhancing his characterization by using a Portugese accent Tracy was wonderful as the virile simple hard-working fisherman. The illustrious supporting cast included Lionel Barrymore and Mickey Rooney. In addition to Tracy's Oscar this immensely popular movie received Academy Award nominations for Best Picture and Best Screenplay.

Un Carnet De Bal (1937) FRANCE, DIRECTOR – JULIEN DUVIVIER

This film starring Marie Bell, Françoise Rosay, Louis Jouvet, Raimu, Harry Baur, Fernandel, and Pierre Blanchar was an enormous worldwide success. Duvivier's reputation for poetic realism was already well-established by the time he made the film and *Un Carnet de Bal* reveals the director at the apex of his powers. A dance program becomes the vehicle for linking together several separate stories in this romantic gem about a wealthy widow who attends a ball. The film provides fine roles for its marvelous cast and their performances still impress. The film's success brought Duvivier to Hollywood where he created a new version of *Un Carnet de Bal* titled *Lydia*.

43

Casablanca

(1942) USA, DIRECTOR – MICHAEL CURTIZ

The cast list of this Oscar winning movie is pure gold and the song 'As Time Goes By' is golden, too. Enormously famous this romantic idealistic and humorous masterpiece may be the best movie ever made. Based on an unproduced play *Everybody Comes To Rick's* the movie's central character is a Spanish Civil War hero turned cynic portrayed by Humphrey Bogart, who runs a café in Casablanca called Rick's. Into his life a second time comes Ingrid Bergman. But she's married to a vital leader of the underground played by Paul Henreid. The noble gesture of sacrificing his love for the sake of the cause redeems Bogart. Bergman and Henreid escape from Casablanca thanks to Bogart and he goes off to fight the Nazis, accompanied by Claude Rains, the venal chief of police who has also redeemed himself. One of the glories of the film is the supporting cast: Sydney Greenstreet as Señor Ferrari, the owner of the Blue Parrot, Peter Lorre as the rogue Ugarte, S Z Sakall as the waiter Carl, Leonid Kinsky as the bartender Sascha and Dooley Wilson as Sam the piano player who plays 'As Time Goes By.'

Captain Reynaud (Claude Rains) calls for a roundup of the usual suspects in *Casablanca* (42) while Rick (Humphrey Bogart), Victor Lazslo (Paul Henreid) and Ilsa (Ingrid Bergman) wait.

Le Casque D'Or

(1952) FRANCE, DIRECTOR – JACQUES BECKER

Sensuous and luminous this melodrama is a period love story noted for its atmospheric quality. When it was first shown it seemed steeped in a golden glow and it is still considered one of the finest examples of tragic romance ever filmed. Set in the slums of Paris in 1898 it stars the magnificent Simone Signoret and Serge Reggiani who turns in the premiere performance of his career. The movie, also known as *Golden Marie*, is the masterpiece of famed director Becker who captures the texture of French low-life in this tale of a gangster's passion, and eventually his execution for murder. Notable, too, is the screenplay by Becker and the cinematography of Robert Le Fèbvre.

The Cat And The Canary

(1939) USA, DIRECTOR – ELLIOTT NUGENT

The first version of *The Cat And The Canary* was a 1927 silent film. Remade for sound under the title *The Cat Creeps* in 1931 the movie was filmed again with Bob Hope, Paulette Goddard, and Gale Sondergaard. Hope is wonderfully funny in this comic thriller set in a creepy old house where a group of people gather for a midnight reading of a will. The movie was a hit and Hope and Goddard made *The Ghost Breakers* the following year. In 1978 the by now ubiquitous *The Cat And The Canary* was remade again in color.

Cat On A Hot Tin Roof   (1958) USA, DIRECTOR – RICHARD BROOKS

Director Richard Brooks also wrote the screenplay for this film version of the classic Tennessee Williams play. The film focuses on a rich plantation owner called Big Daddy, strongly played by Burl Ives, who is dying of cancer and the stormy relationships brewing in the cauldron of his money loving family. Sexy, worried Maggie the Cat is played by Elizabeth Taylor. The source of Maggie's worry, the husband who won't sleep with her, is played by Paul

Newman. The dialogue, much of it straight from the play, crackles and Taylor's sensuality and Newman's brooding portrayal of Brick create amazing chemistry. However, the movie loses some of the play's impact by minimizing Brick's latent homosexuality.

Burl Ives and Elizabeth Taylor await a response from the brooding Brick (Paul Newman) in *Cat on a Hot Tin Roof* (58).

The Champp   (1931) USA, DIRECTOR – KING VIDOR

An enormous commercial success this three-handkerchief tear-jerker features two engaging talents, Wallace Beery and Jackie Cooper. The homely but lovable Beery plays a hard-drinking washed-up prize fighter who goes into the ring one more time for the sake of his son, Jackie, who has still faith in his father. The film did a lot for Cooper's career

and Beery won a Best Actor Oscar, sharing the prize with Fredric March who also won Best Actor for *Dr Jekyll And Mr Hyde*. A 1952 remake titled *The Clown* starred Red Skelton. A 1979 remake, again called *The Champ* starred Jon Voight, Faye Dunaway and Ricky Schroder.

Chariots Of Fire   (1981) GREAT BRITAIN, DIRECTOR – HUGH HUDSON

Visually beautiful, and reminiscent of old-fashioned inspirational movies *Chariots Of Fire* boasts a fine script, excellent performances, a thrilling musical score and a glimpse into recent history. Two British athletes, one a deeply religious Scot, one a wealthy Jew struggling against the confines of religious bigotry, run for honor, glory, and a gold medal at the Olympics of 1924. Ian Charleson and Ben Cross star as the runners. Ian Holm, who played Cross's trainer, received an Oscar nomination for Best Supporting Actor. Hudson was nominated for direction. The film won the Oscar for Best Picture.

Ian Charleson is carried by his teammates after winning his race in *Chariots of Fire* (81).

Un Chien Andalou   (1928) FRANCE, DIRECTOR – LUIS BUÑUEL

Un Chien Andalou/An Andalusian Dog began when director Buñuel and artist Salvador Dali spent three days discussing their dreams and fantasies. Then together they wrote the script for a surrealistic short film. Running only twenty-four minutes the movie consists of a series of shocking images, seemingly unrelated. A woman's eyeball is methodically cut by a razor. In another 'scene' a hand is apparently eaten by ants. Dead donkeys are revealed on a piano. The movie was initially shown at a special Paris screening and today it can be seen at film festivals.

Luis Buñuel's *Un Chien Andalou* (28) was bizarre and surrealistic.

Chinatown   (1974) USA, DIRECTOR – ROMAN POLANSKI

Sharp dialogue and a complex plot go a long way towards making *Chinatown* a stylish tribute to the tough-guy movie of the 1930s and 1940s. Jack Nicholson starred as the private eye, and John Huston costarred as the rich and greedy Noah Cross who is involved in a fraudulent scheme to become even richer. Faye Dunaway played the beautiful and mysterious widow who meets with a tragic and violent death. Lustful passion is as important in *Chinatown* as lust

for power and incest is a key element in the film. Polanski's direction keeps the film's suspense high and the cinematography with its vivid use of orange is striking. The picture received numerous Oscar nominations and won an Academy Award for Best Screenplay.

Roman Polanski holds a knife on private eye Jack Nicholson in *Chinatown* (74).

Citizen Kane   (1941) USA, DIRECTOR – ORSON WELLES

Orson Welles created *Citizen Kane*, described by Welles as 'a portrait of a public man's private life.' Based on the career of newspaper magnate William Randolph Hearst, this remarkable movie consists of a series of interviews and flashbacks revealing the transformation of Charles Foster Kane (Orson Welles) from a young idealist to a disillusioned old man whose dying word 'Rosebud', the name of his boyhood sled, recalls lost innocence. Technically *Citizen Kane* broke all the old rules and established some new ones. In addition to Welles himself

cinematographer Gregg Toland deserves praise as does Welles's co-scriptwriter Herman J Mankiewicz. The cast, which included Joseph Cotten, Agnes Moorehead, Dorothy Comingore, George Coulouris and Ruth Warrick, members of Welles's Mercury Theater Company, was wonderful. Oscar nominations abounded but the only Award was for the screenplay.

Left: Dorothy Comingore in Xanadu's Great Hall: *Below,* Orson Welles as *Citizen Kane* (41) with reporter Joseph Cotten.

City Lights   (1931) USA, DIRECTOR – CHARLES CHAPLIN

Though sentimental by modern standards the movie remains a masterpiece. Chaplin is brilliant as the tramp mistaken for a millionaire who falls in love with a blind flower girl (Virginia Cherrill). The Depression-era film is deeply compassionate and humanistic. It is also superbly comic. The film's artistic success is not surprising. What is surprising is the film's initial box office success since it is a silent movie made during the age of sound. Essentially a balletic mime Chaplin resisted sound as long as possible. *City Lights* does have a score, composed and conducted by Chaplin, who also wrote, directed, and starred in the film.

Civilization   (1916) USA, DIRECTOR – THOMAS HARPER INCE

This is the most ambitious film by the only American director of the period as technically adept and original as D W Griffith. Ince was a visionary of even greater depth than Griffith as proved by this silent pacifist allegory which was made in support of President Woodrow Wilson's peace efforts. It was Ince's hope that the United States would not become involved in the war raging in Europe. In the film a war is started by a mythical nation. A vision of Christ in human form intervenes and a peace treaty is signed. Some critics suggest that several directors actually worked on the film with Ince only overseeing operations. But the style and ideas are his.

A Clockwork Orange   (1971) GREAT BRITAIN, DIRECTOR – STANLEY KUBRICK

Bleakly pessimistic and utterly terrifying this brilliantly directed film, based on a novel by Anthony Burgess, takes audiences into a nihilistic and violent Britain of the future where anarchism reigns, gruesome crime is commonplace, and the young have lost all moral ties. Malcolm McDowell was unforgettable as a young criminal who rapes and murders without a qualm and who goes to prison only to be released after submitting to experimental brainwashing designed to decriminalize him. Outside he finds the world more violent than ever. A savage indictment of society the film was nominated for Best Picture. Kubrick, too, received nominations for writing and directing.

Malcolm McDowell played the sinister, Beethoven-loving murderer and rapist, Alex, in *A Clockwork Orange* (71).

Scientists and the extra-terrestrials in *Close Encounters of the Third Kind* (77).

Close Encounters Of The Third Kind   (1977) USA, DIRECTOR – STEVEN SPIELBERG

Basically, there are two kinds of science fiction films, those that claim things are out to get us and those that claim things are out to ennoble us. *Close Encounters* definitely belongs in the latter category. UFO's are seen over Indiana and a combination of brains and intuition leads Richard Dreyfuss to the landing site of the aliens. A fine movie with mystical overtones it features thrilling special effects. In 1980 a 'special edition' of the movie was released with additional footage. Composer John Williams, Spielberg and actress Melinda Dillon also received Oscar nominations. Cinematographer Vilmos Zsigmond won the award.

Coal Miner's Daughter   (1980) USA, DIRECTOR – MICHAEL APTED

The authorized version of the life of country and western singer and song writer Loretta Lynn, the film shines because of its star, Sissy Spacek whose talent, Southern drawl, and impish charm are perfect for this role. Spacek even sang all the songs herself, and won the Best Actress Oscar portraying a heroine who represents enduring rural values. The movie's strengths lie in its evocation of rural life; the beauty of Kentucky, the importance of family, and the dignity of people usually derided as hillbillies. But the movie also concerns singer Lynn's complex marriage and the alienation, breakdowns, and eventual healing that accompanied her rise to the top in show business. Tommy Lee Jones costars as Lynn's husband, and Beverly D'Angelo gives a remarkable performance as country singer Patsy Cline, but Levon Helm and Phyllis Boyens almost steal the film as Spacek's parents.

Sissy Spacek as Loretta Lynn in *Coal Miner's Daughter* (80).

51

The Colditz Story   (1954) GREAT BRITAIN, DIRECTOR – GUY HAMILTON

A superb cast including John Mills, Eric Portman, Christopher Rhodes, Lionel Jeffries, Ian Carmichael, and Theodore Bikel plus the craftsmanship of director Hamilton make this one of the most believable movies about British Prisoners of War ever made. Based on a book by P R Reid the movie depicts the adventures of POWs held in a maximum security prison in the castle at Colditz in Saxony, during World War II. Daily life means boredom and monotony for the POWs but there is suffering and even humor as well as the adventure and danger of attempted escape. The movie led to a television series which debuted in 1972.

The Covered Wagon   (1923) USA, DIRECTOR – JAMES CRUZE

This silent western classic influenced not only the western film genre but documentaries and historic costume pictures as well. Based on a novel by Emerson Hough the movie is one of the best-known works of director Cruze. It is certainly the most famous of his silent films. A vigorous telling of the legendary western story of pioneers crossing America by wagon train the movie is meticulously done though plot and character seem weak by modern standards. The film stars Ernest Torrence, Tully Marshall, J Warren Kerrigan, Lois Wilson and Alan Hale. Cinematographer Karl Brown deserves special mention for the real star of this movie is the camera.

The wagon train circles to camp in *The Covered Wagon* (23).

The Crowd   (1928) USA, DIRECTOR – KING VIDOR

One of the finest American films to emerge in the silent era, the barren life of a city clerk is the theme which allows director Vidor to make his point that city life is drab, depressing, and anonymous. The movie is famed for its stark realism, technical virtuosity, and essential humanism. Several camera shots have become positively legendary, for example the scene where the camera scans a skyscraper, then takes the audience through a window and into a large impersonal crowded office, halting at last at the hero's desk. The powerful movie stars James Murray, Eleanor Boardman (Vidor's wife at the time) Bert Roach, and Estelle Clark.

The Cruel Sea   (1952) GREAT BRITAIN, DIRECTOR – CHARLES FREND

The outstanding writer of suspense thrillers Eric Ambler received an Oscar nomination for his screenplay based on Nicholas Monserrat's bestselling novel. Jack Hawkins was at his best in this movie about naval life aboard a corvette in the North Atlantic during World War II. In no way does this film present a romantic view of war. Rather it is a realistic portrayal of the tragedy and violence inherent in warfare and it is this very realism which makes it a moving and powerful experience. The excellent cast includes Donald Sinden, Stanley Baker, John Stratton and Denholm Elliott. In addition to being an artistic success the movie was a smash hit at the box office.

The crew is forced to abandon ship in *The Cruel Sea* (52).

Dames (1934) USA, DIRECTOR – RAY ENRIGHT

This delectable froth is the last movie Busby Berkeley choreographed before the Hollywood Code and budget cutting at Warner Bros studio forced him to restrain his admiration for 'those beautiful dames.' Joan Blondell, Dick Powell, Ruby Keeler, Guy Kibbee, and Zasu Pitts are five good reasons for seeing the movie but comic wisecracks and romance are only part of the fun. As with all Busby Berkeley pictures spectacular scenes of chorus girls dancing in geometric patterns are the real joy of the film. The plot is similar to the Gold Digger films, Powell plays an aspiring songwriter who needs a backer to put on his show. All the songs work but the 'I Only Have Eyes For You' number set in the New York subway is especially delicious.

The Damned (1969) WEST GERMANY/ITALY, DIRECTOR – LUCHINO VISCONTI

Though at the start of his career this major director was an early adherent to neorealism later he crafted elaborately decorative films frequently choosing as his subject the moral disintegration and decay of society as seen through the disintegration of a particular family. Presumably based on Germany's Krupp dynasty *The Damned/Gotterdammerung* is a baroque, even operatic study of rotting decadence which depicts a family of munitions manufacturers during the Nazi rise to power. Family members turn against each other and the family is destroyed. Dirk Bogarde heads a cast which includes Ingrid Thulin, Helmut Berger and Charlotte Rampling.

The Damned (69) explored the decadence of the Third Reich.

Dark Victory   (1939) USA, DIRECTOR – EDMUND GOULDING

A vehicle for Bette Davis *Dark Victory* is one of her most famous films, a classic Hollywood melodrama. Davis plays Judith Traherne a fun-loving socialite who learns she is dying of a brain tumor and who is ultimately ennobled by her courage in coming to grips with the impending tragedy. She received an Oscar nomination for her performance and the movie was nominated for Best Picture. Remade in 1963 as *Stolen Hours*, starring Susan Hayward, *Dark Victory* was also filmed as a made-for-television movie in 1975, starring Elizabeth Montgomery. Neither remake could compare to the original. *Dark Victory* will always belong to Bette Davis and George Brent, who played the doctor who loves and marries her. Humphrey Bogart and Geraldine Fitzgerald costar.

Fitzgerald, Davis and Cora Witherspoon in *Dark Victory* (39).

Darling   (1965) GREAT BRITAIN, DIRECTOR – JOHN SCHLESINGER

Julie Christie gave a fine performance as a beautiful, bored, and totally self-absorbed model who uses men and then discards them, indifferent, even oblivious to the trouble she stirs up in her wake. Her list of conquests includes a journalist, a director, a photographer, and an Italian prince. Schlesinger directed this tale of the empty lives of mid-1960s swingers with style and panache. *Darling* received a nomination for Best Picture as did Schlesinger. Scriptwriter Frederic Raphael won the Academy Award and so did Christie giving her career a considerable boost. Dirk Bogarde and Laurence Harvey are also in the cast.

David Copperfield   (1935) USA, DIRECTOR – GEORGE CUKOR

One of the best film versions of a great novel ever made, the casting was brilliant, the sets immaculate, and the movie's spirit truly Dickensian. W C Fields was cast in the role of Mr Micawber after Charles Laughton backed out. Equally good were Basil Rathbone as Mr Murdstone, his first role as a villain and Roland Young as Uriah Heep, his only role as a villain. Freddie Bartholomew plays young David, and Frank Lawton is David grown up. Edna May Oliver as Aunt Betsey Trotwood, Maureen O'Sullivan, Lionel Barrymore, Elsa Lanchester, Hugh Walpole who also co-wrote the script and Arthur Treacher are just some of the performers who make this movie still a delight fifty years later.

David (Frank Lawton) and Mr Micawber (W C Fields) listen to the villain Uriah Heep (Roland Young) in *David Copperfield* (35).

The Dawn Patrol (1930) USA, DIRECTOR – HOWARD HAWKS

From *Wings* to *Hell's Angels* there are many movies about World War I flyers but this stark early talkie which evokes an aura of hopelessness is one of the best. Stationed in France, a group of officers in the Royal Flying Corps are waiting to take off on dangerous missions from which they may never return. Writer John Monk Saunders received an Oscar nomination for his taut, incisive, and economical script. The aerial footage is superb for its time and was actually reused in the 1938 remake of the film starring Errol Flynn and Basil Rathbone. The 1930 film stars Richard Barthelmess, Douglas Fairbanks Jr and Neil Hamilton. Originally titled *Flight Commander* the movie is sometimes seen on television under that name.

D Fairbanks Jr and R Barthelmess bail out into the French trenches in *The Dawn Patrol* (30).

The Dawn Patrol (1938) USA, DIRECTOR – EDMUND GOULDING

One of the few remakes to equal the film it is based on this picture stays remarkably close to the 1930 original. Errol Flynn plays ace flyer Captain Courtney while an all-British cast includes Basil Rathbone, David Niven and Donald Crisp. It is World War I and the Fifty-ninth Squadron of the Royal Flying Corps in France fights valiantly with antiquated planes and equipment. The movie's mood is one of utter futility and the squadron officers form a fellowship of the doomed while their commanding officer must deal with the pain of sending his friends perhaps to their deaths. This is one of the last action films of the era with an anti-war bias as the onslaught of World War II made such films untenable.

A Day At The Races (1937) USA, DIRECTOR – SAM WOOD

There's a blue-tinted ballet sequence in this inspired and inspiring comedy with Groucho, Chico and Harpo because unlike earlier Marx Brothers classics this movie was given a decent budget by MGM. It doesn't make any difference. It's the usual wonderful stuff and some people may even miss the cheap tricks and junky old sets. The Marx Brothers get help from that reliable matron who always plays it straight, Margaret Dumont, and from Maureen O'Sullivan, Allan Jones, Douglass Dumbrille, Esther Muir and Sig Ruman. There's a damsel in distress, a sanatorium on the skids and a racehorse in this one plus extra romance and music but despite the respectable touches the Marx Brothers are best when they are out of control. The *All God's Chillun Got Rhythm* number sung by Ivie Anderson and the Crinoline Choir is an unfortunate stereotype.

Day For Night (1973) FRANCE, DIRECTOR – FRANÇOIS TRUFFAUT

Truffaut was writer, director and star of this movie, a valentine to the film industry which takes audiences behind the scenes and shows them how movies are made. It's also a comic, affectionate view of the charming but temperamental people who work in the industry. Everything that can go wrong does go wrong as actors and crew gather to make a romantic movie in Nice but creativity wins out and the film within the film turns out just fine despite fits of ego, love affairs, and a sad accident. Jacqueline Bisset, Valentina Cortese, and Jean-Pierre Aumont star with Truffaut. The movie won the Best Foreign Film Oscar and brought much deserved nominations to Truffaut and Cortese.

The great French director François Truffaut appeared in the film within a film *Day For Night* (73).

The inquisitor interrogates a witch in the torture chamber of *Day of Wrath* (43).

Day Of Wrath   (1943) DENMARK, DIRECTOR – CARL DREYER

This slow, somber, depressing, yet fascinating film set in the seventeenth century is a pictorial masterpiece. An old woman is burned as a witch. Her accuser dies and further accusations of witchcraft follow. Every scene in this study of a witch hunt is sketched by cinematographer Carl Andersson in the shading and form of a Rembrandt painting. Director Dreyer, the greatest creative figure in the history of Danish Cinema was fascinated by psychology and *Day of Wrath* is a monumental drama of faith and human passion. Because the film contains allusions to the Nazi occupation of Denmark, Dreyer was forced to flee to Sweden where he remained for the rest of World War II.

Days Of Wine And Roses   (1962) USA, DIRECTOR – BLAKE EDWARDS

Jack Lemmon's career as a serious dramatic actor really took off after his performance in this fine film about alcoholism. Lemmon plays a public relations man who becomes hooked on drinking and Lee Remick plays his wife who learns to drink along with him. They become alcoholics and he loses his job. She continues to deteriorate. In the end Lemmon quits drinking but Remick can't. Both Lemmon and Remick received Oscar nominations and the popular title song by Henry Mancini and Johnny Mercer won the Academy Award. The show was originally done as a teleplay with Cliff Robertson and Piper Laurie.

Dead End   (1937) USA, DIRECTOR – WILLIAM WYLER

This is the movie which gave birth to the Dead End Kids, originally played by Billy Halop, Leo Gorcey, Bernard Punsley, Huntz Hall, Bobby Jordan, and Gabriel Dell. In the beginning they were tough little hoods but their popularity and the censors turned them into comedians in a string of movies first as the Dead End Kids, and later The East Side Kids and The Bowery Boys. Lillian Hellman wrote the screenplay for this film based on the play by Sidney Kingsley about a gangster returning to the old neighborhood. Joel McCrea, Sylvia Sidney, Humphrey Bogart, Wendy Barrie, Claire Trevor, Marjorie Main and Ward Bond make this highly theatrical movie a winner.

Dead Of Night   (1945) GREAT BRITAIN, DIRECTORS – ALBERT CAVALCANTI, CHARLES CRICHTON, ROBERT HAMER, BASIL DEARDEN

Arguably the finest supernatural film ever made, the movie consists of a succession of stories which succeed through good writing, fine performances, and the evocation of a nightmarish mood rather than through garish and gratuitous violence. An architect who suffers from a recurring dream finds himself living the dream as a group of people describe macabre incidents that have occurred to them. Each of the incidents becomes more suspenseful and terrifying. Murder occurs and the ending has a brilliant disturbing twist. The script is by John Baines and Angus Macphail with some stories based on the works of H G Wells and E F Benson. The best known excerpt stars Michael Redgrave as a ventriloquist whose life is taken over by his dummy.

Allen Jeyes and Michael Redgrave in *Dead of Night* (45).

Death Of A Salesman   (1951) USA, DIRECTOR – LASLO BENEDEK

Arthur Miller wrote the play which is now considered an American classic and Stanley Roberts wrote the screen adaptation. *Death Of A Salesman* tells the story of a little guy who believes in the American Dream but whose life is really hollow, empty, and filled with self-deception. When the world closes in on him he kills himself. Fredric March starred as the flawed pathetic salesman and tragic victim, Willy Loman, and received an Oscar nomination for his performance. Other Oscar nominees in the cast are Kevin McCarthy as Willy's son Biff and Mildred Dunnock as Willy's wife. The movie itself was nominated for Best Picture.

The Deer Hunter   (1978) USA, DIRECTOR – MICHAEL CIMINO

Winner of five Academy Awards including Best Picture and Best Director this movie running three hours in length was extremely controversial when first released. Critics denounced its graphic violence and racial stereotypes. Defenders paised the cinematography of Vilmos Zsigmond and the extraordinary acting performances of a cast which includes Robert DeNiro, John Savage, Christopher Walken, John Cazale, and Meryl Streep. Three Pennsylvania steelworkers are smalltown buddies who shoot pool together and hunt together. The movie cuts abruptly to a Vietnam Prisoner of War camp where the friends, now prisoners, are forced to play Russian roulette. The overall mood of the movie is deliberately surrealistic.

Robert DeNiro, John Savage, Christopher Walken, John Cazale and Meryl Streep starred in *The Deer Hunter* (78).

The Defiant Ones   (1958) USA, DIRECTOR – STANLEY KRAMER

Tony Curtis and Sidney Poitier costar in this movie about a black convict and a white convict who escape from a chain gang and who must co-operate because of the chains which bind them together. An important advance in films about racial tension and prejudice this melodrama with its powerful message about brotherhood features plenty of action. Hollywood gave the popular film plenty of recognition. Screenwriters Nathan E Douglas and Harold Jacob Smith won an Oscar as did cinematographer Sam Leavitt. *The Defiant Ones* also received a Best Picture nomination. Stanley Kramer was nominated for direction and performers Curtis, Poitier, Theodore Bikel and Cara Williams were also nominated.

Sidney Poitier and Tony Curtis in *The Defiant Ones* (58).

The Desert Fox (1951) GREAT BRITAIN, DIRECTOR – HENRY HATHAWAY

Based on a book by Desmond Young and with an excellent screenplay written by Nunnally Johnson this is a vivid film account of the last years of German general Erwin Rommel. After meeting defeat in North Africa Rommel returns to Germany disillusioned and becomes involved in a plot against Hitler. Actor James Mason is superb as Rommel. The fine cast includes Jessica Tandy, Cedric Hardwicke, Luther Adler as Hitler, Leo G Carroll and George Macready. Well directed with beautiful cinematography by Norbert Brodine, the movie is the first major film to begin with an action sequence rather than the credit titles, a now common device.

Destry Rides Again (1939) USA, DIRECTOR – GEORGE MARSHALL

Comedy, drama, and music combine to make this unusual western great fun. Marlene Dietrich is wonderful as the tough saloon hostess who sings 'See What The Boys In The Back Room Will Have' with flair and gusto and who shines in a knock-down brawl with Una Merkel. James Stewart costars as the meek and mild sheriff who means to clean up the town of Bottle Neck. Stewart and Dietrich find time for a little romance and horseplay in the midst of some fast-paced action. A 1932 early sound version starred Tom Mix. A 1954 remake, *Destry*, starred Audie Murphy. A variation of *Destry Rides Again* titled *Frenchie* (1950) starred Joel McCrea and Shelley Winters.

Marlene Dietrich with Una Merkel in *Destry Rides Again* (39).

La Diable Au Corps (1947) FRANCE, DIRECTOR – CLAUDE AUTANT-LARA

A romantic love story tinged with sorrow set during World War I, this movie was an enormous box office success internationally and it shot handsome appealing Gerard Philipe to instant stardom. Philipe portrays an awkward adolescent boy who falls in love with an older woman. Micheline Presle plays the married woman who returns his love while her husband is off at war and who dies bearing Philipe's child. *La Diable Au Corps/Devil In The Flesh* is based on a novel by Raymond Radiguet. The gifted actor and director Jacques Tati has a minor role in the film.

Wallace Beery scolds his wife Jean Harlow in *Dinner at Eight* (33).

Dinner At Eight (1933) USA, DIRECTOR – GEORGE CUKOR

Producer David O Selznick and director Cukor, assembled a great cast including Marie Dressler, John Barrymore, Wallace Beery, Lionel Barrymore and a young platinum blonde named Jean Harlow to make this movie. Harlow not only kept up with the veterans but stole the picture. Based on the successful play by George Kaufman and Edna Ferber this delicious comedy takes an odd assortment of people to a society dinner party. The dialogue sparkles and the banter is great. Every star has his or her glittering moments and even the bit parts are bright. The movie's glamor and sophistication as well as its humor won it a huge following at the box office.

The Discreet Charm Of The Bourgeoisie   (1972) FRANCE/SPAIN/ITALY, DIRECTOR – LUIS BUÑUEL

Bold social criticism distinguishes this savagely funny surrealistic film. Crafted by the master of black humor and irony, Buñuel who is known primarily for his courageous ideas rather than for technical virtuosity, the movie concerns a group of friends who keep trying to get together for dinner and who are continually frustrated in the attempt. Fernando Rey, Delphine Seyrig, Stéphane Audran, Bulle Ogier, Jean-Pierre Cassel, Paul Frankeur, and Julian Bertheau all give fabulous performances. Buñuel received an Oscar nomination for the script as did co-writer Jean-Claude Carrière. Blisteringly witty and thoroughly iconoclastic, *The Discreet Charm Of The Bourgeoisie/Le Charme Discret de la Bourgeoisie* won the Oscar for Best Foreign Film of 1972.

Divorce Italian Style   (1961) ITALY, DIRECTOR – PIETRO GERMI

Marcello Mastroianni stars as a Sicilian nobleman eager to shed his unappetizing wife for another woman, his young and beautiful cousin. Divorce being illegal in Italy at the time he concocts a scheme to get rid of her which involves seduction and murder. It's all a spoof, of course, a comedy satirizing the mores and code of honor of Southern Italy. Director Germi and actor Mastroianni both received Oscar nominations for the film which won international attention and Germi shared a writing Academy Award with co-writers Ennio de Concini and Alfredo Gianetti. The entire cast, especially Daniela Rocca as the unloved wife, Stefania Sandrelli, and Leopoldo Trieste give delightful performances.

Dr Jekyll And Mr Hyde   (1932) USA, DIRECTOR – ROUBEN MAMOULIAN

Robert Louis Stevenson's horror and mystery novella about the two characters of one man received its finest film treatment at the hands of director Mamoulian and cinematographer Karl Struss. The use of light and shadow is impressive while on-camera transformation of March thanks in part to imaginatively designed make-up is a technical tour de force. The movie relies on sexual tension and emotional impact rather than mere horror. March and Miriam Hopkins gave excellent performances and March received an Oscar for his dual role. The 1941 version with Spencer Tracy and Ingrid Bergman has some merit, but most of the later sequels and variations on *Dr Jekyll and Mr Hyde* are just plain awful.

Fredric March won an Oscar for his convincing portrayal of *Dr Jekyll and Mr Hyde* (32).

Doctor No   (1962) GREAT BRITAIN, DIRECTOR – TERENCE YOUNG

The first of the enormously successful James Bond films takes British secret service agent 007 to the West Indies. A winning blend of heroics, gadgetry, sex, humor and glamour make this movie one of the best of the genre and it set the tone for the series to come. Voluptuous Ursula Andress costarred in *Doctor No* and the movie's massive popularity advanced her career. Sean Connery who starred for the first time as Bond became a major star thanks to the film. Richard Mailbaum, Johanna Harwood and Berkeley Mather wrote the screenplay based on the best-selling novel by Ian Fleming.

Dr Strangelove   (1963) GREAT BRITAIN, DIRECTOR – STANLEY KUBRICK

Subtitled *How I Learned To Stop Worrying And Love The Bomb* this brilliantly macabre film is one of the gifted director's greatest masterpieces. A nightmare of pessimism and despair underlie the movie's sharp humor and black comedy. A crazy American general launches a nuclear war. Despite a bumbling attempt made to stop it, Armageddon arrives. Peter Sellers is marvelous playing three roles, a British airforce officer, the President and the mad German scientist Strangelove whose arm automatically makes Nazi salutes. George C Scott costars as the ultimate Jingo, General Turgidson, and Sterling Hayden is the crazed general Jack D Ripper. Slim Pickens is the pilot who rides to earth on the bomb whooping and waving his ten-gallon hat.

Peter Sellers as the German scientist *Dr Strangelove* (63).

Doctor Zhivago   (1965) USA, DIRECTOR – DAVID LEAN

Based on Boris Pasternak's novel this sweeping epic about a Russian doctor caught up in the turmoil of World War I and the Russian Revolution was a spectacular box office success. Omar Sharif starred as the young doctor who is also a poet, and in love with two women. Also in the glittering cast were Julie Christie, Geraldine Chaplin, Rod Steiger, Alec Guinness, Ralph Richardson, Tom Courtenay and Siobhan McKenna. Tom Courtenay received a nomination for Best Supporting Actor as did director Lean, and the picture itself. Scriptwriter Bolt won an Oscar as did cinematographer Frederick A Young whose craftsmanship makes this film a treat for the eye. Maurice Jarre also received an Oscar for his dramatic score.

Omar Sharif and Julie Christie, one of the two women he loves, attend to the wounded in *Doctor Zhivago* (65).

La Dolce Vita (1960) ITALY/FRANCE, DIRECTOR – FEDERICO FELLINI

Never has decadence been more fun than in *La Dolce Vita/The Sweet Life* directed by the grand master of Italian films. Essentially autobiographical with Marcello Mastroianni playing Moraldo, a character based on Fellini himself, the movie concerns a journalist who left his home to seek a better life in Rome and who becomes a big success. Though disgusted by Rome's shallow glitter he is seduced by it, joining the ranks of the rich and self-indulgent. The movie is filled with beautiful women, orgies, wonderful performances and so much joy in life one envies rather than condemns Moraldo. The movie, though controversial in Italy, was a smash hit there and elsewhere.

Anita Ekberg celebrates her divorce in *La Dolce Vita* (60), one of Federico Fellini's masterpieces.

Double Indemnity (1944) USA, DIRECTOR – BILLY WILDER

The movie is one of the finest examples of *film noir* ever to hit the screen. The excellent script by director Wilder and mystery writer Raymond Chandler is based on James M Cain's novel. Fred MacMurray plays the insurance agent who falls for scheming Barbara Stanwyck. Together he and Stanwyck murder her husband for his insurance. Edward G Robinson costars as the investigator who traps them. The movie is steamily sexy despite the conventions of the time and it captures the cynicism, weariness, and urban grittiness essential to the genre. *Double Indemnity* received lots of Oscar nominations but the only performer nominated was Barbara Stanwyck.

The scheming lovers Fred MacMurray and Barbara Stanwyck in *Double Indemnity* (44).

Down To The Sea In Ships   (1923) USA, DIRECTOR – ELMER CLIFTON

A young Clara Bow had a minor role in this silent movie about whaling and she even masqueraded as a boy to stow away, but the main plot involved the romantic triangle of Marguerite Courtot, Raymond McKee and Patrick Hardigan. The movie was made, in part, aboard the *Charles W Morgan*, the last whaler, which is now on exhibit at Mystic Seaport in Connecticut and has an air of reality later films made aboard sailing ships seem to be missing. Clifton began his film career assisting D W Griffith and then struck out on his own, achieving success until the sound era relegated him to low budget films. *Down To The Sea In Ships* (1948) stars Lionel Barrymore and Dean Stockwell in an adventure movie about a whaling captain who wants his grandson to carry on the seafaring tradition.

Dracula   (1931) USA, DIRECTOR – TOD BROWNING

Lots of actors including Christopher Lee and Frank Langella have played Dracula but the most famous Dracula is Bela Lugosi and his is the classic version of the tale of the Transylvanian vampire, who comes to England in search of immortality. The movie is based on the late nineteenth-century novel by Bram Stoker. In addition to Lugosi the movie stars Helen Chandler, David Manners, Dwight Frye as Renfield the real-estate agent who goes mad and Edward Van Sloan as Dr Van Helsing. Lugosi brought wit and style to the character of the Count and indelibly stamped him with his own Hungarian accent. The immortal *Dracula* has spawned countless sequels.

Lugosi mesmerizes Helen Chandler in *Dracula* (31).

Die Dreigroschenoper   (1931) GERMANY, DIRECTOR – G W PABST

Famed director Pabst did an outstanding job of directing this screen adaptation of the Bertolt Brecht/Kurt Weill musical play *Die Dreigroschenoper/The Threepenny Opera* though Brecht objected to some of the changes and sued the production company. The essential story is taken from John Gay's eighteenth century *The Beggar's Opera* but the play and movie are set in nineteenth century London where Mack The Knife, the brutal amoral hero, makes his way in a corrupt dehumanized society where everything and everybody is for sale. Lotte Lenya and Rudolph Forster star. The movie was made in both German and French. The French version, titled *L'Opéra de Quat'sous* stars Albert Prejean.

Louis Calhern is suspicious of Chico and Harpo Marx in *Duck Soup* (33).

Duck Soup (1933) USA, DIRECTOR – LEO McCAREY

Only sixty-eight perfect minutes long this is a whimsical beautifully directed Marx Brothers picture with Margaret Dumont and Louis Calhern. Groucho portrays Rufus T Firefly, leader of Fredonia who declares war on a neighboring country. Zeppo is Groucho's aide-de-camp. Harpo and Chico are enemy spies. The movie differs from other Marx Brothers films in that Harpo doesn't play the harp, Chico doesn't play the piano, and there is no romantic interlude. Groucho zings out a steady barrage of one-liners though and the film contains some of the best known scenes featuring the Marx Brothers, notably the famous mirror sequence and the lemonade stall, a classic Groucho–Chico confrontation.

Dumbo (1941) USA, DIRECTOR – BEN SHARPSTEEN, WALT DISNEY STUDIO

This full-length (64 minutes) animated technicolor cartoon feature introduces one of Disney's most enduring anthropomorphic animals, a flying circus elephant named *Dumbo*. For pure melodrama the movie's hard to beat as the little elephant strives to overcome the handicap of his huge ears. Scenes between baby Dumbo and his mother are genuinely tender. There's a wonderful drunken nightmare sequence, some very rude and irreverent crows, enough cruelty to sadden any pro-elephant audience and a happy ending. The score by Frank Churchill and Oliver Wallace was nominated for an Academy Award and contains several wonderful songs, including 'Baby Mine' and 'Pink Elephants on Parade'. Along with Disney's *Bambi* this movie helped raise the public's awareness of animals as living creatures deserving of humane treatment.

E.T.   (1982) USA, DIRECTOR – STEVEN SPIELBERG

A worldwide success of almost mythic proportions *E.T. The Extra-Terrestrial* is a sci-fi fantasy which has been compared to the 1939 masterpiece, *The Wizard Of Oz*. Originally titled *A Boy's Life*, *E.T.* is about a lovable toddler-sized creature from outer space stranded in a Los Angeles suburb. Three children protect E.T. from a hostile adult world which would mistreat him in the name of science.

After numerous adventures and hair's breadth escapes E.T. is finally allowed to return to his own planet. Dee Wallace as the children's mother, Henry Thomas, Peter Coyote, Drew Barrymore as the children and Robert MacNaughton star. It remains Spielberg's best film to date.

The lost alien of *E.T.* (82) was designed by Carlo Rambaldi.

Earth   (1930) USSR, DIRECTOR – ALEXANDER PETROVICH DOVZHENKO

The director's greatest film and a triumph of silent cinema, *Earth/Zemlya* is a lyric visual poem about the glories of nature, and the rhythms of life, love and death in a rustic world. The movie is set in a Ukranian village and the basic plot concerns a landowner who refuses to yield his property to a collective farm. The fine cinematography is the work of Danylo Demutsky. Dovzhenko was steeped in his subject. Though patriotic and a Communist Party member he was the son of a Ukranian peasant. But despite his politics and credentials the movie was attacked as counterrevolutionary in the USSR and several key scenes were cut from the original version.

East Of Eden   (1955) USA, DIRECTOR – ELIA KAZAN

The legendary James Dean had his first starring role in this fascinating melodrama based on John Steinbeck's novel which echoes biblical themes. In a rural California valley during World War I two sons compete for their father's love. Raymond Massey played the father Adam while Dean starred as the troublesome son Cal. Abra, the girl loved by both brothers was played by Julie Harris and Oscar winner Jo Van Fleet gave a brilliant performance as the boys' mother, who while believed dead, has become the tough durable madame of a brothel. Dick Davalos costarred as the innocent brother Aron who is destroyed when Cal tells him the truth about their mother. Writer Paul Osborne, director Kazan, and actor Dean all received Oscar nominations.

James Dean, Julie Harris, Richard Davalos – *East of Eden* (55).

Easter Parade (1948) USA, DIRECTOR – CHARLES WALTERS

Gene Kelly was originally slated to play the lead in this colorful musical but when he broke his ankle he suggested Fred Astaire replace him. Astaire took the part, appearing opposite Judy Garland with Ann Miller, Peter Lawford, Clinton Sundberg, and Jules Munshin adding to the fun. The simple plot about a dancer quarreling with his partner and finding another is really just an excuse for the wonderful Irving Berlin numbers which include Ann Miller 'Shaking the Blues Away' and Astaire and Garland dressed up as bums singing 'We're A Couple of Swells.' This movie is the only time Garland and Astaire appeared together on screen.

Easy Rider (1969) USA, DIRECTOR – DENNIS HOPPER

After years of appearing in horror films, Jack Nicholson got his big break in this quintessential 1960's film playing a lawyer who drops out of the system, and earned an Oscar nomination for the role. Made for a pittance and grossing millions the film follows a couple of drop-outs portrayed by Peter Fonda and Dennis Hopper on a motorcycle odyssey across America during the era of Vietnam War protests. It touched all the bases in its youth-oriented presentation of a society seen through the eyes of the alienated. Popular music of the era, Easter mysticism, the celebration of drugs, freedom, and communes all have their place in the film. *Easy Rider* captures a certain aspect of the romance envisaged in the idea of dropping out.

Drop-outs Peter Fonda and Dennis Hopper are ambushed by rednecks during their trip in *Easy Rider* (69).

Eight And A Half (1963) ITALY, DIRECTOR – FEDERICO FELLINI

Fellini considered *Otto e Mezzo/8½* his eighth and a half production, hence the odd title. It was Fellini's seventh solo effort while three prior collaborations he counted as a half each. Self-analytical, unorthodox, confessional and wonderfully inventive, the autobiographical film, part fact and part fantasy, concerns a successful movie director who in Fellini's own words is 'trying to pull together the pieces of his life and make sense of them.' Marcello Mastroianni portrays the director. The women in his life are Claudia Cardinale, Anouk Aimée, Sandra Milo, Rosella Falk, Barbara Steele, and Madeleine Lebeau. Winner of a Best Foreign Film Oscar the movie formed the basis of a 1982 hit Broadway musical called *Nine*.

Les Enfants Du Paradis   (1945) FRANCE, DIRECTOR — MARCEL CARNÉ

Arletty is a vision of beauty and femininity in this great masterpiece of cinema, the evocative creation of a brilliant and poetic duo of artists, director Carné and screenwriter Jacques Prévert. Richly detailed with stunning sets and outstanding cinematography *Les Enfants du Paradis/ Children of Paradise* is a romantic pictorial epic set in the Paris theatre world in the 1840s which tells the tale of a mime who falls in love. The superb cast also includes Jean-Louis Barrault, Pierre Brasseur, Marcel Herrand and Maria Casares. Prévert received an Oscar nomination for his witty and poignant script.

Maria Casares gazes at Jean-Louis Barrault who gave a stunning portrayal of the love-struck mime in *Les Enfants du Paradis* (45).

The Exorcist   (1973) USA, DIRECTOR — WILLIAM FRIEDKIN

William Blatty wrote the Oscar-winning screenplay based on his own best-selling novel. Max Von Sydow and Jason Miller played the priests conducting the exorcism on the young girl possessed by a demon, played by Linda Blair. Oscar nominations showered down on this movie whose scary and sickening special effects are incredibly vivid. Nominees included Blair, Ellen Burstyn who played the thankless role of the possessed girl's mother, director Friedkin, cinematographer Owen Roizman, and actor Miller. Mercedes McCambridge provided the voice of the demon. A 1977 sequel starring Blair, Von Sydow and Richard Burton was so bad one wonders what possessed anyone to make it.

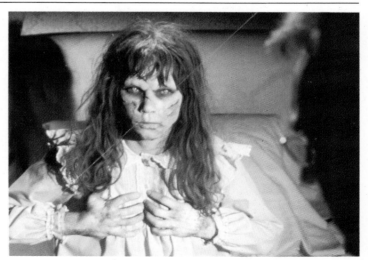

Priest Max von Sydow confronts Linda Blair as the young girl possessed by a demon in *The Exorcist* (73).

The Face/The Magician   (1958) SWEDEN, DIRECTOR – INGMAR BERGMAN

Directorial genius Bergman and master cameraman Gunnar Fischer crafted this film about a nineteenth-century mesmerist who when partially exposed as a fraud takes a surrealistic revenge. It is a darkly disturbing film, centering on a confrontation between a skeptical and rational doctor brilliantly played by Gunnar Bjornstrand and the magician played by Max Von Sydow in a bravura performance. Other outstanding members of the cast include Ingrid Thulin, Naima Wifstrand, Ake Fridell, Lars Ekborg and Bengt Ekerot. Many critics consider the film to be an allegorical vision of Christianity and its survival.

Fanny And Alexander   (1982) SWEDEN/FRANCE/WEST GERMANY, DIRECTOR – INGMAR BERGMAN

A beautiful fantasy about childhood complete with magic, villainy and melodrama, *Fanny and Alexander* is a work of art revealing the director's great range, his compassion, and a rare inspired sense of joy. Set in the early part of the century, the movie tells the story of a brother and sister from a warm, loving, and colorful theater family. Ugliness and danger enter this enchanting little world in the guise of a wicked and puritanical churchman who becomes the children's stepfather. The fairy tale quality of the movie increases as adventures multiply. It's a near miss but Fanny and Alexander escape and the movie ends happily. The cast which includes Pernilla Allwin, Bertil Guve and Erland Josephson is splendid and Sven Nykvist's cinematography which won an Academy Award superb. The film was honored as Best Foreign Language Film of 1983, and won Academy Awards for Costume and Art Direction as well.

Pernilla Allwin and Bertil Guve played the children in *Fanny and Alexander* (82).

Fantasia   (1940) USA, WALT DISNEY

Visual cartoon images combined with classical music make this one of the most original and creative films ever produced by the Walt Disney Studio. Leopold Stokowski conducts the Philadelphia Orchestra and radio commentator Deems Taylor introduces each selection. Credit for this imaginative and cinematic work must go to the over one thousand members of the Disney staff who put this series of animated selections together as well as Disney himself with special honors going to production supervisor Ben Sharpsteen. The film is enormously varied and includes Mickey Mouse as Paul Dukas' 'The Sorcerer's Apprentice', balletic hippos and ostriches in Hamilcare Ponchielli's 'The Dance of the Hours' and a visually hypnotic supernatural version of Modest Mussorgsky's 'Night on a Bare Mountain.'

Right: Mickey Mouse as Paul Dukas' 'The Sorcerer's Apprentice', in the enchanting Walt Disney masterpiece *Fantasia* (40).

Farewell My Lovely   (1944) USA, DIRECTOR – EDWARD DYMTRYK

Dick Powell made a stunning and highly successful transition from playing boyish crooners in movie musicals to playing tough guys on screen thanks to this fine *film noir* with a screenplay by John Paxton based on the novel by Raymond Chandler. Powell, Claire Trevor, Mike Mazurki, and Otto Kruger costar in this tale of a private eye searching for an ex-con's missing girl friend. Harry J Wild was responsible for the excellent cinematography which captures the seediness of the original novel. Roy Webb crafted the musical score that sets the right mood. A more than decent remake was released in 1975 starring Robert Mitchum as Philip Marlowe.

La Femme Du Boulanger   (1938) FRANCE, DIRECTOR – MARCEL PAGNOL

The wonderful script was written by director Pagnol who viewed all film as a means of capturing stage plays for posterity and getting plays into wider circulation via the screen. This bit of photographed theater stars the great actor Raimu in a peasant fable about a baker who loses interest in making good bread once his wife proves unfaithful. The country folk set things straight by putting an end to the wife's misbehavior. A fond look at village life the movie received worldwide critical acclaim. With Raimu in *La Femme du Boulanger/The Baker's Wife* are Ginette Leclerc, Charles Moulin, Charpin and Maximilienne.

Rudolph Valentino tangoes in *The Four Horsemen of the Apocalypse* (21).

The Four Horsemen Of The Apocalypse   (1921) USA, DIRECTOR – REX INGRAM

Love, war and death all have their place in this exotic silent movie about a young Argentinian who fights for France during World War I. Best known as the movie that made Rudolph Valentino a star, it is still an exciting spectacle. Until *The Four Horsemen Of The Apocalypse* Valentino was little more than a bit player. The lead role came to him thanks to the efforts of the movie's screenwriter June

Mathis who lobbied hard on his behalf. Seemingly overnight Valentino became the sex symbol of the decade, the image of mysterious eroticism to women, the image of foppish ludicrousness to red-blooded American men. The movie, based on a book by Vincente Blasco-Ibanez, was remade in 1961 with Glenn Ford.

Frankenstein   (1931) USA, DIRECTOR – JAMES WHALE

Director Whale's seminal masterpiece, a trail blazer in the genre of horror films, stars Boris Karloff as the monster and Colin Clive as Dr Frankenstein with Mae Clark, Edward Van Sloan, Frederick Kerr and Dwight Frye in archetypal roles. Despite the heavy makeup applied by Jack Pierce, Karloff's monster is no mere thing but a tormented creature who arouses pity as well as fear and the performance is a sensitive *tour de force*. The movie is

one in a long line of man as monster films and it was heavily influenced by German silents, notably *The Golem* (1920). But it was this version of Mary Shelley's novel about a scientist creating life from dead flesh that set the tone for the innumerable sequels that followed.

Left: Boris Karloff played the fearsome but also pitiful monster in the original version of *Frankenstein* (31).

Freaks   (1932) USA, DIRECTOR – TOD BROWNING

Many of the stars of *Freaks* were freaks which is why the movie is macabre and horrifying yet wakens sympathy. The movie was originally conceived of as MGM's answer to Universal's successful horror film *Frankenstein* (1931) but *Freaks* was thought to be so gruesome it was finally disowned by MGM and banned in many places. Set in a traveling circus it focuses on a beautiful trapeze artist (Olga Baclanova) who agrees to marry a midget (Harry

Earles) because she wants his money. When she tries to poison the midget the freaks take their revenge by turning her into the most hideous freak of all. This one-of-a-kind movie is based on a 1923 magazine story called *Spurs* by Tod Robbins.

Olga Baclanova, once a beautiful trapeze artist, becomes the most hideous freak of all in *Freaks* (32).

The French Connection   (1971) USA, DIRECTOR – WILLIAM FRIEDKIN

Gene Hackman starred as tough Detective Jimmy (Popeye) Doyle and costar Roy Scheider played Hackman's partner in this movie with a semi-documentary look which shows New York police in hot pursuit of a smooth French drug dealer portrayed by Fernando Rey. Based on a book by Robin Moore about a real case the movie features real life French Connection participants

Eddie Egan and Sonny Grosso in small roles and uses real New York locales. The movie boasts an amazing chase scene involving a car and an elevated train. Winner of five Academy Awards including Best Picture the movie brought Hackman and director Friedkin Oscars and Scheider received a nomination. A sequel, *French Connection II*, followed four years later.

Deborah Kerr and Burt Lancaster in *From Here to Eternity* (53).

From Here To Eternity   (1953) USA, DIRECTOR – FRED ZINNEMANN

Based on James Jones' novel, this movie about soldiers and the women in their lives is set in Hawaii at the time of Pearl Harbor. Burt Lancaster heads a cast which includes Deborah Kerr, Frank Sinatra, Donna Reed, Ernest Borgnine and Montgomery Clift, who was outstanding as the tough Southerner, Robert E Lee Prewitt. Heavy on sex, soap opera, and sentimentality the movie took the public by storm. Sinatra won an Oscar for Best Supporting Actor for his role as Maggio, reviving his sagging career. Kerr became a sex symbol thanks to the notorious beach scene with Lancaster. Reed won an Oscar for stepping out of character to play the 'hostess' of a popular 'hangout'. The film also won the Oscar for Best Picture and Zinnemann, Best Director.

The Front Page   (1931) USA, DIRECTOR – LEWIS MILESTONE

Nobody quite knew how to handle sound till this fast-paced comedy with the crackling dialogue showed Hollywood how to make talkies. Bartlett Cormack and Charles Lederer adapted Ben Hecht's and Charles MacArthur's stage play set in a Chicago newsroom brilliantly. Pat O'Brien stars as the ace reporter who thinks he wants marriage and a quiet life, and Adolphe Menjou costars as the tough editor who will go to any lengths to keep his best man on the job. The movie was remade in 1940 as *His Girl Friday* with Rosalind Russell as the reporter and Cary Grant as her boss. It was remade again in 1974 with Jack Lemmon and Walter Matthau.

Funny Girl   (1968) USA, DIRECTOR – WILLIAM WYLER

This film version of the 1964 Broadway hit musical introduced dynamic superstar Barbra Streisand to the moviegoing public, instantly winning her hordes of new fans and an Academy Award. Streisand recreates the role she played in the Broadway original, as Fanny Brice, a homely Jewish girl from New York who became one of the best loved comediennes in show business. Handsome Omar Sharif plays Brice's husband Nickey Arnstein, known for his shady business deals. The romanticized version of the stormy Brice/Arnstein marriage gives Streisand plenty to sing about, including 'My Man' and 'Don't Rain on My Parade.' A sequel, *Funny Lady*, with James Caan as Brice's second husband Billy Rose, was released in 1975.

Barbra Streisand played the title role in *Funny Girl* (68).

Gallipoli   (1981) AUSTRALIA, DIRECTOR – PETER WEIR

Gallipoli starring Mark Lee and Mel Gibson, is a good example of the high quality of Australian films. The movie is generally about the stupidity and barbarism of war in general but is also presents a critical view of the British role in the Gallipoli campaign during World War I where Australians died in excessive numbers. The movie concerns two friends who enlist in 1915. En route from Perth they learn about life and the audience learns about Australia. The movie ends tragically with the futile death of one of the young men in the Dardanelles.

Gandhi   (1982) GREAT BRITAIN, DIRECTOR – RICHARD ATTENBOROUGH

In Ben Kingsley producer/director Attenborough found the perfect actor to play the title role in this vast epic biography with its cast of thousands which includes Candice Bergen, Edward Fox and Trevor Howard. Kingsley won the Best Actor Oscar for his portrayal of the great leader of the Indian non-violent revolutionary movement, aging on screen with remarkable skill. Kingsley, in his debut screen performance was not the only winner. The movie swept the Academy Awards, bringing Oscars to screenwriter John Briley and Attenborough among others. Though it is never truly inspirational *Gandhi*, partly funded by the Indian government, is a grand and impressive portrait of an extraordinary human being and his times.

Ben Kingsley won an Oscar for his portrayal of *Gandhi* (82).

The Garden Of Allah   (1936) USA, DIRECTOR – RICHARD BOLESLAWSKI

Realism isn't the strong point of this elegant romance. Color photography is, thanks to Oscar-winning cinematographer W Howard Greene. *The Garden of Allah* was a giant step forward for technicolor, an elegant film about a beautiful sophisticated woman who falls in love in the Algerian desert. She marries the man she loves who alas turns out to be a renegade Trappist monk. Marlene Dietrich, Charles Boyer and a great lush score by Max Steiner make the movie a treat for film buffs. Two silent versions of *The Garden Of Allah* preceded this film, the first in 1917 with Tom Santschi and Helen Ware and the second in 1927 starring Ivan Petrovich and Alice Terry.

Gaslight   (1944) USA, DIRECTOR – GEORGE CUKOR

In 1940 a British movie called *Gaslight* was released in the United States under the title *Angel Street* starring Diana Wynyard and Anton Walbrook. MGM bought the film and destroyed most of the prints and negative, then remade *Gaslight* with Ingrid Bergman as the lovely young wife and Charles Boyer as the suave but wicked husband trying to drive her mad. Joseph Cotten costars as the Inspector from Scotland Yard who believes her. Making her film debut was Angela Lansbury, as an impudent Cockney maid. The movie is highly suspenseful and the fog-swept streets and ornate sets evoke a romanticized Victorian atmosphere. Bergman won an Oscar for her role in the film, and Lansbury received a nomination. In Britain the movie is sometimes titled *The Murder In Thornton Square*.

Ingrid Bergman keeps a wakeful eye on her manipulative husband, Charles Boyer, in the American version of *Gaslight* (44).

Gate Of Hell   (1953) JAPAN, DIRECTOR – TEINOSUKE KINUGASA

Gate of Hell/Jigokumon, a traditional film in its homeland, helped create a vogue for Japanese films in the west. Formal visual style combined with a glorious use of color make this adaptation of a medieval legend, based on a novel by Kan Kikuchi, an esthetic experience. The movie, set in the twelfth century, tells the story of that ever popular Japanese hero, a samurai, who requests a particular woman as his reward at the end of a war, but the woman is married. The movie stars Machiko Kyo, Kazuo Hasegawa and Isao Yamagata. Kohei Suziyama is the masterful cinematographer. The movie won a Best Foreign Film Oscar.

The Gay Divorcee   (1934) USA, DIRECTOR – MARK SANDRICH

After Fred Astaire and Ginger Rogers impressed audiences as minor characters in *Flying Down To Rio* RKO decided to give them a picture all their own. The show RKO chose was a musical that Astaire had done on Broadway called *Gay Divorce*. Hollywood's Hays office demanded a change in title, divorce being a tabu word. Divorcee was allowed. In the film Astaire plays dancer Guy Holden while Rogers plays the divorcee Mimi Glossop. The movie has more laughs than dances but the big number is 'The Continental'. Edward Everett Horton does a dandy number himself called 'Lets K-nock K-nees' with a pretty unknown blonde named Betty Grable. Costars Erik Rhodes and Eric Blore had also appeared in the Broadway show.

The General   (1926) USA, DIRECTOR – BUSTER KEATON

This splendid comedy loaded with some of the most ingenious sight gags was director Keaton's own favorite. The great stone faced clown of silent films also stars in the cleverly conceived and astonishingly well executed tale of an engineer of a Confederate train during the Civil War who loses both his train and his girl to the Union side temporarily. Marion Mack and Glen Cavander appear with Keaton and there's action and adventure as well as laughs before Keaton retrieves both the train and the girl. The movie is roughly based on a true Civil War incident which also formed the basis of a straight adventure film made by Walt Disney in 1956 called *The Great Locomotive Chase*.

Buster Keaton salutes Marion Mack in *The General* (26).

Il Generale Della Rovere (1959) ITALY/FRANCE, DIRECTOR – ROBERTO ROSSELLINI

Director Rossellini's once brilliant and innovative career had been in decline for several years. This film went a long way towards restoring his reputation. Set during World War II, the film tells of an opportunistic con man who impersonates a dead general, grows to accept his ideals and becomes a hero by choosing to face a firing squad rather than betray his code of honor. Vittorio de Sica is magnificent as the imposter. The screenplay written by Sergio Amedei, Diego Fabbri, Indro Mantanelli and Rossellini received an Oscar nomination. The director's brother Renzo Rossellini scored the film.

Vittorio de Sica starred as the imposter in Roberto Rossellini's *Il Generale Della Rovere* (59).

Ghostbusters

(1984) USA, DIRECTOR – IVAN REITMAN

Boasting dazzling special effects and a spirit akin to Bud Abbott/Lou Costello movies of the 1940s this film was a monumental smash hit. Bill Murray plays the wise-cracking cynic, Harold Ramis the weirdo, and Dan Akroyd the fool to end all fools in this humorous tale of pseudoparapsychologists armed with high tech weapons who pursue ghosts but who are just as likely to be pursued by them. After struggles in the New York Public Library and an apartment house on Central Park West, the film culminates in the return of an ancient god who sends a giant marshmallow man rampaging through Manhattan. Sigourney Weaver plays the woman with the haunted apartment, a role reminiscent of the sort Dorothy Lamour played in the road movies with Bob Hope and Bing Crosby.

Bill Murray, Dan Akroyd and Harold Ramis as the *Ghostbusters* (84) stake out an apartment on the West Side of New York for ghosts but meet instead an ancient god who threatens the destruction of the city.

The Ghost Goes West

(1936) GREAT BRITAIN, DIRECTOR – RENÉ CLAIR

One of the all-time charmers this movie is a whimsical delight which stars Robert Donat in a dual role. An American millionaire buys a Scottish castle and moves it stone by stone to his native land. Where the castle goes so goes the rakish ghost who haunts it. Donat plays both the ghost and ghost's descendant. Despite the Scottish jokes the guiding genius behind the film is the Frenchman René Clair, at the top of his form crafting this witty fantasy. Jean Parker as the millionaire's daughter who marries the ghost's descendant, Eugene Pallette as the millionaire, Elsa Lanchester, Ralph Bunker, Patricia Hilliard and Morton Shelton adroitly round out the cast.

Gigi (1958) USA, DIRECTOR – VINCENTE MINNELLI

Shot almost entirely in Paris *Gigi* based on a story by Colette concerns a young girl (Leslie Caron) raised to be a courtesan who gains the heart of a bored Parisian played by Louis Jordan. Instead of merely snagging him as a lover Gigi is asked to become his wife. Betty Wand did the vocals for Leslie Caron while Maurice Chevalier did his own singing including 'Thank Heaven For Little Girls'.

Hermione Gingold, Isabel Jeans, Jacques Bergerac, Eva Gabor and John Abbot round out the cast. Alan Jay Lerner and Frederick Loewe's music and Cecil Beaton's glorious *fin de siecle* costumes and lavish sets helped make this a hit. *Gigi* received numerous Oscar nominations and won nine of them including Best Picture.

Gilda (1946) USA, DIRECTOR – CHARLES VIDOR

This *film noir* exemplified the cynical movies which emerged right after World War II and which seemed all the more decadent at the time because wartime Hollywood had concentrated so heavily on screen sweetness and light. *Gilda* concerns a gambler in South America who rediscovers a woman he's known before. Their torrid love-hate relationship is rekindled but the woman is now the wife of the gambler's treacherous new boss and mentor. Rita Hayworth's Gilda is lushly sexy. Her rendition of the song 'Put The Blame On Mame' is legendary. Glenn Ford, George Macready, Steve Geray and Joseph Calleia costar. Marion Parsonnet's script, Vidor's direction and Rudolph Maté's strong black-and-white cinematography are first-rate.

Rita Hayworth in the title role is best remembered for her sexy rendition of 'Put the Blame on Mame' in *Gilda* (46).

The Godfather (1972) USA, DIRECTOR – FRANCIS FORD COPPOLA

Images of family life are strikingly interspersed with scenes of graphic violence in this saga of the Mafia in America, an Oscar-winning movie based on Mario Puzo's best-selling novel. Brilliantly directed the film traces the rise of Michael Corleone, played by Al Pacino, in the family business which is organized crime. Marlon Brando gave a magnificent performance as Pacino's father the old Don, Vito Corleone and won the Oscar for Best Actor. A major

achievement in the genre of Hollywood gangster films *The Godfather* also features outstanding performances by Robert Duvall, James Caan, Diane Keaton, Alex Rocco, Sterling Hayden, Talia Shire, John Cazale and the entire cast.

Marlon Brando won an Oscar for his performance as Don Vito Corleone, Al Pacino's father, in *The Godfather* (72).

The Godfather, Part II (1974) USA, DIRECTOR – FRANCIS FORD COPPOLA

The sequel to *The Godfather* this movie rounds out the story of the Corleone family. Robert De Niro plays Vito Corleone in his early days in Italy and later in America. After Don Vito Corleone's death the movie picks up the tale of his son Michael where the first movie left off. A fine epic about corruption the movie won the Oscar for Best Picture and brought Oscars to Coppola and De Niro. Oscar

nominations went to Al Pacino as Michael, Lee Strasberg, Michael V Gazzo and Talia Shire. A videocassette version of the original film and the sequel merged and running in chronological order was released as *The Godfather Saga – 1902-1958* with a running time of seven and a half hours.

Going My Way (1944) USA, DIRECTOR – LEO McCAREY

Bing Crosby plays a young priest assigned to the parish of Barry Fitzgerald. The two overcome their differences and bring sweetness and light to a New York slum parish in this incredibly popular sentimental comedy. *Going My Way* won the Best Picture Academy Award and Crosby, Fitzgerald and McCarey also won Oscars. Winners, too, were songwriters James Van Heusen and Johnny Burke

who took Oscars for their now classic song, 'Swinging On A Star'. Crosby's character, Father O'Malley, the singing priest, proved such a hit with moviegoers that Crosby played him again in the *The Bells Of St. Mary's* (1945). Appearing with Crosby in *The Bells Of St Mary's* was Ingrid Bergman as a nun.

The famous 'Shadow's Waltz' sequence in *Gold Diggers of 1933* (33).

Gold Diggers Of 1933 (1933) USA, DIRECTOR – MERVYN LeROY

The original *The Gold Diggers* was a play done in 1919. The light hearted plot was based on the idea that rich men like chorus girls and chorus girls like rich men. A variation of this essential theme cropped up in a 1929 silent early technicolor film called *Gold Diggers Of Broadway*. Then came the 1933 sound version of chorines in search of golden wedding bands. This one's the best, outshining the rest of the series that followed. *Gold Diggers of 1933* has

beautiful girls in songs like 'We're In The Money' and 'Pettin' In The Park' by Busby Berkeley. Joan Blondell, Aline MacMahon and Ruby Keeler are the chorus girls. Dick Powell plays a rich young man who wants to prove himself as a songwriter. Guy Kibbee and Warren William costar. Though pure escapism the movie weaves the depression right into its plot, through Joan Blondell's rendition of 'My Forgotten Man.'

The Gold Rush (1925) USA, DIRECTOR – CHARLES CHAPLIN

Perhaps it was his impoverished childhood which gave Chaplin the material he needed to create sympathetic characters on the bottom of the social heap trying to survive in a brutal world, characters which made audiences laugh and cry. *The Gold Rush* beautifully combines Chaplin's ability to express pathos, tenderness, humor, and social awareness and many critics consider it his finest work. The movie is about a prospector in the Yukon who encounters other prospectors, dancehall girls and adventure. Perfectionist Chaplin at the top of his form as a clown and mime slowly constructs a rising crescendo of sight gags in this silent film. A sound version was released in 1942.

Charles Chaplin – a starving prospector in *The Gold Rush* (25).

Der Golem (1920) GERMANY, DIRECTOR – PAUL WEGENER

Wegener made his screen debut in 1913 and a year later appeared in and co-directed his first film version of *Der Golem*. He created another version in 1917. Later other directors in other countries would bring the ancient and mystical Jewish legend to the screen. But Wegener's third version made in 1920 is a definitive one. Wegener co-wrote the script and also played the monster in this tale of a sixteenth-century Jewish rabbi in Prague who brings a clay monster to life to save his people from a pogrom. The medieval sets, make-up, Karl Freund's cinematography, and the acting performances are superb. The movie heavily influenced numerous Hollywood films especially *Frankenstein* (1931).

Paul Wegener played the made-of-clay monster *Der Golem* (20) which was based on a sixteenth century Jewish legend.

Gone With The Wind

(1939) USA, DIRECTORS – VICTOR FLEMING, GEORGE CUKOR, SAM WOOD

A legend in its own time and a legend today this vast technicolor epic based on Margaret Mitchell's novel of a woman's coming of age against the background of the American Civil War is also a love story packed with adventure. British actress Vivien Leigh made her American debut in the movie, winning an Academy Award for her perfect portrayal of the beautiful and willful Southern belle Scarlett O'Hara. Clark Gable costarred as the notorious blockade runner Rhett Butler. Olivia de Havilland played the virtuous Melanie and Leslie Howard the dreamer, Ashley Wilkes. Black actress Hattie McDaniel won an Academy Award for her performance as Mammy. Awards were also won by the film itself, screenwriter Sidney Howard and director Victor Fleming.

Below: Clark Gable, Vivien Leigh and Olivia de Havilland look on as Ashley (Leslie Howard) has his wound attended by Dr Meade (Harry Davenport). *Right:* Rhett Butler and Scarlett O'Hara.

Terry Kilburn and Robert Donat in *Goodbye, Mr Chips* (39).

Goodbye, Mr Chips (1939) GREAT BRITAIN, DIRECTOR – SAM WOOD

This engaging sentimental biography of a shy schoolmaster stars Robert Donat in the title role. The movie follows the life of Mr Chips from his first job to his death and Donat ages on screen from twenty-five to eighty-three, a remarkable performance, which won him an Academy Award. Sentimental, gently humorous, and immensely popular the movie was the creation of MGM's British studio. Actress Greer Garson made her screen debut in *Goodbye, Mr Chips*, as Chips' wife, and she, director Wood, the movie itself, and the script received Oscar nominations. The movie was remade in 1969 as a musical starring Peter O'Toole and Petula Clark. A BBC TV serial with Roy Marsden was made in 1983.

The Gospel According To St Matthew (1964) ITALY/FRANCE, DIRECTOR – PIER PAOLO PASOLINI

Writer/director Pasolini combined radical Marxism with unorthodox religious beliefs and his provocative films frequently got him into trouble with the authorities. In 1962 he was arrested in Italy on the charge of having insulted the Catholic Church in the movie *Rogopag*. What Pasolini had done was parody biblical extravaganzas. The arrest gave him the idea of making his own straightforward version of a biblical film. *Il Vangelo Secondo Matteo/The Gospel According To St Matthew* presents the life of Christ almost as a documentary, simply and realistically. Most of the film's roles are played by non-professional actors with Pasolini's mother as the Virgin Mary.

The Graduate   (1967) USA, DIRECTOR – MIKE NICHOLS

Dustin Hoffman got his first starring role in this gentle satire about American values, which won the Academy Award for Best Picture. Hoffman played a recent college graduate, aimless and insecure, who is seduced by an older woman (Anne Bancroft) who is the wife of his father's business partner and then falls in love with her daughter portrayed by Katharine Ross. Everything about this movie is delicious from the acting which brought Hoffman, Bancroft, and Ross Oscar nominations to the direction, which won the talented Nichols an Oscar. The music of Simon and Garfunkel helped popularize the film.

Dustin Hoffman cautiously eyes the fine legs of Anne Bancroft, the older woman who seduces him in *The Graduate* (67).

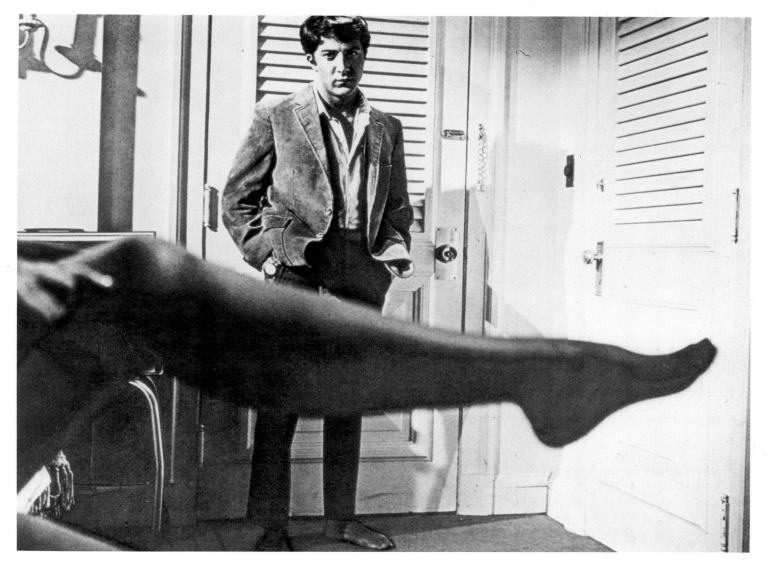

Grand Hotel   (1932) USA, DIRECTOR – EDMUND GOULDING

Set in a grand hotel in Berlin where guests and staff find their lives intertwined the movie is an episodic series of interlocking dramas. MGM received an Oscar for the film which was one of the earliest to feature top talent ensemble acting. The cast includes Greta Garbo as the dancer, John Barrymore who falls in love with her, Lionel Barrymore as the dying clerk, Kringelein, Joan Crawford as the stenographer Flaemmchen and Wallace Beery as the financier Preysing. The movie really captures the feel of a great European meeting place successfully aided by the beautiful Art Deco sets of Cedric Gibbons. The movie was remade as *Weekend At the Waldorf* in 1945 with Ginger Rogers, Van Johnson, Walter Pidgeon and Lana Turner.

Joan Crawford, Wallace Beery and John Barrymore in *Grand Hotel* (32).

La Grande Illusion   (1937) FRANCE, DIRECTOR – JEAN RENOIR

Jean Renoir co-wrote as well as directed this restrained magnificently constructed anti-war film which is set in a German Prisoner Of War camp in 1917. The film stars Pierre Fresnay and Jean Gabin as two of the French prisoners. Erich Von Stroheim whose silent film *Foolish Wives* influenced Renoir deeply plays the camp's German commandant. The film's tragic force and potent impact do not result from the dramatic theme alone nor does the film's power come from the heroism of the captured prisoners. The movie's strength is due to its brilliant examination of the personal relationships of the characters and the way they are affected by nationalism and social class. The internationally acclaimed film received a nomination for Best Picture.

The Grapes Of Wrath   (1940) USA, DIRECTOR – JOHN FORD

Oscar winning director John Ford directed this Oscar winning American classic based on the novel by John Steinbeck. Henry Fonda starred as the unjustly convicted ex-con Tom Joad, and Oscar-winner Jane Darwell played Joad's strong enduring mother in this tale of a family of poor farmers who migrate from the midwestern dustbowl to the valleys of California during the depression. The movie represents the highest flowering of social compassion and concern for social problems to emerge in those troubled times. Gregg Toland's stark cinematography, Nunnally Johnson's moving script, Ford's brilliant direction and Alfred Newman's musical score are notable achievements. Besides Fonda and Darwell, John Carradine and Charley Grapewin turn in superb performances.

The Great Dictator   (1940) USA, DIRECTOR – CHARLES CHAPLIN

Chaplin plays two characters, a Jewish barber and Adenoid Hynkel, dictator of Tomania, in this satire on Adolf Hitler and the Nazis while Jack Oakie plays Benzini Napaloni, the dictator of Bacteria, a spoof of Mussolini. Henry Daniell and Bill Gilbert costar as Hynkel's aides Garbitsch and Herring. The movie, Chaplin's first talkie, represented a departure for the artist who generally worked with an incomplete screenplay and a very long shooting schedule. *The Great Dictator* follows a tight script and was completed in twelve weeks. Chaplin addressed the audience directly as himself in the last seven minutes of the movie to plead against man's inhumanity to man. The film marks the last time Chaplin used the little tramp characterization.

The Great Escape

(1963) USA, DIRECTOR – JOHN STURGES

Humor, action, suspense and a great chase scene all play a part in this epic cinemascope adventure film with the tragic ending. The movie concerns a group of Allied prisoners who plan a major escape from a Prisoner Of War camp, partly with the idea of pulling Germans away from the front to aid in the recapture of the prisoners. Based on a true incident recounted in the book by Paul Brickhill *The Great Escape* boasts super cinematography by Daniel Fapp and an excellent musical score by Elmer Bernstein. The cast includes James Garner, Donald Pleasance, James Coburn, Charles Bronson, Richard Attenborough, David McCallum and Steve McQueen who performed most of his own motorcycle stunts including jumping a ten-foot barbed wire fence. Of the sixty-three prisoners who escaped, fifty were shot after capture. The film is dedicated to the fifty.

Steve McQueen is caught in the barbed wire inches away from the Swiss border, after he had jumped another ten-foot barbed-wire fence in his own motorcycle stunt in *The Great Escape* (63).

Great Expectations (1946) GREAT BRITAIN, DIRECTOR – DAVID LEAN

A superb film adaptation of Charles Dickens's novel the movie is beautifully acted with great attention devoted to mood, atmosphere, and detail. The central character is a young man who since childhood has considered a wealthy eccentric woman to be his benefactor only to discover that the person who helps him make his way in life is an escaped convict he aided when he was a boy. John Mills stars and the cast includes Valerie Hobson, Finlay Currie, Martita Hunt as Miss Havisham, Alec Guinness as Pocket with Jean Simmons as young Estella, the proud beauty reared to disdain men.

Martita Hunt played the recluse Miss Havisham and Valerie Hobson the adult Estella in *Great Expectations* (46).

The Great Train Robbery   (1903) USA, DIRECTOR – EDWIN S PORTER

Marie Murray, Broncho Billy Anderson and George Barnes appear in this movie milestone. One of the longest films of its day, twelve full minutes, with what was then a huge cast consisting of forty performers, *The Great Train Robbery* made box office history. A fast paced, clearly delineated silent western, describing the robbery of a train and the pursuit of the bandits by a posse the movie did not originate new techniques so much as utilize what was available with brilliance. The movie ends with the famous close-up of a bandit firing a pistol at the audience. Enormously influential the movie remained the best-known and profitable film until D W Griffith's *The Birth Of A Nation* (1915).

The Great Train Robbery (03) was a landmark in its day. A full twelve minutes long, the movie was filmed in New Jersey.

Greed   (1923) USA, DIRECTOR – ERICH VON STROHEIM

Adapted from Frank Norris's novel *McTeague* this extraordinarily realistic and dramatic silent movie about a man who murders his greedy wife and later is killed by her ex-fiancé was written as well as directed by the erratic genius Von Stroheim, and represents his most controversial work. The film which stars Gibson Gowland, Zasu Pitts, and Jean Hersholt ran nearly nine hours in the original uncut version. Reluctantly, Von Stroheim allowed the film to be cut from forty-two to twenty-four reels. Against his wishes others cut it further, undermining the movie's power by disrupting its sequential structure. Reviews were mixed though the few who have seen the original acclaim it a remarkable study of human degradation.

Kirk Douglas, Burt Lancaster, John Hudson and De Forrest Kelly in *Gunfight at the OK Corral* (57).

Gunfight At The OK Corral   (1957) USA, DIRECTOR – JOHN STURGES

Burt Lancaster starred as Wyatt Earp and Kirk Douglas played Doc Holliday in this lavish and colorful western which brings a touch of psychology and motivation to the legendary tale of the battle at a Tombstone, Arizona, livery stable where the Clanton gang met their match. Jo Van Fleet, Rhonda Fleming, John Ireland, Frank Faylen, Kenneth Tobey and Earl Holliman round out the cast. The screenplay was written by Leon Uris, and the cinematographer was Charles B Lang. Credit for the musical score goes to Dimitri Tiomkin. The pairing of Lancaster and Douglas was and still is movie magic and this is the most famous Earp/Holliday screen duo.

Gunga Din   (1939) USA, DIRECTOR – GEORGE STEVENS

Joel Sayre, Fred Guiol, Ben Hecht and Charles MacArthur wrote the script for this exciting and comical adventure movie based on Rudyard Kipling's poem about an Indian water carrier. Sam Jaffe played the title role of the *bhisti* who wanted to be a soldier. Cary Grant, Douglas Fairbanks Jr and Victor McLaglen play three sergeants in the British Army, characters based on those in Kipling's *Soldiers Three*. In the course of the film they fight a monomaniac villain (Eduardo Ciannelli), discover temples with golden towers and romance (Joan Fontaine) before the final charge in which Gunga Din proves his courage and is killed.

Cary Grant, Victor McLaglen, Douglas Fairbanks Jr and Sam Jaffe are shown the enemy's position by the evil Gura (Eduardo Ciannelli) in *Gunga Din* (39).

Hail The Conquering Hero   (1944) USA, DIRECTOR — PRESTON STURGES

This wartime movie celebrates American small town life but teases it gently at the same time. Director Sturges is in top form so there's plenty of slapstick comedy and sentiment in this tale of a nervous marine portrayed by Eddie Bracken who when discharged from service because he has hay fever can't face telling his father, World War I hero, Hinky Dinky Truesmith. His buddies see to it that Bracken's hometown thinks he's a hero and Bracken winds up running for mayor. A good cast includes William Demarest, Ella Raines, Franklin Pangborn, Raymond Walburn and Alan Bridge.

Hamlet   (1948) GREAT BRITAIN, DIRECTOR — LAURENCE OLIVIER

Several actors have played Shakespeare's Hamlet on screen including Sir Johnston Forbes Robertson and Asta Nielsen in the silent era but Olivier's is the most famous characterization. The movie, which is a distinctly Freudian and Oedipal interpretation of Shakespeare won the Academy Award for Best Picture and a Best Actor Oscar for Olivier. Other outstanding members of the cast of *Hamlet* include Eileen Herlie as Gertrude, Basil Sydney as Claudius, Felix Aylmer as Polonius, Jean Simmons as Ophelia and Stanley Holloway, incomparable as the gravedigger. Desmond Dickinson's fine cinematography which leads the audience along murky castle corridors sets the right tone for the tragedy of the Danish prince who wishes to avenge his father's death. The brilliant score by Sir William Walton added the correct note of pageantry.

Hannah And Her Sisters   (1986) USA, DIRECTOR — WOODY ALLEN

One of Woody Allen's most critically acclaimed films this sweet serious comedy has a lot to say about the way people hurt one another and help one another grow and change. Mia Farrow plays Hannah, the seemingly stable center of her family. Diane Wiest and Barbara Hershey play her sisters. Lloyd Nolan and Maureen O'Sullivan portray the actor parents of Hannah and her sisters. Michael Caine, Sam Waterston, Carrie Fisher, Daniel Stern, Tony Roberts and Joanna Gleason also appear in this film about complex relationships in the complex city of New York. Max Von Sydow is marvelous as the reclusive artist married to Barbara Hershey and the fine cinematography is by Carlo Di Palma.

A Hard Day's Night   (1964) GREAT BRITAIN, DIRECTOR — RICHARD LESTER

The Beatles seem to embody everything that's best about being young in this fresh charming movie filled with comedy and music. The movie takes the rock stars through a madcap twenty-four hours but for all the fame and fan adoration they seem immensely sane, likeable and innocent. Director Lester brings out each of the Beatles' individuality by refusing to shackle them to anything remotely resembling a plot. The film is realistic, silly and absurd in turns, loaded with slapstick and parody. Gilbert Taylor's cinematography is super and Wilfrid Brambell, Norman Rossington, and Victor Spinetti also turn in fine performances. Scriptwriter Alun Owen and musical director George Martin received Oscar nominations.

George Harrison, Paul McCartney, Ringo Starr and John Lennon with Victor Spinetti in *A Hard Day's Night* (64).

James Stewart introduces Harvey to a worried Josephine Hull in *Harvey* (50).

Harvey (1950) USA, DIRECTOR – HENRY KOSTER

This charming film stars James Stewart as the boozy but amiable Elwood P Dowd whose best friend happens to be a six foot three white rabbit invisible to all but Dowd himself. Attempts to have Dowd put in a sanitarium fail fortunately and he and Harvey are free to go their merry yet gentle way. Oscar Brodney wrote the screenplay with Mary C Chase, the author of the original play. Josephine Hull won an Oscar for her fine performance as the sister anxious to have Dowd committed and Stewart, perfect as the small-town-middle-American looney, received an Oscar nomination. Stewart also played Dowd on stage and on television.

Heaven Can Wait (1943) USA, DIRECTOR – ERNST LUBITSCH

Based on the play *Birthday* by Lazlo Bush-Fekete this Oscar-nominated movie, adapted for the screen by Samson Raphaelson, reveals the famed Lubitsch touch at its surest. Don Ameche stars as the recently deceased gentleman who confesses his youthful peccadilloes to a very elegant Satan played by Laird Cregar. Satan is definitely a sympathetic man of the world and since Ameche is really a decent fellow he is sent upstairs to heaven. Edward Crongjager's technicolor cinematography is lovely and the film's sets and costumes evoke a magic 1890s. Gene Tierney costars as Ameche's wife. Warren Beatty used the title *Heaven Can Wait* when he remade the 1941 movie *Here Comes Mr Jordan* in 1978.

The Heiress (1949) USA, DIRECTOR – WILLIAM WYLER

This extremely decorative movie set in the 1890s is based on Henry James' novella *Washington Square*. Composer Aaron Copland won an Academy Award for his musical score and Olivia de Havilland won one for her portrayal of Catherine Sloper, the wealthy but unattractive heiress who falls in love with a fortune hunter but renounces him at the film's end. Montgomery Clift costarred as the elegant fortune hunter, Morris Townsend. Ruth and August Goetz wrote the successful play based on James's work and adapted it for the screen. A fine cast includes Ralph Richardson, who was nominated for an Oscar, as Dr Sloper and Miriam Hopkins.

Hell's Angels   (1930) USA, DIRECTOR – HOWARD HUGHES

A lavish spectacle about World War I flying aces on both
sides of the war *Hell's Angels* boasts great combat footage,
thanks to the 87 planes and 137 pilots who were involved
in the stunt work, and includes a thrilling zeppelin raid
over London. Ben Lyons and John Darrow star as two of
the fliers. The film was begun as a silent in 1927, and the
heroine was played by the Swedish actress Greta Nissen.
When Hughes reshot the film with sound in 1930, he cast
an American in Nissen's role. Her name was Jean Harlow.
The wonderful cinematography was by Tony Gaudio,
Harry Perry and E Burton Steene. As an action adventure,
this Oscar-nominated film is a milestone in the history of
motion pictures.

Ben Lyons as a World War I flying ace and his beloved Jean
Harlow in *Hell's Angels* (30).

Henry V   (1944) GREAT BRITAIN, DIRECTOR – LAURENCE OLIVIER

Arguably the best film version of a Shakespearean play
ever made, this lively technicolor drama was the first
movie to be directed by Olivier who also produced it and
played the title role. The quality of the film is all the more
remarkable because it was made during World War II
when movie equipment, costumes, props and color film
were in short supply in Great Britain. Though in no sense a
filmed play, *Henry V* begins in the Globe theatre as it
would have been produced originally and moves back to
the reign of the king, but never losing, until the battle, its
essential theatricality. The sets, in proportion and design
are drawn from fifteenth century miniatures. The battle of
Agincourt, the most realistic scene in the film (shot on the
Powerscourt estate in neutral Ireland) is incredibly
stirring. Olivier is superb as the heroic young king and the
outstanding cast includes Robert Newton as Ancient Pistol,
Leslie Banks as the Chorus, Esmond Knight as Fluellen and
Leo Genn as the Constable of France. The stirring score
was composed by William Walton. Olivier was awarded a
special Oscar in 1946 for his total contribution 'in bringing
Henry V to the screen.'

Laurence Olivier as Henry V courts the Princess of France
(Renee Asherson) in his own production of *Henry V* (44).

Here Comes Mr Jordan   (1941) USA, DIRECTOR – ALEXANDER HALL

One of the best fantasy/comedy movies ever to emerge from Hollywood the film stars Robert Montgomery as a boxer, amateur saxophonist, and airplane-crash victim who is taken to heaven by mistake. He returns to earth only to discover that his body has been cremated and he is forced to inhabit another. A fine cast includes Claude Rains as the ministering administrative Mr Jordan. This film was based on the play *Halfway to Heaven* by Harry Segall and was remade by Warren Beatty in 1978 but was retitled *Heaven Can Wait* not to be confused with *Heaven Can Wait* (1943) which starred Don Ameche.

High Noon   (1952) USA, DIRECTOR – FRED ZINNEMANN

John W Cunningham wrote a story called *The Tin Star* and Carl Foreman adapted it for the screen, earning an Oscar nomination, as did director Zinnemann and the picture itself. Dimitri Tiomkin won an Oscar for the famous title song. Gary Cooper won an Academy Award, too, for his role as Will Kane the brave sheriff who must face ruthless killers alone, after the cowardly townspeople abandon Cooper to his fate and his Quaker bride (Grace Kelly) threatens to leave him if he meets violence with violence. Ironically, writer Foreman was blacklisted just after he completed *High Noon's* taut script, and he went into self-imposed exile in Britain, writing under various pseudonymns.

Sheriff Will Kane (Gary Cooper) is left alone to fight the ruthless killers who terrorize his town in *High Noon* (52).

Ida Lupino pleads with Humphrey Bogart in *High Sierra* (41).

High Sierra   (1941) USA, DIRECTOR – RAOUL WALSH

If any film can be described as Bogart's break out of the gangster mould this is it. True, he plays a gangster, but this time he is not a mere thug. He's an anti-hero with soul. John Huston and W R Burnett wrote the screenplay based on Burnett's novel of the same name. The combination of Huston and Bogart would prove an exciting mix in years to come when Huston turned to directing. A fine cast includes Ida Lupino, Joan Leslie and Arthur Kennedy. Bogart's performance, as well as the excitement and suspense overlaid by a sense of doom and futility make the picture memorable. It was remade in 1955 as *I Died A Thousand Times* with Jack Palance and Shelley Winters.

Holiday   (1938) USA, DIRECTOR – GEORGE CUKOR

Katharine Hepburn plays the rich tomboy who falls in love with her sister's fiancé played by Cary Grant. Both stars shine in this delightful depression comedy which has a more serious theme than most of the screwball comedies of the era since Grant portrays a character who cares more about enjoying life than making money and who frowns on the values of the rich and snobbish. Donald Ogden Stewart wrote the fine script based on a play by Philip Barry and a super cast includes Lew Ayres and Edward Everett Horton, who also appeared in the 1930 film version of *Holiday* starring Ann Harding.

Horse Feathers   (1932) USA, DIRECTOR – NORMAN Z McLEOD

The delightfully irreverent Marx Brothers ridicule higher education in this zany surrealistic film which is even wilder, less focused, and more anarchistic than other Marx Brothers films. Groucho plays Quincey Adams Wagstaff, president of Huxley College, merrily telling the world in song that whatever his faculty wants he's against it. What Groucho wants is a winning football team and he gets one thanks to the bizarre efforts of Chico and Harpo. Zeppo plays Groucho's son. Thelma Todd is the woman Groucho takes canoeing. Bert Kalmar, Harry Ruby, S J Perelman, and Will B Johnstone wrote the script for this gag-a-minute movie punctuated by nice musical interludes.

The Hound Of The Baskervilles (1939) USA, DIRECTOR – SIDNEY LANFIELD

This is the first picture to pair Basil Rathbone and Nigel Bruce as Sherlock Holmes and Dr Watson. The highly atmospheric movie, with a script by Ernest Pascal, was based on the novel by Arthur Conan Doyle. The famous sleuth and his loyal friend travel to Dartmoor to investigate a presumably supernatural hound which is the family curse of a hapless baronet played by Richard Greene. A solidly good cast includes Wendy Barrie, Lionel Atwill, John Carradine, and E E Clive. The historic film spawned numerous sequels and made Rathbone's cerebral characterization of Holmes and Bruce's doddering characterization of Watson the prototypes for decades.

The House On 92nd Street (1945) USA, DIRECTOR – HENRY HATHAWAY

Time Magazine and producer Louis de Rochemont created an important and popular documentary/newsreel called *The March of Time* in 1935 and de Rochemont used the same basic 'shot on location' format when he produced this influential espionage and mystery thriller which raised Hollywood movies to a new level of realistic technique. Presumably based on a true story *The House On 92nd Street* is about a group of Nazi spies in New York during World War II who are foiled in their attempt to steal atomic secrets. William Eythe, Lloyd Nolan, Signe Hasso, and Leo G Carroll star. Barre Lyndon, Charles G Booth and John Monks Jr, wrote the excellent script.

How Green Was My Valley (1941) USA, DIRECTOR – JOHN FORD

This Academy Award winning film brought Oscars to noted director Ford, actors Walter Pidgeon and Donald Crisp, and to cinematographer Arthur Miller. Based on Richard Llewellyn's novel the movie presents a nostalgic view of the joys and sorrows of a family in a Welsh mining town. The cast includes Maureen O'Hara, Roddy McDowall, Sara Allgood, and Barry Fitzgerald. Great care was shown for detail and the movie's elaborately constructed set of a mining village was used in several later movies. A great success at the time and still a touching evocation of childhood, *How Green Was My Valley* has been criticized for being the movie that 'stole' the Oscar from Orson Welles's masterpiece *Citizen Kane*.

How Green Was My Valley (41) was famous for its beautiful and elaborate set of a mining village.

Brandon deWilde and Paul Newman in *Hud* (63).

Hud   (1963) USA, DIRECTOR – MARTIN RITT

Paul Newman plays the charming but worthless son of a decent rancher played by Melvyn Douglas in this exceptional western which relies on drama rather than cliches to keep the audience involved. There are no traditional shoot-em-up brawls but there is a superb performance by Patricia Neal as the family housekeeper mistreated by the arrogant immoral Newman who lacks a sense of decency or compassion. Douglas and Neal won Oscars. Cinematographer James Wong Howe also won an Oscar. Irving Ravetch and Harriet Frank wrote the spare bitter screenplay based on Larry McMurty's novel *Horseman Pass By*.

The Hunchback Of Notre Dame   (1939) USA, DIRECTOR – WILLIAM DIETERLE

The film is based on the classic Victor Hugo novel set in medieval Paris, in which Quasimodo, a deaf and deformed bell ringer saves the life of a gypsy girl Esmeralda, who has been unjustly convicted of murder. The story has been adapted for the screen many times but the 1939 version starring Charles Laughton as the hunchback, and Maureen O'Hara as the gypsy girl may be the best. Laughton's make-up is grotesque, almost overpowering, and he has few intelligible lines, yet his acting was widely praised. This version is lavish requiring crowd scenes with over 3000 extras. Some film buffs prefer the 1923 silent version with Lon Chaney as Quasimodo.

Quasimodo (Charles Laughton) gives the beautiful Esmeralda (Maureen O'Hara) a bird in a cage in *The Hunchback of Notre Dame* (39).

I Am A Fugitive From A Chain Gang (1932) USA, DIRECTOR – MERVYN LeROY

One of the earliest and best of the socially conscious Hollywood films of the 1930s this movie boasts a stunning performance by Paul Muni as an innocent man falsely convicted of a crime who winds up on a chain gang where he is treated brutally. He escapes and becomes a criminal to survive. Both Muni and the picture itself received Oscar nominations. Sol Polito gets the credit for the fine cinematography and the excellent script was written by Sheridan Gibney, Brown Holmes, and Robert E Burns. Filmed in semi-documentary style the movie so shocked audiences it led to the reform of several prison systems.

I Am A Fugitive From A Chain Gang (32) starred Paul Muni in a convincing and powerful performance.

I Married A Witch (1942) USA, DIRECTOR – RENÉ CLAIR

A witch burned at the stake in Salem in the seventeenth century, and her sorcerer father come back to life to haunt the descendant of the Puritan who condemned them. The film is not a horror story, but a delightful romantic comedy-fantasy. Much of the film's success is due to a very lively and sexy performance by Veronica Lake, at the top of her form, as the witch. Fredric March plays the very conventional descendant. The special effects are dandy. Humorist Thorne Smith, who wrote *Topper* also wrote the story on which this film was based.

I Was A Male War Bride (1949) USA, DIRECTOR – HOWARD HAWKS

Cary Grant stars with Ann Sheridan, Hollywood's sassy 'oomph girl' in this genuinely funny farce about a WAC in war-torn Europe who marries a French officer. It takes a lot of machinations to get him home including a stint in skirts for Cary as he pretends to be a Frenchwoman. Only the unflappable Cary Grant can get away with slapstick and still wind up looking handsome and elegant with dignity intact. Marion Marshall and Randy Stuart costarred. The amusing script was written by Leonard Spiegelgass.

If . . . (1968) GREAT BRITAIN, DIRECTOR – LINDSAY ANDERSON

A creator of socially conscious documentaries and films director Anderson turned his attention to the British public schools in this allegorical movie which Anderson also co-produced. Starring Malcolm McDowell, David Wood, Richard Warwick and Christine Noonan, *If . . .* describes a rebellion in a boys' public school but of course it is also about injustice and violence in a wider social context. Surrealistic in tone the movie moves back and forth between color and black and white. Unusual cutting, pacing, and early use of full frontal nudity made *If . . .* a highly influential film and it initiated a wave of surrealistic movies. The interesting script was written by David Sherwin.

Malcolm McDowell as Travis leads the school rebellion in *If . . .* (68).

I'm No Angel (1933) USA, DIRECTOR – WESLEY RUGGLES

This pre-Legion of Decency movie starring Mae West made so much money it saved financially troubled Paramount Pictures from bankruptcy. As the carnival dancer who tames a lion in *I'm No Angel*, the buxom, lusty, confident Mae West is in top form dropping her inimitable one-liners all over the set while ogling a handsome young, susceptible Cary Grant. The cast also includes Edward Arnold and Gregory Ratoff. In addition to starring in the movie Miss West wrote the screenplay or took credit for writing the dialogue anyway. Musical numbers include 'They Call Me Sister Honky Tonk', 'No One Loves Me Like That Dallas Man' and the title song.

Mae West with her maid Libby Taylor in *I'm No Angel* (33).

The Importance Of Being Earnest (1952) GREAT BRITAIN, DIRECTOR – ANTHONY ASQUITH

Essentially a filmed play in exquisite technicolor this movie, adapted by the director from the comedy of manners by Oscar Wilde, boasts a cast which includes such luminaries of the British theatre as Michael Redgrave, Michael Denison, Edith Evans, Margaret Rutherford, Joan Greenwood, Miles Malleson, Dorothy Tutin and Walter Hudd. The dazzling wit of Oscar Wilde is captured in this on screen presentation of the famous comedy of manners about the wickedly clever rich of the 1890s and one young man of unknown parentage in particular who is eager to be Ernest. The cinematography is thanks to Desmond Dickinson.

In Which We Serve (1942) GREAT BRITAIN, DIRECTORS – NOEL COWARD, DAVID LEAN

Noel Coward, produced, wrote, scored and starred in as well as co-directed this brilliant and inspirational propaganda film made during the dark hours of World War II. Coward plays the captain of a torpedoed destroyer who along with other survivors shares memories of life at home and on the sea. The cast includes Bernard Miles, John Mills, Richard Attenborough, Celia Johnson, Joyce Carey and Michael Wilding. Coward astonished both critics and the public by the depth of his performance and the totality of his achievement and the movie received a special Academy Award. It marked the first really major saga of the sea to emerge during the war.

Noel Coward played the destroyer's captain in *In Which We Serve* (42).

The Informer (1935) USA, DIRECTOR – JOHN FORD

RKO was against Ford's filming a version of (his cousin) Liam O'Flaherty's fatalistic novel so the movie was given a tiny budget and Ford was forced to work with a meager set. But the results were magnificent with Joseph H August's cinematography a remarkable study in light and shadow. Victor McLaglen is marvelous as the simple-minded, primitive hanger-on who betrays an IRA leader during the troubles for money and is then tortured by his conscience and tormented by the other rebels, redeeming himself only in death. Ford actually allowed McLaglen to improvise freely during the memorable trial scene. Ford and McLaglen won Oscars as did Max Steiner for his haunting musical score.

Victor McLaglen as Gypo Nolan threatens J M Kerrigan during the troubles in Ireland – *The Informer* (35).

Inherit The Wind   (1960) USA, DIRECTOR – STANLEY KRAMER

Producer/director Kramer was at his best filming this fictional rendition of the famous 1925 Scopes 'Monkey Trial' when a teacher was brought to trial for teaching evolution in a Tennessee public school. Based on a play by Jerome Laurence and Robert E Lee, the movie starred Spencer Tracy as Henry Drummond, the liberal lawyer based on Clarence Darrow while Fredric March was brilliant as Matthew Harrison Brady, Tracy's opponent who was based on the creationist and populist leader

William Jennings Bryan. Gene Kelly played E L Hornbeck the cynical reporter modeled on H L Mencken. Dick York costarred as the young teacher Bertram T Cates. Dramatic confrontational trial scenes characterize the movie. Memorable, too, is the way the film captures the mood of a small Southern town in the heat of summer.

Governess Deborah Kerr interrogates Pamela Franklin, whom she suspects is possessed, in *The Innocents* (61).

The Innocents   (1961) GREAT BRITAIN, DIRECTOR – JACK CLAYTON

Based on the Henry James novella, *The Turn Of The Screw*, the script for this film was worked on by two strong writers, Truman Capote and John Mortimer as well as William Archibald who had based a play on James' story. It is the story of a governess whose two young charges may or may not be possessed by the evil spirits of Miss Jessel, the former governess and her brutal lover Quint. The ghosts may be conjured up out of the mind of the

frustrated governess. Some critics complain the interpretation is too Freudian, but the film works at any level. Deborah Kerr stars as the repressed and nervous governess and the two children are brilliantly played by Martin Stephens and Pamela Franklin. Shot in black and white, the film is filled with images at once beautiful and frightening. Even the musical score by George Auric is haunting.

Intermezzo (1939) USA, DIRECTOR – GREGORY RATOFF

A beautiful Swedish actress named Ingrid Bergman made her American debut in this classic love story. Leslie Howard played the famous violinist who, though married, cannot resist the charms of a lovely young pianist. Bergman appeared in the original 1936 Swedish version of *Intermezzo*, opposite Gösta Ekman, which was written and directed by Gustav Molander. The Swedish movie caught the attention of producer David O Selznick and Bergman was invited to America, the start of an illustrious Hollywood film career. The cast of *Intermezzo* includes John Halliday, Edna Best, Cecil Kellaway and credit for the music goes to Robert Henning, Heinz Provost and Lou Forbes.

Intolerance (1916) USA, DIRECTOR – D W GRIFFITH

Griffith was reputedly stunned by the accusation that his 1915 epic *Birth Of A Nation* condoned bigotry and it may have been the controversy caused by that film which made him decide to make *Intolerance*, a massive expensive epic dwarfing all his prior works which he wrote as well as directed. Subtitled *Love's Struggle Through The Ages* the film consists of four historical tales revealing man's inhumanity to man visually linked by the image of a mother and baby 'out of the cradle, endlessly rocking.' The Babylonian sequence is the most impressive, the modern sequence the most interesting. The episodes on the life of Christ, known as the Judaean Story, and the French story about the St Bartholomew's Day Massacre are not truly developed. The enormous cast features many of Griffith's regular performers, including Lillian Gish, Mae Marsh, Robert Herron and Constance Talmadge. The movie deeply influenced the Russian director Sergei Eisenstein.

Right: The battle during the formidable Babylonian sequence in D W Griffith's epic *Intolerance* (16).

Intruder In The Dust (1951) USA, DIRECTOR – CLARENCE BROWN

William Faulkner's novel about an innocent black threatened by a terrifying lynch mob was brought to the screen with remarkable skill. No mere moral tract the film throbs with action and drama. Filmed on location in Oxford, Mississippi the movie stars Juano Hernandez in his first on screen role as the proud black man aided by an indomitable old woman portrayed by Elizabeth Patterson. David Brian, Claude Jarman Jr, Porter Hall and Will Geer all give fine performances. Ben Maddow's script is first-rate and Robert Surtees's cinematography is excellent. In an era when movies with racial themes were generally timid or poorly done this stands out as a major film achievement.

Invasion Of The Body Snatchers (1956) USA, DIRECTOR – DON SIEGEL

In a typical American small town, friends, relatives and people on the street look the same, but their behavior is subtly different. That's hardly surprising since they have been replaced by exact duplicates hatched out of 'pods' from outer space. Can Kevin McCarthy and Dana Wynter escape replacement before it's too late? Based on Jack Finney's novel *Sleep No More*, this very scary film generates an atmosphere of genuine paranoia. A 1978 remake with Donald Sutherland is almost as effective as the original. Kevin McCarthy played his original part as a cameo in the remake.

The Invisible Man (1933) USA, DIRECTOR – JAMES WHALE

After his success with *Frankenstein* director Whale turned to the H G Wells story of a scientist who discovers a formula for turning himself invisible, and is driven mad in the process. The part of the scientist was offered to Boris Karloff, who turned it down because he didn't like a film in which he appeared on screen only in the final scene. So the part was played by a little known British actor named Claude Rains, who, as the voice of a man going insane, is highly effective. Equally effective are the special effects, a dramatic and witty script and a fine cast of mostly British supporting actors. Though there have been several remakes and sequels, none has been as well-done.

Though his face was only seen briefly in death, Claude Rains became a star after his performance as *The Invisible Man* (33).

The Iron Horse   (1924) USA, DIRECTOR – JOHN FORD

This archetypal silent western about the first transcontinental railroad represented a milestone in the career of Ford. The film stars George O'Brien, Madge Bellamy, Cyril Chadwick, and Fred Kohler, and the screenplay was written by Charles Kenyon and John Russell. The breathtaking cinematography was by George Schneidermann. Big productions were the order of the day in the American motion picture industry by 1924 and studios vied with one another to prove that bigger was better, an adage that proved true at the box office at any rate. *The Iron Horse* quite literally boasts a cast numbering in the thousands.

It Happened One Night   (1934) USA, DIRECTOR – FRANK CAPRA

A madcap comedy about a spoiled heiress on the run who meets a handsome reporter and discovers real life, this film turned out to be box office magic. Scenes in buses and motels, views of America during the Depression, sexiness, sparkling dialogue and good chemistry between the stars Clark Gable and Claudette Colbert are the movie's selling points. The movie was a real sleeper. Gable had been loaned out to Columbia by MGM to make the film as a punishment for demanding a raise, and Colbert had to be persuaded to appear. Scriptwriter Robert Riskin, director Capra, the picture itself, Gable and Colbert all won Oscars. A 1956 remake *You Can't Run Away From It* starred June Allyson and Jack Lemmon.

Clark Gable teases a prudish Claudette Colbert on the other side of the wall of Jericho in *It Happened One Night* (34).

It's A Wonderful Life   (1946) USA, DIRECTOR – FRANK CAPRA

This wonderful fantasy, vintage Capra and vintage James Stewart, is still one of the best and most heartwarming films ever made. Stewart earned an Oscar nomination for his role as a decent man overwhelmed by financial problems caused partly by his own generosity. Rescued from suicide by an angel played by Henry Travers, Stewart is shown what the lives of his friends and loved ones would have been like if he'd never been born. Stewart learns the power of love and solid small town values and the movie ends on an incredibly hopeful note. The fine cast includes Donna Reed, Lionel Barrymore and Thomas Mitchell. A 1977 made-for-television version called *It Happened One Christmas* stars Marlo Thomas.

James Stewart and Donna Reed are reunited on Christmas Eve in *It's a Wonderful Life* (46).

Ivan The Terrible (1942-1946) USSR, DIRECTOR – SERGEI M EISENSTEIN

Originally conceived as a three-part epic about the sixteenth century Tsar Ivan IV, only two parts of the film known in the Soviet Union as *Ivan Groznyi*, which consumed the brilliant Eisenstein for several years, were completed. Part I, noted for its vivid imagery and magnificent coronation scene, describes the intrigues of the Muscovite court during the regency of the young king, the establishment of his central power, the war with the Tartars culminating in the capture of the city of Kazan and his temporary self-exile. Actor Nicolai Cherkasov plays the adult Tsar, changing from an eager boy to a calculating autocrat. Part I of the film proved a popular success, and

was compared in style and scope to grand opera thanks in part to the music of Sergei Prokoviev. Part II, subtitled 'The Boyars' Plot', allows the Tsar to outwit the nobles of his court, as he creates a private army, the Oprichniki, in his struggle to unify the diverse Russian territories into one Empire. Stalin objected to the depiction of the Tsar as weak and vacillating and the second portion of the film was banned in the USSR until 1958.

Ivan The Terrible (Nicolai Cherkasov) is given the last rites when he believes he is dying, in Part I of *Ivan the Terrible* (42-46).

Jane Eyre (1943) USA, DIRECTOR – ROBERT STEVENSON

This quintessential Gothic movie stars Joan Fontaine in the title role but the movie really belongs to Orson Welles, who was magnificent as Mr Rochester the brooding master of Thornfield Hall, a Yorkshire mansion hiding a tragic secret. Peggy Ann Garner plays young Jane who manages to survive the horrors of a Victorian boarding school. Welles' style permeates every aspect of the film including camera angles. The screenplay based on Charlotte Bronte's novel, is by Aldous Huxley, Robert Stevenson and John Houseman. The cast includes Henry Daniell, Elizabeth Taylor, Agnes Moorehead and John Abbott. Three silent versions of *Jane Eyre* were filmed as well as a sound version in 1934, a 1972 version with Susannah York and George C Scott, and one made by BBC Television with Timothy Dalton and Zelah Clarke.

Jaws (1975) USA, DIRECTOR – STEVEN SPIELBERG

A blockbuster success, this movie stars Roy Scheider, Robert Shaw, Richard Dreyfuss and a remarkable mechanical shark (known as Bruce) which scared audiences out of their wits. But the movie's real star was its gifted director. Based on the best-selling novel by Peter Benchley the Oscar-nominated film is set at an East Coast resort town which is being beseiged by a great white shark. John Williams received a much deserved Oscar for his musical score which includes the famous menacing *Jaws* theme. The fine underwater cinematography was by Bill Butler. Two sequels, *Jaws 2* (1978) and *Jaws 3D* (1983) proved disappointing.

Susan Backlinie is attacked while swimming in *Jaws* (75).

Al Jolson in blackface sings 'Mammy' in *The Jazz Singer* (27).

The Jazz Singer   (1927) USA, DIRECTOR – ALAN CROSLAND

Famous for being the first talking feature movie in reality this film which stars the dynamic Al Jolson is mostly silent. Still, when Jolson uttered the words 'You ain't seen nothin' yet' on screen, movie history was made. Based on a play by Samson Raphaelson, with a screenplay by Alfred A Cohen, *The Jazz Singer* is a three-handkerchief tear jerker about a cantor's son who opts for a career in show business. The movie was remade in 1953 with Danny Thomas, Peggy Lee and Mildred Dunnock. The movie was remade again in 1980 with Neil Diamond, Laurence Olivier and Lucie Arnaz. Despite its sentimentality the Jolson version, which also stars May MacAvoy and Warner Oland, is the best.

Les Jeux Interdits   (1952) FRANCE, DIRECTOR – RENÉ CLEMENT

Brigitte Fossey, Georges Poujouli, Amédée, Laurence Badie, Jacques Marin, Suzanne Courtal and Lucien Hubert appear in this perceptive and powerful anti-war movie. In 1940, after seeing her parents killed, a little girl is taken in by a family of peasants. She makes friends with a young boy who helps her bury her dead puppy and together they invent an elaborate imaginary world about death. Their imaginary world is innocent; the real world corrupt. *Les Jeux Interdits/Forbidden Games* is based on a novel by Francois Boyer, film script by Jean Aurenche and Pierre Bost. The movie won the Academy Award for Best Foreign Film.

Brigitte Fossey and Georges Poujouli in *Les Jeux Interdits* (52).

Jew Süss (1934) GREAT BRITAIN, DIRECTOR – LOTHAR MENDES

Based on an anti-Nazi novel written by Jewish author Leon Feuchtwangler this satiric film stars Conrad Veidt and Benita Hume. Set in old Wurtemberg, *Jew Süss* is about a Jew who becomes powerful in order to assist his people, only to discover that he is really a Gentile. The film underscores the point that racial and ethnic differences really don't matter. The more famous version of *Jew Süss* was filmed in 1940 in Germany, directed by Veit Harlan, Goebbel's protegé. The leading exponent of Nazi ideology on screen Harlan's version libels the Jew as an evil and dangerous figure who rapes Aryan women before he is ultimately destroyed. The film which Harlan helped write, stars Ferdinand Marian and Kristina Soderbaum, Harlan's wife.

Conrad Veidt (right) played Süss, in the English version of Leon Feuchtwangler's novel on race distinctions – *Jew Süss* (34).

Jezebel (1938) USA, DIRECTOR – WILLIAM WYLER

This vehicle for Bette Davis was a consolation prize meant to soften the pain of losing the plum role of Scarlett O'Hara in *Gone With The Wind* or so legend has it. Based on a play by Owen Davis Sr, with screenplay by Clements Ripley, Abem Finkel, and John Huston *Jezebel* is a romance set in New Orleans before the Civil War. Bette Davis stars as the headstrong scheming Julie Morrison in love with Henry Fonda. When Fonda marries another (Margaret Lindsay) Davis weds George Brent. Davis makes up for her selfishness by nursing Fonda through yellow fever and letting him return, cured to his own wife. Bette Davis and Fay Bainter won Oscars and the movie received a Best Picture nomination.

Bette Davis flirts with George Brent to spite her true love Henry Fonda in *Jezebel* (38).

Johnny Belinda   (1938) USA, DIRECTOR – JEAN NEGULESCO

Jane Wyman won an Academy Award and rose to stardom thanks to her touching performance as the sensitive young deaf-mute who is raped and bears a child. The movie, set in a remote fishing village, represented an advance by treating a rape victim with compassion. The fine cast includes Lew Ayres as the kind doctor who helps Wyman, Charles Bickford as Wyman's father, Agnes Moorehead as Wyman's aunt, and Stephen McNally as the man who rapes

Wyman and later attempts to steal her baby. Despite its ultimate success Jack Warner of Warner Bros disliked the movie and held up release for a year. Ted McCord's cinematography and Max Steiner's musical score are among the film's strengths.

Jane Wyman beautifully played the deaf mute who is raped and Charles Bickford played her father in *Johnny Belinda* (38).

The Jolson Story   (1946) USA, DIRECTOR – ALFRED E GREEN

Al Jolson was so popular entertaining troops during World War II that Columbia Pictures decided to film his life story. The movie was an enormous hit. Larry Parks played the cantor's son who becomes a star but learns life has its share of troubles. Though the movie is sanitized and sentimental, it's entertaining and Jolson's voice does the actual singing while Parks lip synchs with verve. Morris

Stoloff won an Oscar for the lively musical score. Cinematographer Joseph Walker, actors Parks and William Demarest who plays a vaudevillian received Oscar nominations. Evelyn Keyes portrays a character modeled on Jolson's third wife, dancer Ruby Keeler. A sequel, *Jolson Sings Again*, was released in 1949.

Le Jour Se Leve   (1939) FRANCE, DIRECTOR – MARCEL CARNÉ

Romantic fatalism permeates *Le Jour Se Leve/Daybreak*, one of the foremost examples of the French school of 'Poetic Realism'. The script was written by Jacques Viot and the poet Jacques Prévert. The movie which stars Jean Gabin, Arletty and Jules Berry tells the tragic tale of a man who, for good reason, commits a murder and who is

trapped in an attic room by the police. The man walks about, smokes, contemplates his past during the night and in the morning shoots himself. Almost all the prints of this critically acclaimed movie were destroyed when RKO bought it to film a 1947 remake called *The Long Night* starring Henry Fonda and Barbara Bel Geddes.

Jules Et Jim (1961) FRANCE, DIRECTOR – FRANÇOIS TRUFFAUT

This film about a *ménage à trois* stars Oskar Werner, Jeanne Moreau and Henri Serre. Director Truffaut concentrates on character and atmosphere rather than technical camera work in this interesting tale of a young woman who can't decide between a French and German student, so switches from one to the other until after World War I ends when the trio meet again and the triangle forms once more but on an ever shifting basis.

Written by Truffaut and Jean Grualt the film is based on the novel by Henri-Pierre Roche. The movie has great charm and Moreau is marvelous. A 1980 Hollywood remake called *William and Phil* stars Michael Ontkean, Margot Kidder and Ray Sharkey.

Jeanne Moreau starred as the woman in love with two men, Oskar Werner and Henri Serre (left) in *Jules et Jim* (61).

Julia (1977) USA, DIRECTOR – FRED ZINNEMANN

Based on an episode from the book *Pentimento* by Lillian Hellman this movie stars Jane Fonda as Hellman, Jason Robards as Dashiell Hammett, Hellman's lover and Vanessa Redgrave as the idealistic and courageous Julia, a member of an anti-Nazi resistance movement within Germany who is subsequently murdered by the Nazis. Redgrave and Robards won Academy Awards for their magnificent performances, screenwriter Alvin Sargent

also won an Oscar, and nominations deservedly showered down on this exceptional film in which actress Meryl Streep debuted in a small role. The characterizations are complex and interesting and *Julia* evokes the *zeitgeist* of the 1930s brilliantly. The movie manages to be compelling and informative at the same time, a rare mix.

Right: Jane Fonda played Lillian Hellman in *Julia* (77).

Julius Caesar (1953) USA, DIRECTOR – JOSEPH L MANKIEWICZ

A straight forward film version of Shakespeare's political tragedy, *Julius Caesar* starred James Mason as Brutus and John Gielgud as the 'lean and hungry' Cassius, with Louis Calhern as Caesar. The great surprise in casting was Marlon Brando who played Mark Anthony and gave a believable performance, having abandoned Method Acting for coaching by Gielgud. Best of all was Edmond O'Brien as a nervous, sweating Casca. Though the film

lacks the magic of Olivier's *Henry V*, it is probably the best Hollywood adaptation of Shakespeare and was both a critical and financial success. A color remake starring Jason Robards, Richard Johnson and Charlton Heston was filmed in 1969.

Louis Calhern as Julius Caesar, Morgan Farley as the blind seer Artemidorus and John Gielgud as Cassius in *Julius Caesar* (53).

Kameradschaft (1931) GERMANY, DIRECTOR – G W PABST

This movie proved politically controversial at the time it was released because it called for solidarity of workers across national lines. The great director Pabst used the device of a mine disaster on the French/German border to make his point. Though their employers forbid it, German mine workers put nationalism and national interest aside

in *Kameradschaft/Comradeship* to go to the aid of their French brethren trapped in the mine. The screenplay is by Laszlo Vajda, Karl Otten and Peter Martin Lampel and the film stars Ernst Busch and Alexander Granach. Despite the left-wing message of the film Pabst spent all of World War II in Germany and made two films for the Nazi regime.

La Kermesse Heroique (1935) FRANCE, DIRECTOR – JACQUES FEYDER

La Kermesse Heroique/Carnival In Flanders was an international hit without peer when first released, winner of countless awards. A clever politically sophisticated farce the movie stars Feyder's wife, the famous French actress Françoise Rosay. The cast also includes Louis Jouvet, Jean Murat, Alfred Adam and André Alerme. Feyder wrote the screenplay, with Charles Spaak, author of the original novel. The deliciously absurd plot concerns the Spanish invasion of a Flemish town in the year 1616. The conquerors arrive only to find that the men of the town are nowhere in sight but the women are very much in evidence. The sexually provocative movie is still sprightly and polished.

Françoise Rosay and the women of a Flemish town speed the Spanish invaders on their way in *La Kermesse Heroique* (35).

Key Largo   (1948) USA, DIRECTOR – JOHN HUSTON

The gifted John Huston not only directed this brooding yet exciting film but co-wrote the screenplay, adapted from the play by Maxwell Anderson, with Richard Brooks. The fine cinematography is by Karl Freund. Edward G Robinson stars as the brutal gangster who intimidates a group of essentially decent people trapped in a Florida hotel during a hurricane. Humphrey Bogart plays a veteran back from the war. Lauren Bacall and Lionel Barrymore costar. But the supreme acting performance in the film is by Claire Trevor who won an Oscar for her poignant portrayal of Robinson's alcoholic mistress.

Left: Lauren Bacall and Humphrey Bogart join together to fight the mobster Edward G Robinson in *Key Largo* (48).

Kind Hearts And Coronets   (1949) GREAT BRITAIN, DIRECTOR – ROBERT HAMER

Set in the Edwardian era this delightful film stars Dennis Price as a poor but elegant member of the D'Ascoyne family who decides to murder eight of his relatives in order to inherit the D'Ascoyne title and estate. He proceeds to do just that with great ingenuity but is thwarted at the end. His eight relatives (male and female) are all portrayed by one actor, the incomparable Alec Guinness. The rest of the fine cast includes Valerie Hobson, Joan Greenwood, Miles Malleson and Arthur Lowe. The screenplay by Hamer and John Dighton is based on the novel *Noblesse Oblige* by Roy Horniman.

Alec Guinness as Lady Agatha D'Ascoyne at the funeral of Henry D'Ascoyne, in *Kind Hearts and Coronets* (49).

The King And I (1956) USA, DIRECTOR – WALTER LANG

This tale of east meets west began with Anna Leonowens' autobiography about her experiences as a governess at the exotic court of Siam. Margaret Landon wrote a book based on Leonowens' autobiography called *Anna And The King Of Siam*. Rex Harrison starred as the king of the movie *Anna And The King Of Siam* (1946) with Irene Dunne as Anna. Richard Rodgers and Oscar Hammerstein II turned it into a musical for Gertrude Lawrence, whose King was played by Yul Brynner. When the musical version was filmed Brynner again played the King and won an Academy Award for the part. Deborah Kerr played Anna, although her vocals were dubbed by Marni Nixon. The choreography, including the charming ballet, 'The Small House of Uncle Thomas', was by Jerome Robbins and Irene Sharaff designed the wonderful costumes.

Yul Brynner as the King of Siam toasts Deborah Kerr as Anna Leonowens, the teacher of his children in *The King and I* (56).

King Kong

(1933) USA, DIRECTORS – MERIAN C COOPER, ERNEST B SCHOEDSACK

The tale of the giant ape from Skull Island who falls in love with a little blonde and dies during a battle with biplanes on the top of the Empire State Building is familiar to everyone who has ever seen a movie. Fay Wray starred as the blonde, Robert Armstrong played the director Carl Denham and Bruce Cabot was the clean cut hero. The real hero was Willis O'Brien whose stop-motion animation of Kong and the other film monsters provided special effects unequaled for decades. There have been many sequels and ripoffs of the original. A 1976 remake with Jessica Lange as the blonde and the World Trade Center replacing the Empire State Building was an embarrassing flop.

On top of the Empire State Building King Kong fights off the biplanes in *King Kong* (33).

King Of Hearts   (1966) FRANCE/ITALY, DIRECTOR – PHILLIPE DE BROCA

Set during World War I this delightful fantasy is brightly eccentric, bold, joyously irreverent, and visually beautiful. It has a lot to say about the madness of the world, the evil of war, and the sanity and sensitivity of those society deems lunatics. Alan Bates plays a Scottish soldier who discovers a town abandoned by all but the lunatics of the town's asylum who make him their king. They also charm an invading army, at least for a while. When the lunatics return to their asylum Bates contrives to join them permanently. The film's fine cinematographer is Pierre Lhomme. The cast includes Genevieve Bujold, Jean-Claude Brialy and Françoise Christophe.

King Solomon's Mines   (1950) USA, DIRECTOR – COMPTON BENNETT

Stewart Granger and Deborah Kerr starred in this romantic and adventurous technicolor fantasy based on H Rider Haggard's novel. Robert Surtees is the Oscar-winning cinematographer and the movie takes audiences on an epic tour through Africa in quest of treasure and Kerr's missing husband. The 1936 version of *King Solomon's Mines*, directed by Robert Stevenson, which sticks closer to Haggard's original plot stars Cedric Hardwicke as Allan Quartermain the great white hunter and Paul Robeson as Umbopa the chief returning from exile. The ever popular tale was revived again in *Watusi* (1959) which has Allan Quartermain's son following in his father's footsteps and used much of the outdoor footage shot by Surtees. A 1975 remake of the original is titled *King Solomon's Treasure* and Richard Chamberlain played Quartermain in a slapstick version in 1986.

Kiss Me Kate   (1953) USA, DIRECTOR – GEORGE SIDNEY

This great movie version of Cole Porter's clever hit Broadway musical, which was shot in 3-D, spoofs a lot of things including Shakespeare. Kathryn Grayson and Howard Keel play a husband and wife living apart who appear together on stage in *Taming Of The Shrew*. Complications such as an invasion of assertive gangsters makes the couple's backstage life as violent and funny as their onstage life. Ann Miller as Bianca, Keenan Wynn and James Whitmore as the gangsters who steal the film with their rendition of 'Brush Up Your Shakespeare' and the rest of the super cast add to the movie's madcap mood. Hermes Pan choreographed the film with some help from Bob Fosse who also appeared on screen.

Kathryn Grayson and Howard Keel quarrel while gangsters Wynn and Whitmore keep an eye on them in *Kiss me Kate* (53).

123

Klute   (1971) USA, DIRECTOR – ALAN J PAKULA

Jane Fonda won a much deserved Oscar for her unsentimental, unsensationalized portrayal of a prostitute. The movie works on several levels, as an interesting study of character, as a suspense thriller, and as a complex love story. As a call girl Fonda's world is dangerous in part because of the fantasies she encourages. But the movie doesn't preach either. Donald Sutherland plays the detective who doesn't 'rescue' Fonda so much as offer her an alternative, one she's not at all sure she wants. Andy K Lewis and Dave Lewis wrote the excellent screenplay. The cast includes Charles Cioffi, Roy Scheider and Rita Gam.

Roy Scheider threatens prostitute Jane Fonda in *Klute* (71).

The Knack   (1965) GREAT BRITAIN, DIRECTOR – RICHARD LESTER

This hilarious movie from the swinging 1960s, with a screenplay by Charles Wood, is based on Ann Jellicoe's play about sex but the film works best when it forgets the play and gives itself over to running gags and visually creative scenes shot in the streets of London. David Watkin is the outstanding cinematographer. Lester's direction is free, spontaneous, joyful, even anarchistic. The cast, which includes Michael Crawford, Ray Brooks, Rita Tushingham and Donal Donnelly, is loaded with verve. The plot, such as it is, concerns a sexually frustrated teacher who lets out one room in his house to an innocent young woman and another to a Don Juan.

Knife In The Water   (1962) POLAND, DIRECTOR – ROMAN POLANSKI

Knife In the Water/Noz w Wodzie is talented director Polanski's first feature-length film. It is a subtle work which reveals the director's favorite themes, fear and obsession. *Knife In The Water* is about a young couple who invite a stranger to join them on their yacht. Violence and sexual passion simmer beneath the surface as the psychology of the trio is explored. Polanski wrote the screenplay with Jerry Skolimowski and Jakub Goldberg. Leon Niemszyk, Jolanta Umecka and Zygmunt Malanowicz star. The movie, which won the Best Foreign Film Oscar, established Polanski as a major director and he left Poland to pursue his career in France, Britain and Hollywood.

Kramer Vs Kramer   (1979) USA, DIRECTOR – ROBERT BENTON

Dustin Hoffman, Meryl Streep, Jane Alexander and eight-year-old Justin Henry all give outstanding performances in this Oscar-winning movie written as well as directed by Benton, based on a novel by Avery Corman. Hoffman, Streep, Alexander and Henry all received Oscar nominations. Hoffman and Streep won. Streep plays a woman who leaves her husband, then returns to reclaim their son, while Hoffman plays a competitive ambitious man who changes radically as he cares for his child. The popular movie caught the tenor of the times when the women's liberation movement and divorce were changing the roles and images of both men and women.

Dustin Hoffman and Meryl Streep in *Kramer vs Kramer* (79).

The Lady Eve (1941) USA, DIRECTOR – PRESTON STURGES

Written as well as directed by the inimitable Preston Sturges who combined a style worthy of Lubitsch with a gift for irreverent satire this movie about a cardsharp's daughter (Barbara Stanwyck) and a millionaire bachelor (Henry Fonda) is a wonderful treat. Farce meets romance in this second on-screen pairing of Stanwyck and Fonda which, despite the slapstick and pratfalls, is very sophisticated. Charles Coburn, marvelous as Stanwyck's father, and a fine supporting cast which includes Eugene Pallette, William Demarest and Eric Blore add to the frenzied pace. A 1956 remake, *The Birds And The Bees* stars George Gobel, Mitzi Gaynor and David Niven.

The Lady Vanishes (1938) GREAT BRITAIN, DIRECTOR – ALFRED HITCHCOCK

This charming and riveting suspense drama is a masterpiece. Set almost entirely on a train the movie concerns a woman (Margaret Lockwood) who discovers that an elderly lady, actually a British spy, appears to have vanished into thin air. There's some question as to whether she even exists. The only person who believes her is a young musician (Michael Redgrave). The witty clever script by Sidney Gilliat and Frank Lauder is based on Ethel Lina White's novel *The Wheel Spins*. The entire cast is superb including Dame May Whitty, Paul Lukas and Basil Radford and Naunton Wayne as cricket fans Charteris and Caldicott. A remake in 1980 starring Cybill Shepherd and Elliot Gould was not a success.

Dame May Whitty, Margaret Lockwood, Basil Radford and Michael Redgrave in *The Lady Vanishes* (38).

The Ladykillers (1955) GREAT BRITAIN, DIRECTOR – ALEXANDER MACKENDRICK

A wonderful comedy with a great performance by British actress Katie Johnson, then well into her seventies, who plays an old lady whose innocence is more than a match for a ruthless gang of criminals. Alec Guinness shines as the mad genius who takes a room in Katie Johnson's house and plans a robbery. Peter Sellers is a comic delight as a member of the motley gang. The rest of the fine cast includes Cecil Parker, Herbert Lom, Danny Green, and Jack Warner. Screenplay writer William Rose received an Oscar nomination for his clever script.

Lassie Come Home (1943) USA, DIRECTOR – FRED M WILCOX

The very first of the Lassie series shows the noble collie at her (really his since the character was played by a male dog) heartwarming best. When the poor family that owns her is forced to sell her the loyal and intelligent dog goes through a series of dangerous and remarkable adventures on her journey home. Much of the movie's popularity was due to its being a wartime film which provided audiences with a much needed emotional lift and escape. Adapted from the novel by Eric Knight the movie boasts a fine cast including Roddy McDowall, Donald Crisp, Nigel Bruce and Elizabeth Taylor. A string of Lassie movies followed and the dog was the star of a 1950s television series and a 1970s television cartoon series.

Roddy McDowall with Lassie, the noble and intelligent collie who suffers many adventures in *Lassie Come Home* (43).

The Last Laugh   (1924) GERMANY, DIRECTOR – F W MURNAU

The Last Laugh/Der Letzte Mann is a silent movie starring the great Emil Jannings, a massive presence on screen as on stage. A milestone in the history of film the movie dispenses with subtitles allowing the story to tell itself strictly pictorially. Cinematographer Karl Freund's use of camera movement was nothing short of revolutionary. Brilliantly written by scriptwriter Carl Mayer the movie is a poignant and incisive study of an old doorman of a luxury hotel demoted to lavatory attendant. Unfortunately, the movie has an unconvincing happy ending. A 1955 German remake stars Hans Albers.

Karl Freund used multiple exposures in *The Last Laugh* (24).

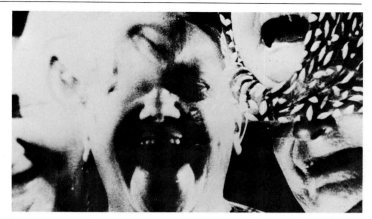

The Last Picture Show   (1971) USA, DIRECTOR – PETER BOGDANOVICH

This excellent movie about coming of age in a small dreary Texas town in the early 1950s catapulted director Bogdanovich to the top though he has not lived up to the promise shown in this film. Larry McMurty's novel forms the basis of the movie, with the screenplay adapted by McMurty himself and co-written by Bogdanovich. Timothy Bottoms, Jeff Bridges, Cybill Shepherd, Oscar-winner Ben Johnson, Oscar-winner Cloris Leachman, and Ellen Burstyn star. The film is rich in detail, characterization and nostalgia. The film was a huge box office success and enormously influential. The outstanding black and white cinematography is by Robert Surtees.

The Last Wave   (1977) AUSTRALIA, DIRECTOR – PETER WEIR

A sophisticated Sydney lawyer, played by Richard Chamberlain is hired to defend a group of urban, slum-dwelling aborigines accused of murdering one of their companions. He slowly realizes that the murder was not a mere street brawl, but a ritual killing and that the aborigines are descendants of an ancient tribe whose homeland lies just beneath the city. There are visions, magic, fantastic discoveries and an apocalyptic ending. Just what is actually going on is never clear, but the eerie and dreamlike images, and an excellent performance by the aborigine actor David Gulpilil make this a thoroughly fascinating film. *The Last Wave* was one of the first Australian films to have an impact in the United States.

Laura   (1944) USA, DIRECTOR – OTTO PREMINGER

This exquisite mystery and love story stars beautiful Gene Tierney in the title role as a girl presumed murdered who turns out to be very much alive. Dana Andrews plays the detective who falls in love with Laura thanks in part to her captivating portrait. As murder suspects Vincent Price and Dame Judith Anderson are simply super. Best of all is Clifton Webb, on screen for the first time since the silent era, who portrays the eccentric Waldo Lydecker. Preminger's direction shows a delicate touch. The fine spare script is by Jay Dratler, Samuel Hoffenstein and Betty Reinhardt from Vera Caspary's novel. Cinematographer Joseph La Shelle won a much deserved Oscar. The movie's haunting and romantic theme song became a classic.

Clifton Webb, Gene Tierney, Vincent Price and Dame Judith Anderson meet at a party in *Laura* (44).

The Lavender Hill Mob   (1950) GREAT BRITAIN, DIRECTOR – CHARLES CRICHTON

One of the finest British comedies ever made this delightful caper movie stars Alex Guinness as a mild bank clerk who decides to pull off an amazing bullion theft and puts together the most unlikely gang possible to carry out his scheme. The fine cast includes Sidney James, Alfie Bass, Marjorie Fielding, Edie Martin, John Gregson and Gibb McLaughlin while Stanley Holloway practically steals the film as Guinness's chief co-conspirator. Scriptwriter T E B Clarke won a much deserved Oscar. A charming unknown, Audrey Hepburn, plays a bit part.

Alec Guinness and Sidney James in *The Lavender Hill Mob* (50).

Lawrence Of Arabia   (1962) GREAT BRITAIN, DIRECTOR – DAVID LEAN

A massive expansive Oscar-winning epic about the British adventurer T E Lawrence, this film features a spectacular performance by Peter O'Toole in the title role. Notable, too, are cast members Omar Sharif, Arthur Kennedy and Alec Guinness as Prince Feisal. Cinematographer Frederick A Young captures the beauty of the desert as well as extraordinary crowd scenes and scenes of battle in this tale of an eccentric but heroic figure's life during World War I and the Arab Revolt. The movie's grandeur and excitement won Lean and Young Oscars and also brought one to Maurice Jarre for the stirring, romantic musical score. O'Toole and Sharif received nominations.

Peter O'Toole starred as the enigmatic *Lawrence of Arabia* (62).

The League Of Gentlemen   (1960) GREAT BRITAIN, DIRECTOR – BASIL DEARDEN

This is an outstanding caper film. A down on his luck ex-army colonel, played by Jack Hawkins, blackmails a group of disreputable former officers to pull off a big bank heist. The film is ingeniously plotted, written with great wit and played with verve not only by Hawkins, but by Nigel Patrick, Roger Livesey, Richard Attenborough, Bryan Forbes, Kieron Moore, Robert Coote and Nanette Newman. Actor Forbes also wrote the script, based on the novel by John Boland.

The Letter   (1940) USA, DIRECTOR – WILLIAM WYLER

Based on Somerset Maugham's story this movie tells the tale of a wife of a rubber plantation owner who kills a man in apparent self-defense. Actually the dead man was her lover and the murder is a crime of passion. An incriminating letter leads to blackmail. A moralistic ending required by the Hays Office was tacked on to the movie, violating the spirit of the story. Bette Davis as the wife is superb in this study of deceit and hypocrisy. Herbert Marshall plays Davis's husband. Interestingly, he played the lover in the 1929 version starring Jeanne Eagels. The movie was remade and retitled *The Unfaithful*, starring Ann Sheridan in 1947 and Lee Remick starred in a made-for-television-version in 1982.

Bette Davis gave a superb performance as the wife who shoots her lover and is mysteriously blackmailed in *The Letter* (40).

The Life And Death Of Colonel Blimp   (1943) GREAT BRITAIN, DIRECTORS – MICHAEL POWELL, EMERIC PRESSBURGER

Written as well as produced and directed by the team of Powell and Pressburger this film concerns a very human and very sympathetic British Officer whose career runs from the Boer War to the London Blitz of World War II. Distinguished British character actor Roger Livesey plays the title role and Deborah Kerr portrays each of the three women in his life. Anton Walbrook costars as Blimp's German friend. The perceptive amiable movie, amazingly free of propaganda for a wartime film, was made in stunning Technicolor and originally ran a full three hours.

The Life Of Emile Zola   (1937) USA, DIRECTOR – WILLIAM DIETERLE

Noted actor Paul Muni gave his finest performance in the title role of this Oscar-winning film, the best of the Warner Bros series of biographical historical dramas which were highly popular in the 1930s. The stirring film focuses on Zola's many fights against injustice, taking him from youth through old age. Joseph Schildkraut won an Oscar for his portrayal of Captain Alfred Dreyfus, the victim of anti-semitism falsely accused of treason whose cause was championed by Zola. The cast includes Gloria Holden as Madam Zola and Gale Sondergaard as Madame Dreyfus.

Paul Muni (right) in *The Life of Emile Zola* (37).

Lilies Of The Field   (1963) USA, DIRECTOR – RALPH NELSON

Sidney Poitier became the first black actor to win a Best Actor Academy Award for his performance as the ex-GI named Homer Smith who goes to work for a group of German nuns in the Arizona desert and helps them build a chapel. James Poe received an Oscar nomination for his screenplay based on the novel by William E Barrett. Nominated, too, were cinematographer Ernest Haller and German actress Lilia Skala who played the Mother Superior in the film. Ralph Nelson wrote and directed a made-for-television sequel called *Christmas Lilies of the Field* (1979) starring Billy Dee Williams.

Sidney Poitier entertains the German nuns (Lilia Skala as the Mother Superior sits at head of table) in *Lilies of the Field* (63).

The Lion In Winter (1968) GREAT BRITAIN, DIRECTOR – ANTHONY HARVEY

The lion of the title is Henry II played with verve by Peter O'Toole. Katharine Hepburn costarred as the tough aging Eleanor of Aquitaine allowed back at her husband's court only for Christmas. James Goldman wrote the screenplay, an adaptation of his original stage play. The movie boasts good dialogue and deliciously meaty roles for its two charismatic leads. Eleanor and Henry mix family troubles with political intrigue as they squabble, compete, reminisce, and play their grown children off against each other. Anthony Hopkins gives a fine performance as Richard the Lion Heart, focus of Eleanor's hopes. John Castle plays Geoffrey, the middle son, and Nigel Terry, Prince John, the son Henry is trying to promote. The movie brought Hepburn her third Oscar and O'Toole a nomination. Goldman and composer John Barry also won Academy Awards.

Katharine Hepburn played the headstrong Eleanor of Aquitaine in *The Lion in Winter* (68).

Little Caesar (1930) USA, DIRECTOR – MERVYN LE ROY

Edward G Robinson became not only a star but the quintessential gangster of Hollywood films thanks to this exciting early talkie about the rise and fall of a character based on Al Capone, with the gang wars of the prohibitionist 1920s providing a backdrop for plenty of action. The movie's last line, 'Is this the end of Rico?' is classic. Screenwriters Francis Faragoh and Robert E Lee received Oscar nominations. Le Roy's direction is first-rate especially considering the technically primitive level of sound equipment at the time. The solid cast includes Douglas Fairbanks Jr and Glenda Farrell.

'No buzzard like you will ever put the cuffs on Rico' – Edward G Robinson in the hard-hitting gangster movie *Little Caesar* (30).

Bill (Bojangles) Robinson and Shirley Temple in *The Little Colonel* (35).

The Little Colonel   (1935) USA, DIRECTOR – DAVID BUTLER

Child actress Shirley Temple was everybody's favorite little girl in the 1930s. She came complete with golden ringlets, dimples, precocious charm, an expressive singing voice and twinkling tapping feet, and this movie really shows her off. Set in Kentucky after the Civil War the film has Shirley portraying a lively short-tempered child. Lionel Barrymore is the lively short-tempered grandfather who has rejected his daughter because she married a Yankee, but granddaughter Shirley brings him around. Little Shirley also solves a lot of other problems along the way. She also does a super dance routine with Bill (Bojangles) Robinson. The movie has one oddity, a one-minute Technicolor party scene.

Little Women (1933) USA, DIRECTOR – GEORGE CUKOR

Louisa May Alcott's famous novel about young girls growing up in nineteenth-century New England worked beautifully when brought to the screen, by scriptwriter Sarah Y Mason. Katharine Hepburn stars as the tomboyish basically feminist Jo. Frances Dee plays Meg, Joan Bennett, Amy and Jean Parker, Beth. The rest of the fine cast includes Paul Lukas, Spring Byington, and Edna May Oliver. The movie was remade in 1949 with a strong dose of sugar added. This version stars June Allyson as Jo, Peter Lawford, Margaret O'Brien, Janet Leigh and Mary Astor. The best performance is turned in by Elizabeth Taylor, beautiful and smug as Amy.

Lives Of A Bengal Lancer (1935) USA, DIRECTOR – HENRY HATHAWAY

Gary Cooper got round his American accent by playing a Canadian in this glorious adventure film set in a fantasy version of India where fabulous sets and elaborate costumes add to the fun. Franchot Tone and Richard Cromwell join Cooper as Bengal Lancers. The plot whizzes along with plenty of action and the picture has everything from a glamorous Russian spy played by Kathleen Burke to a grand palace owned by the fiendish Mohammed Khan played by Douglass Dumbrille who prides himself on quite ingenious methods of torture. The cast includes Guy Standing, C Aubrey Smith and Akim Tamiroff.

Gary Cooper at the head of a troop of lancers in *Lives of A Bengal Lancer* (35).

Local Hero (1983) GREAT BRITAIN, DIRECTOR – BILL FORSYTH

The representative of an oil company (Peter Riegert) is assigned to buy up a small and poor Scottish coastal village which the company needs for a refinery site. The village is delighted, but circumstances complicate the plans. This sounds like one of the Ealing comedies that were being made in Britain in the 1950s, but this one is the product of the special and quirky vision of Scottish writer-director Forsyth. The film is filled with strange and wonderful characters including Burt Lancaster and Fulton McKay. *Local Hero* is a small gem and may be better than Forsyth's better known film *Gregory's Girl*.

Oil executives Peter Capaldi and Peter Riegert rescue a rabbit on their way to a Scottish village in *Local Hero* (83).

Ronald Colman and H B Warner in Shangri-La – *Lost Horizon* (37).

Lost Horizon   (1937) USA, DIRECTOR – FRANK CAPRA

This hugely successful and enormously romantic film, based on the novel by James Hilton, is about five people who discover Utopia in the form of a remote Tibetan valley called Shangri-La. The contrast between the real world and Shangri-La is striking. The glorious mountain fantasyland with a great climate is peaceful and happy. But one of its inhabitants chafes under the perfection and persuades two of the visitors to lead her out. The movie's near perfect cast includes Ronald Colman, Jane Wyatt, H B Warner, Thomas Mitchell, Edward Everett Horton, and Sam Jaffe as the High Lama. Dimitri Tiomkin received an Oscar nomination for the musical score. A musical remake with Peter Finch and Liv Ullman was made in 1973.

The Lost Weekend   (1945) USA, DIRECTOR – BILLY WILDER

A strong but compassionate film about an alcoholic, *The Lost Weekend* represented a giant step forward for Hollywood. Wilder's magnificent treatment of a sensitive subject earned him a scriptwriting Oscar shared with Charles Brackett and the Best Director's Oscar. The movie won Best Picture and Ray Milland also won an Oscar for his outstanding portrayal of the writer driven by drink to pawn his typewriter, hide bottles in secret places, and steal. Cinematographer John F Seitz does a terrific job shooting the seamy side of real New York. Miklos Rozsa's music, played on a theremin enhances the terrible delirium tremor scenes.

Love Me Tonight   (1932) USA, DIRECTOR – ROUBEN MAMOULIAN

An early sound musical phenomenon about a tailor who winds up in high society the movie blends song, comedy, and romance with deft sophistication. The superb cast includes Maurice Chevalier, Jeanette MacDonald, Charles Butterworth, Charles Ruggles, Myrna Loy and C Aubrey Smith. The charming screenplay was written by Samuel Hoffenstein, Waldemar Young and George Marion Jr. Victor Milne's cinematography is a joy to behold. Rodgers and Hart songs like 'Mimi' and 'Isn't It Romantic' add to the movie's glitter. Director Mamoulian's Paris sparkles so brightly many critics believe he outdid René Clair and outshone Ernst Lubitsch in crafting this delightful film.

M (1931) GERMANY, DIRECTOR – FRITZ LANG

Peter Lorre's first, and greatest screen role was as the child-like, child-murderer Hans Beckert. Lorre is able to make this most depraved of all criminals an almost sympathetic character. The murders of little girls in Berlin inspire a massive police manhunt which disrupts normal criminal activity. So the criminals themselves organize a hunt for the killer. Much of the film concerns Lorre's flight from everyone. Finally he is captured by the criminals and brought before their kangaroo court. Lorre's pathetic defense is one of the great performances in film history. Lang's expressionistic directing was never better.

Peter Lorre discovers he has been identified in *M* (31).

Mad Max

(1979) AUSTRALIA, DIRECTOR – GEORGE MILLER

Australia after the apocalypse is dominated by gangs of barely civilized and bizarrely dressed bikers. Max is a member of the police force, the Bronze. First his partner and then his wife and baby are killed by a gang known as the Glory Riders and Max sets out to revenge their deaths. This could have been a fairly standard motorcycle or avenge film, but Miller's vision of people as dehumanized and machine-like, makes it much more. Besides the action is great and the stunts unbelievable. The picture made an international star out of unknown Australian actor Mel Gibson. *Mad Max 2/The Road Warrior* (1981) was more ambitious, and even better than the original but *Mad Max Beyond Thunderdome* (1985) was overstuffed and disappointing.

Maedchen In Uniform   (1931) GERMANY, DIRECTOR – LEONTINE SAGAN

Director Sagan was a noted stage actress and theater director who studied with Max Reinhardt. The internationally acclaimed yet highly controversial *Maedchen In Uniform* was her first film. An anti-Nazi movie with a radically strong lesbian theme the movie is about a student who falls in love with one of her teachers at a rigidly authoritarian girls' school and commits suicide.

The movie stars Dorothea Wieck, Ellen Schwannecke, Hertha Thiele, and Emilie Lunde. Shortly after making *Maedchen In Uniform* Sagan went to Britain where she directed the movie *Men Of Tomorrow*, a comedy set at Oxford starring Maurice Braddell, Joan Gardner, Emlyn Williams, Merle Oberon and Robert Donat.

The Magnificent Ambersons   (1942) USA, DIRECTOR – ORSON WELLES

Orson Welles wrote the screenplay as well as directed this pictorially brilliant evocation of small town American life early in the century. The fine cast includes Joseph Cotton, Dolores Costello, Agnes Moorehead and Tim Holt. Based on the novel by Booth Tarkington the movie begins when the proud Ambersons are at their peak and follows them through their decline focusing on the spoiled young heir to the family's fortune, a fortune that vanishes. Unfortunately RKO did not allow Welles artistic control and key scenes were left out of the movie while other scenes were rearranged without his approval. But the leisurely and beautiful film is still a treasure.

The heir to the Ambersons' fortune, Tim Holt provokes their financial ruin in *The Magnificent Ambersons* (42).

Major Barbara   (1940) GREAT BRITAIN, DIRECTOR – GABRIEL PASCAL

This splendid screen version of George Bernard Shaw's play features a first-rate cast which includes Rex Harrison, Wendy Hiller, Robert Morley, Robert Newton, Marie Lohr, Emlyn Williams, Sybil Thorndike and Deborah Kerr. With a brilliant script adapted by Pascal and Anatole de Grunwal, the movie is about a rich young woman who becomes a leading force in the Salvation Army until she is persuaded by her clever scheming father and an idealistic young man who loves her to resign. The dialogue is, of course, sparkling and Shaw himself wrote some of the additional scenes.

Robert Newton argues with Wendy Hiller of the Salvation Army while Rex Harrison is caught in the middle in *Major Barbara* (40).

The Maltese Falcon   (1941) USA, DIRECTOR – JOHN HUSTON

The one movie that's on every fan's list of favorite films stars Humphrey Bogart as Sam Spade. Based on Dashiell Hammett's novel, *The Maltese Falcon* is about a group of greedy thieves in search of a fabulous treasure. Spade becomes entangled with them when he starts tracking down the murderer of his partner. Mary Astor, Sidney Greenstreet, Elisha Cook Jr, and Peter Lorre are at their best in this movie but every role is perfectly cast and the film's a character actor's *tour de force*. A good version of *The Maltese Falcon* was made in 1931 with Ricardo Cortez and Bebe Daniels and remade in 1936 as *Satan Met A Lady* starring Bette Davis.

Mary Astor hires private detective Sam Spade (Humphrey Bogart) in *The Maltese Falcon* (41). Jerome Cowan as his partner Miles Archer looks on.

A Man For All Seasons (1966) GREAT BRITAIN, DIRECTOR – FRED ZINNEMANN

A beautifully acted film *A Man For All Seasons* depicts Thomas More's struggle of conscience with Henry VIII which culminates over the issue of divorce. More's brave stand led to his martyrdom. The magnificent cast includes Paul Scofield as More, Wendy Hiller as his wife Alice, Susannah York as his daughter Margaret, Robert Shaw as the king and Leo McKern as the wily Cromwell. The screenplay, by Robert Bolt, is a simplified adaptation of his play, but the film's every detail from the sets to the costumes ring true and clear. *A Man For All Seasons* was a major box office success and won the Best Picture Oscar, bringing Academy Awards to Bolt, Zinnemann, cinematographer Ted Moore and Scofield.

Shaw, Nigel Davenport, York, Scofield and Hiller – *A Man For All Seasons* (66).

The Man In The White Suit (1951) GREAT BRITAIN, DIRECTOR – ALEXANDER MACKENDRICK

Alec Guinness is marvelous as the man who invents a fabric so perfect it stays clean no matter what and never wears out or so it seems. Guinness is soon in trouble for creating a product which will cost workers their jobs and capitalists their profits. This delicious satire, with screenplay by Roger Macdougall, John Dighton and Mackendrick, boasts a cast that includes Joan Greenwood, Cecil Parker and Ernest Thesiger. The fine cinematography is by Douglas Slocombe while the good musical score is thanks to Benjamin Frankel. *The Man In The White Suit* was one of the most charming and perceptive movies to emerge from Britain after the war.

The Man Who Came To Dinner (1941) USA, DIRECTOR – WILLIAM KEIGHLEY

George S Kaufman and Moss Hart wrote the play and Julius J Philip and G Epstein the movie as a satire of writer and celebrity Alexander Woolcott. Monty Woolley gave the best performance of his career as the demanding egotist Sheridan Whiteside who is invited to dinner at the home of quite ordinary people in Ohio. Whiteside breaks his hip and is forced to remain with his hosts seemingly forever, intimidating everyone in sight. The movie takes a heartwarming turn as Whiteside manages, despite his gruffness, to do a bit of good along the way. The cast includes Bette Davis, Ann Sheridan and Mary Wickes with Jimmy Durante poking fun at Harpo Marx and Reginald Gardiner poking fun at Noel Coward.

The Man Who Came To Dinner (41) starred Monty Woolley, Ann Sheridan, Richard Travis and Bette Davis.

The Man Who Knew Too Much

(1934) GREAT BRITAIN,

DIRECTOR – ALFRED HITCHCOCK

This early film by the masterful director of suspense is a real winner. A *tour de force* for Peter Lorre who plays a sinister Nazi, the movie's plot concerns a young girl kidnapped by a ruthless gang of spies who plan a political assassination. The girl's father 'knows too much' and so the girl becomes a pawn, her life endangered. The cast includes Leslie Banks and Edna Best. Hitchcock remade the movie in 1956, this time in vivid technicolor starring James Stewart and Doris Day.

Peter Lorre and one of his gang hold Leslie Banks at gunpoint – *The Man Who Knew Too Much* (34).

139

Marty   (1955) USA, DIRECTOR – DELBERT MANN

Originally a television drama this is the first of the plays from TV's golden age of live drama to be translated to the silver screen. Paddy Chayefsky wrote the original television script, and adapted it for the movies. Ernest Borgnine, who had mainly played heavies, literally created a new film career for himself thanks to his role as a lonely unattractive butcher who meets a plain school teacher portrayed by Betsy Blair and falls in love with her. The dialogue is strikingly realistic and the film works beautifully as a compassionate study of the problems of ordinary people.

The ordinary butcher Ernest Borgnine takes schoolteacher Betsy Blair to the movies in *Marty* (55).

*M*A*S*H*   (1970) USA, DIRECTOR – ROBERT ALTMAN

Director Altman's biggest success this anti-war movie about a medical unit of surgeons during the Korean War is hilarious and it spawned a magnificent long-running television series starring Alan Alda. Ring Lardner, Jr wrote the screenplay based on Richard Hooker's novel and won an Oscar for it. Donald Sutherland, Elliott Gould and Tom Skerritt played the anti-establishment doctors. The movie also stars Robert Duvall as Frank Burns with Sally Kellerman playing Hot Lips Houlihan. There's plenty of blood and gore to go around, plus sexual slapstick and raucous language. The actors were allowed, Altman-style, to make up their own dialogue in a number of scenes. The movie received several Oscar nominations including one for Altman and one for Kellerman.

Right: Gould, Skerritt and Sutherland in *M★A★S★H* (70).

The Mask Of Dimitrios   (1944) USA, DIRECTOR – JEAN NEGULESCO

Based on the wonderful thriller *Coffin For Demitrios* by Eric Ambler, this is one time the movie lives up to the book, in which distinctly unheroic Dutch writer learns the truth about a very accomplished spy and criminal. The fine screenplay is by Frank Gruber. Negulesco's stylish direction evokes a mood of international intrigue. The best thing about the movie, however, is its superb cast of character actors with Peter Lorre, Sidney Greenstreet, Victor Francen, Steve Geray, Eduardo Ciannelli, Kurt Katch, Florence Bates and John Abbott in top form. Zachary Scott in his screen debut is fascinating as Dimitrios.

A Matter Of Life And Death/Stairway To Heaven   (1946) GREAT BRITAIN, DIRECTORS – MICHAEL POWELL, EMERIC PRESSBURGER

Powell and Pressburger's collaboration from 1941 to 1956 resulted in several visually impressive and original works, which they produced, co-wrote and co-directed. *A Matter Of Life And Death/Stairway To Heaven* is one of their greatest achievements. The film stars David Niven as an RAF pilot seriously injured in a plane crash who hovers between life and death while his fate is decided by a trial in heaven. An imaginative fantasy shot in black-and-white and spectacular Technicolor the movie's fine cast includes Roger Livesey, Marius Goring and Raymond Massey.

Meet Me In St Louis   (1944) USA, DIRECTOR – VINCENTE MINNELLI

Beginning in the summer of 1903 and ending the following spring this Technicolor movie is a series of vignettes idealizing turn-of-the-century life each season of the year. Nostalgic and sentimental *Meet Me In St Louis* is about a close-knit loving family afraid they may have to leave their mid-western city. They get to stay in the end, just in time for the Louisiana Purchase exposition which was held in St Louis. Based on the novel by Sally Benson the movie stars Judy Garland, Margaret O'Brien, Tom Drake, Marjorie Main and Harry Davenport. The charming score includes 'The Trolley Song', 'Have Yourself A Merry Little Christmas' and 'Under the Bamboo Tree'.

O'Brien and Garland in *Meet Me in St Louis* (44).

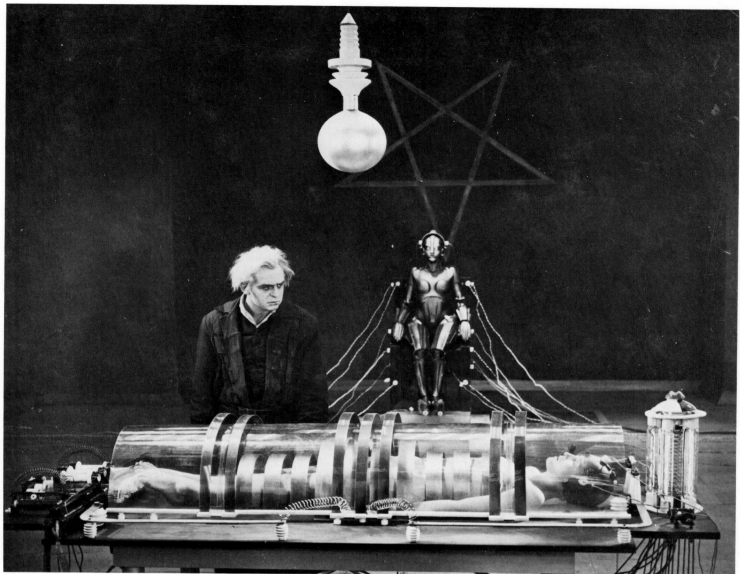

Maria (Brigitte Helm) lies at the mercy of evil Rotwang (Rudolf Klein-Rogge) in *Metropolis* (26).

Metropolis (1926) GERMANY, DIRECTOR – FRITZ LANG

Director Lang got the idea for this great masterpiece on a visit to America when he glimpsed the Manhattan skyline. *Metropolis* is a silent science fiction film set in a city where the workers are slaves, the rulers decadent. Revolution is prevented by the intervention of an angelic young woman until an evil inventor creates a wicked and depraved copy of her with dire results. Though some of the scenes now look silly visually the movie is splendidly imaginative and much of its imagery has never been surpassed. Lang co-wrote the screenplay with Thea Von Harbou. The cinematographer was Karl Freund. In the 1970s the BBC added an electronic music sound track which is excellent.

Midnight Cowboy (1969) USA, DIRECTOR – JOHN SCHLESINGER

One of Hollywood's earliest movies to break through censorship into the new freedom of the late 1960s this film made stars of its two compelling lead actors, Jon Voight and Dustin Hoffman. Voight plays Joe Buck, a country boy from Texas who hopes to make big bucks in New York hustling as a stud, and Hoffman plays Ratso Rizzo, a slimy con artist, suffering from tuberculosis. Despite the demeaning circumstances of their lives they reach out to each other, achieving some humanity and dignity as they pretend to themselves that there's hope for the future. Based on a novel by Leo Herlihy the movie won the Academy Award for Best Picture.

Dustin Hoffman and Jon Voight in *Midnight Cowboy* (69).

Mildred Pierce   (1945) USA, DIRECTOR – MICHAEL CURTIZ

Joan Crawford won an Academy Award for her portrayal of a woman on her own who works her way up from running a neighbourhood pie wagon to owning a chain of restaurants and who is devoted to her utterly selfish and worthless daughter (Ann Blyth). Part love story, part *film noir* murder mystery, the movie is based on a novel by James M Cain. The cast includes Jack Carson, Zachary Scott and Eve Arden. Oscar nominations went to the movie itself, to cinematographer Ernest Haller, and to Arden and Blyth.

Le Million   (1930) FRANCE, DIRECTOR – RENÉ CLAIR

This early sound musical comedy has the exquisite grace you'd expect from a film crafted by the great French director. The movie, about an artist, a con man, and a lost lottery ticket blends song and humor with delicate charm. Clair wrote the screenplay. Georges Van Parys, Armand Bernard, and Philippe Pares composed the musical score. There's great comic timing, plenty of slapstick and there's satire, too, and behind the innocent facade there are the usual profound Clair perceptions awaiting the astute viewer. The movie stars Annabella, Réne Lefevre and Paul Olivier. The movie had a great effect on two important directors, Ernst Lubitsch and Rouben Mamoulian.

René Lefevre with Annabella in René Clair's *Le Million* (30).

The Miracle Of Morgan's Creek   (1944) USA, DIRECTOR – PRESTON STURGES

A glorious farce that was originally filmed in 1942, it was two years before the Hays Office would allow it to be shown. When it finally did get past the censors Sturges was rewarded with an Oscar nomination. Sturges wrote as well as directed the movie, a frantic bit of nonsense which was very daring in its day, a spoof of American wartime values. Eddie Bracken plays Norval Jones, an ordinary guy willing to wed Trudy Knockenlocker, played by Betty Hutton. Knockenlocker is pregnant but can't quite recall who the serviceman she married was. All is forgiven when Knockenlocker has sextuplets.

Trudy Knockenlocker (Betty Hutton) discovers that she is already married, but not to Norval Jones (Eddie Bracken) in *The Miracle of Morgan's Creek* (44).

Miracle On 34th Street   (1947) USA, DIRECTOR – GEORGE SEATON

Seaton wrote as well as directed this whimsical wonder, which has been called the world's favorite Christmas movie. Actor Edmund Gwenn had made his film debut in 1916 but he had to wait until *Miracle on 34th Street* to become a movie star. He was in his seventies at the time. Gwenn plays Kris Kringle who believes he's Santa Claus and who winds up convincing a skeptical little girl played by Natalie Wood, her mother played by Maureen O'Hara, and the man who falls in love with her mother, John Payne. In the end he convinces the audience, too. The movie has charm, humor, and a sharp edge which keeps it from being syrupy. It's also a vintage New York film.

Mr Blandings Builds His Dream House   (1948) USA, DIRECTOR – H C POTTER

This charming gently sentimental comedy caught the post-war mood when an affluent America was about to move *en masse* to the suburbs. Cary Grant plays the Manhattan advertising executive who gets talked into building the house of his dreams in Connecticut. The reality of building a house turns the dream into a nightmare until the end of the film when the house is completed. Myrna Loy plays Grant's loving wife and the rest of the fine cast includes Melvyn Douglas and Reginald Denny. The movie, based on a novel by Eric Hodgkin, has a clever screenplay written by Norman Panama and Melvin Frank.

Mr Deeds Goes To Town   (1936) USA, DIRECTOR – FRANK CAPRA

The first of Capra's socially conscious comedies, the movie makes a strong case for small-town homespun honest values. Capra won an Oscar and actor Gary Cooper received an Oscar nomination for his portrayal of Longfellow Deeds, tuba player, greeting card verse writer, and decent human being who outsmarts the New York sophisticates and teaches them a lesson. Jean Arthur costars as she plays reporter Babe Bennett, posing as a stenographer to get the real story on Deeds. Robert Riskin wrote the delightful screenplay based on the story *Opera Hat* by Clarence Buddington Kelland. A 1969 TV series based on the movie starred Monte Markham.

Lionel Stander keeps an eye on Jean Arthur and Gary Cooper in *Mr Deeds Goes to Town* (36).

Mister Roberts   (1955) USA, DIRECTORS – JOHN FORD, MERVYN LE ROY

Director Ford left the movie halfway through filming but Le Roy stepped in and did a masterful job. A delightful and endearingly sentimental comedy, the movie stars Henry Fonda in the title role, a part Fonda played for years on Broadway and on tour. Mister Roberts is a navy officer yearning for action stuck on a cargo ship. He becomes the crew's champion in their struggle against the ship's obnoxious captain, played by James Cagney. William Powell plays Doc Daneeka, his final screen role. Hollywood underrated Fonda who did not win an Oscar in *Mister Roberts*. Jack Lemmon did, as Ensign Pulver.

Henry Fonda, William Powell and Jack Lemmon in *Mister Roberts* (55).

Mr Smith Goes To Washington   (1939) USA, DIRECTOR – FRANK CAPRA

James Stewart plays an honest politician sent to Washington DC who foils his adversary, the wicked and corrupt Senator Paine, played by Claude Rains. The Oscar-nominated movie, vintage Capra, is a touching tribute to American myths and values, a land where decency wins, democracy lives and innocence triumphs. Stewart received his first Oscar nomination for his fine performance as the awkward good guy Smith. Rains also earned a nomination. The excellent cast includes Jean Arthur, Thomas Mitchell, Edward Arnold and Harry Carey. The movie bears some resemblance to Capra's *Mr Deeds Goes to Town*, starring Gary Cooper.

Greer Garson and Walter Pidgeon and their children endure the Blitz in *Mrs Miniver* (42).

Mrs Miniver (1942) USA, DIRECTOR – WILLIAM WYLER

This Oscar winning movie raised the morale of the American moviegoing public and made viewers conscious of the plight of the British during World War II. Greer Garson won an Oscar for her portrayal of a British housewife minding the home front, pausing only to capture a Nazi pilot (Helmut Dantine) while her husband played by Walter Pidgeon is rescuing the BEF at Dunkirk. Seen in context, as a wartime film, *Mrs Miniver* is powerful and inspiring. The fine cast includes Oscar winner Teresa Wright, Dame May Whitty and Henry Travers.

Modern Times (1936) USA, DIRECTOR – CHARLES CHAPLIN

Only Chaplin could have produced an essentially silent film this late in the sound era. Chaplin also directed the movie, starred in it, wrote the screenplay and composed the musical score. He even sings a song. This is one of Chaplin's most socially incisive creations. The first part of *Modern Times* is about a worker victimized by the assembly line which does its best to dehumanize him. Later he bounces from job to job as factories close down. The gamine he loves is played by Paulette Goddard. *Modern Times* is bitingly satiric despite an overlay of sentimentality while visually it's balletic with impeccably timed sight gags.

Monsieur Hulot's Holiday (1953) FRANCE, DIRECTOR – JACQUES TATI

Jacques Tati not only directed this fascinating comedy, he starred in it, portraying a marvelously warm, lovable and clumsy character who stumbles and bumbles his way through an inhospitable modern world. In *Monsieur Hulot's Holiday/Les Vacances de Monsieur Hulot* the accident-prone Monsieur Hulot takes a vacation near the sea leaving chaos in his wake. The movie, fastidiously constructed, with one well-timed sight gag after another was immensely popular. Tati played Monsieur Hulot again in *Mon Oncle* (1956) which further satirizes the sterility of contemporary society. *Mon Oncle* is about a little boy whose affluent parents are hopelessly dull but whose misfit of an uncle is imbued with the joy of life.

Monty Python And The Holy Grail (1974) GREAT BRITAIN, DIRECTORS – TERRY GILLIAM, TERRY JONES

The immensely popular British television comedy troupe 'Monty Python' made up of Graham Chapman, John Cleese, Eric Idle, Michael Palin and directors Jones and Gilliam brought their brand of inspired lunacy to the big screen in this sendup of the Arthurian legends, the movies and just about everything else although Chapman is a convincing king. Basically the film is a string of typical Python sketches strung together with a medieval theme. The humor is broad, often gross and sometimes surprisingly literate, just as some of the film is surprisingly beautiful. Other Python films include *The Life of Brian* a hilarious religious satire which offended all religions, as was intended.

Morocco (1930) USA, DIRECTOR – JOSEF VON STERNBERG

The incomparable Marlene Dietrich made her American debut in this movie, fascinating audiences with her steamy sexuality and icy aloofness. She plays a cabaret singer in North Africa. Gary Cooper, one of the few silent picture stars to make the transition to talkies successfully, costars as the Foreign Legionnaire Dietrich falls in love with. Director Von Sternberg, cinematographer Lee Garmes and Dietrich all received Oscar nominations. Jules Furthman wrote the screenplay based on Denno Vigny's novel *Amy Jolly*.

Marlene Dietrich and Gary Cooper starred in *Morocco* (30).

The Music Man (1962) USA, DIRECTOR – MORTON DA COSTA

A vivid all-American musical, music and lyrics by Meredith Wilson, the movie is a faithful adaptation of the Broadway hit. Robert Preston, who also starred in the Broadway version, plays a con-artist who makes the people of River City, Iowa, believe he can teach their children to play in a marching band, when in fact he can't tell one note from another. But magic does happen and his real dreams come true thanks to the town librarian (Shirley Jones) who falls in love with him. At the end of the movie he leads a brightly uniformed band down the street. Music director Ray Heindorf received an Oscar.

The people of River City are charmed by Robert Preston – *The Music Man* (62).

Charles Laughton and Clark Gable in *Mutiny on the Bounty* (35).

Mutiny On The Bounty   (1935) USA, DIRECTOR – FRANK LLOYD

Charles Laughton is spectacular as Captain Bligh, the sadistic bullying villain who drives the crew of HMS *Bounty* to mutiny in this Oscar-winning screen adaptation of the novel by Charles Nordhoff and James Norman Hall. Clark Gable costars as the manly and decent master's mate Fletcher Christian. Set in the eighteenth century and based on a true historical incident the movie's fine cast includes Franchot Tone and Dudley Digges. The movie was remade in 1962 with Trevor Howard as Bligh and Marlon Brando as Christian. A 1984 Australian version *The Bounty* stars Anthony Hopkins as Bligh and Mel Gibson as Christian.

My Fair Lady   (1964) USA, DIRECTOR – GEORGE CUKOR

Julie Andrews who created the role of Eliza on Broadway in the musical version of Bernard Shaw's *Pygmalion*, but Audrey Hepburn starred in the film version as the cockney flower seller who is trained by an arrogant elocutionist (Rex Harrison) to behave as a gentlewoman. Marni Nixon dubbed Audrey Hepburn's singing voice. There was reportedly a move to replace Rex Harrison with Cary Grant, but Grant refused. Harrison won an Oscar for his Henry Higgins. Others in the cast include Stanley Holloway as Eliza's father and Wilfred Hyde White as Colonel Pickering. The elegant film, with glorious costumes and sets by Cecil Beaton won the Academy Award for Best Picture. It's not as good as the stage version but the score by Alan Jay Lerner and Frederick Loewe, and George Bernard Shaw's ideas, still make this an extremely entertaining film.

Jeremy Brett and Rex Harrison accompany Eliza (Audrey Hepburn) to the races in *My Fair Lady* (64).

My Little Chickadee   (1939) USA, DIRECTOR – EDWARD CLINE

This comic western stars W C Fields as Cuthbert J Twillie, a cardsharp and Mae West as Flower Belle Lee, a shady lady, who band together against a villain. The two remarkable talents clashed from the start, each jealous of the other's penchant for stealing scenes, each used to being the sole star of his or her own vehicle. They even fought over whose script to use and in the end screenplay credit was given to both. Despite or because of their obvious on-screen competitiveness *My Little Chickadee* has a quirky eccentric charm. Too bad the Hays Office kept such a close eye on Mae though. She's always as her best when nobody's holding the reins.

Mae West and W C Fields starred in *My Little Chickadee* (39).

My Man Godfrey   (1936) USA, DIRECTOR – GREGORY LA CAVA

A Depression era screwball comedy, this movie stars William Powell as a poor tramp who is picked up on a scavenger hunt by a bored rich girl. Though actually a millionaire, he becomes the butler in her family's household, the one decent, honorable, sane person in the midst of a bunch of spoiled lunatics. Carole Lombard is simply wonderful as a zany society girl. So is the rest of the cast which includes Alice Brady, Eugene Pallette and Mischa Auer. The movie, the script, the director, Lombard, Powell and Auer all received Oscar nominations but the picture didn't win a single Academy Award. A 1957 remake starring June Allyson and David Niven isn't in the same league with the original.

Mystery Of The Wax Museum   (1933) USA, DIRECTOR – MICHAEL CURTIZ

Lost for twenty-five years this horror film developed the reputation of being a masterpiece. When a print was finally discovered, it turned out the picture wasn't as good as many had imagined. Still the tale of the disfigured and crazed model maker who turns living people into wax dummies has some very effective moments. Lionel Atwill, usually a supporting player in B-films, gives his strongest performance as the madman. Fay Wray plays the girl who bears a dangerous resemblance to Marie Antoinette. The film was remade as *The House of Wax* in color and 3-D in 1953 with Vincent Price as the mad model maker. *The House of Wax* was the most popular 3-D film of the era.

The Naked City   (1948) USA, DIRECTOR – JULES DASSIN

This film ends with the narrator's famous line 'There are eight million stories in the naked city. This has been one of them.' Director Dassin made a highly influential semi-documentary thriller about a young girl who is brutally murdered in New York, and the police hunt for her killer. Shot on location the film looks real, and the finale on the Williamsburg Bridge is truly exciting. In the cast are Barry Fitzgerald, Don Taylor, Howard Duff and Dorothy Hart. Cinematographers William Daniels and Paul Weatherwax won an Oscar for their work. The film was the basis for a TV series.

Nanook Of The North   (1927) USA, DIRECTOR – ROBERT FLAHERTY

Nanook is a historic and highly influential documentary by the director who is considered the 'father' of documentary films. Flaherty, who had already spent some time among the Eskimos, managed to get modest financial backing from a company of fur dealers and made this remarkable record of the struggles of an Eskimo and his family against the hostile forces of nature. In fact, Nanook died of starvation on the ice two years after the film was made. At first distributors didn't want to handle the film but it turned out to be a resounding commercial success, which encouraged many more documentaries, particularly about 'exotic' people.

The eskimo Nanook harpoons a seal in *Nanook of the North* (27).

Napoleon   (1927) FRANCE, DIRECTOR – ABEL GANCE

This last great epic of the silent era was almost swept into obscurity by the coming of sound. In 1981 it was painstakingly restored to its original length and glory by film historian Kevin Brownlow, and given a debut with full orchestra accompaniment at Radio City Music Hall in New York City. Gance's innovations were astounding, as early as 1927 he was experimenting with split-screen photography, hand held and mobile cameras, color tinting, and rapid-fire editing. His greatest innovation was the use of three-screen Polyvision for the finale. The film which stars Albert Dieudonné covers and romanticizes Napoleon's career from his years as a teenager in military college in 1780 to his triumphs as commander-in-chief of the French army in 1796.

Albert Dieudonné as the French general *Napoleon* (27).

National Lampoon's Animal House   (1978) USA, DIRECTOR – JOHN LANDIS

Written by three former *National Lampoon* writers, Harold Ramis, Douglas Kennedy and Chris Miller this is one of the wildest and funniest anti-establishment movies ever made. Gross to the core *Animal House* takes audiences inside a fraternity in the early 1960s whose inmates excel at food fights, toga parties and flunking out while practicing constant warfare against the respectable fraternity on campus and the college administration. John Belushi turns in a super performance as the most animal denizen of *Animal House* and the rest of the cast which includes Donald Sutherland, Peter Riegert, Kevin Bacon, Tim Matheson, Tom Hulce and Karen Allen are terrific. Unfortunately the movie spawned a series of inferior imitations.

National Velvet   (1944) USA, DIRECTOR – CLARENCE BROWN

Elizabeth Taylor had her best juvenile role as Velvet Brown the girl who disguises herself as a boy in order to ride her horse in England's Grand National steeplechase, in one of the best horse races ever put on film. Mickey Rooney plays the footloose jockey who helps her train her horse. Anne Revere won the Best Supporting Actress Oscar for her role as Velvet's supportive but long-suffering mother. Angela Lansbury appears as Velvet's boy-crazy teenage sister. The script was adapted from a popular novel by Enid Bagnold. Although the setting looks authentically English, the film was made on the MGM soundstages and the California coast during the war. *International Velvet* is a disappointing 1979 sequel.

Mickey Rooney cuts Elizabeth Taylor's hair to help her pass as a boy and ride in the Grand National in *National Velvet* (44).

Network   (1976) USA, DIRECTOR – SIDNEY LUMET

Ex-television writer Paddy Chayefsky turned on his old medium with a vengeance in this ferocious satire about a raving mad anchorman who becomes enormously popular. Peter Finch plays the anchorman whose catch phrase 'I'm mad as hell and I'm not going to take it anymore' became a popular saying at the time. The Motion Picture Academy awarded this hilarious exercise in television bashing with four Oscars, Chayefsky for his screenplay, Finch (posthumously) for Best Actor, Fay Dunaway, Best Actress for her role as a ruthless program executive, and Beatrice Straight Best Supporting Actress. William Holden costarred as the craggy and relatively ethical chief of the news department.

Peter Finch played the suicidal anchorman in *Network* (76).

The Niebelungen   (1924) GERMANY, DIRECTOR – FRITZ LANG

Inspired by the legend of Siegfried that also inspired Richard Wagner's operatic Ring Cycle, this slow, stately two-part film (Part I – *'Siegfried'*, Part II *'Kriemheld's Revenge'*) tells the story of the Teutonic hero and his fierce bride Brunhilde. The spectacle and decor of the film remains fascinating, but the controversy that has surrounded the film also remains. Some saw it as a foreshadowing of the Nazi superman idea, and the film, *The Niebelungen*, was said to be among Hitler's favorites. Lang insisted it was meant only to counteract pessimism that had engulfed post Imperial Germany by reaching to its legendary past.

Paul Richter as Siegfried is murdered in *The Niebelungen* (24).

A Night At The Opera   (1935) USA, DIRECTOR – SAM WOOD

In an attempt to attract a wider audience the Marx Brothers slowed down their zaniness a bit to provide time for songs from Kitty Carlisle and Allan Jones, and musical solos from Harpo and Chico. Fortunately they don't slow things down too long, and this film contains some of their best routines including the famed scene where everybody tries to cram into Groucho's tiny stateroom. Groucho plays Otis P Driftwood, who is trying to convince the wealthy Mrs Claypool (Margaret Dumont) to invest her money in the New York Opera. Of the many wonderful lines this is a favorite. Groucho and Chico are trying to negotiate a contract, but Chico objects to the sanity clause 'Because there ain't no Sanity Claus'. The screenplay was by George S Kaufman and Morrie Ryskind, and the executive producer was Irving Thalberg who brought the Marx Brothers to MGM when their Paramount contract expired.

The famous stateroom scene in *A Night at the Opera* (35).

Night Of The Hunter (1955) USA, DIRECTOR – CHARLES LAUGHTON

James Agee adapted Davis Grubb's novel about a psychopathic preacher on the trail of two children who know the whereabouts of hidden money. The film was Laughton's directorial debut in which he borrowed from D W Griffith and the German Expressionists. Robert Mitchum starred as the hypnotic and terrifying preacher with Lillian Gish as the children's protector. Stanley Cortez's photography is outstanding and unique. The result is a gothic horror story, fairytale, and religious parable that is absolutely fascinating. The image of the preacher riding through the night in pursuit of the two innocents singing 'Leaning On The Everlasting Arms' is one of the most haunting in film history.

Lillian Gish starred as the children's protector in the haunting parable of good and evil, *Night of the Hunter* (55).

Ninotchka

(1939) USA, DIRECTOR – ERNST LUBITSCH

The publicity for this film read 'Garbo Laughs'. It was the great Garbo's first and only real comedy (indeed she retired after her next film). Garbo plays Nina Yakushova, an emotionless Soviet envoy in Paris who is looking for three missing commissars (Sig Ruman, Felix Bressart and Alexander Granach). She meets Count Leon d'Algout (Melvin Douglas) a frivolous ladies' man who is trying to recover the jewels of Grand Duchess Swana (Ina Claire) which the commissars are also after. Improbably Leon and Nina fall in love. The famous Lubitsch touch is evident in the scenes of Paris, and the script by Billy Wilder, Charles Brackett and Walter Reisch is witty. Garbo's performance is intelligent and genuinely funny. The film has been adapted as *Comrade X* (1940), *The Iron Petticoat* (1956). Cole Porter turned it into a Broadway musical *Silk Stockings* in 1955, and Hollywood turned the musical back into a film in 1957.

Norma Rae

(1979) USA, DIRECTOR – MARTIN RITT

Sally Field, formerly Gidget and the Flying Nun, surprised just about everyone with her well-deserved Oscar-winning performance as the spirited woman who helps organize a union in a Southern textile mill. She is recruited to the union cause by a brash Jewish union organizer from New York (Ron Liebman). She has trouble with her bosses, her minister, even her new husband, Beau Bridges. In the film's most moving scene, Field, who has been harassed by management stands up on a table at the mill with a sign that reads 'Union', and one by one the workers shut down their machines. The Oscar-winning song 'It Goes Like It Goes' is sung by Jennifer Warnes.

Sally Field played a textile worker in *Norma Rae* (79).

North By Northwest (1959) USA, DIRECTOR – ALFRED HITCHCOCK

This film is not only one of Hitchcock's most suspenseful works, it is one of his funniest and most enjoyable. Cary Grant plays Roger O Thornhill (ROT, for short) a New York advertising man who is mistaken for a secret agent, and pursued cross country by a group of foreign spies headed by James Mason, and the police who think that he has murdered a UN employee. Grant is befriended by a beautiful stranger (Eva Marie Saint) who is actually a double-agent. The film contains some of Hitchcock's most famous scenes, including Grant being pursued across the Indiana fields by a murderous crop-dusting plane and a cliff-hanging ending (literally) on Mt Rushmore.

Left: Cary Grant runs from a plane in *North by Northwest* (59).

Nosferatu (1922) GERMANY, DIRECTOR – F W MURNAU

The names were changed, reputedly to beat Bram Stoker's copyright, but this is the first film adaptation of *Dracula*. The Dracula character here called Graf Orlok, is a bizarre looking, bald, rat-faced creature, not at all like the elegant Middle-European aristocrat made famous by Bela Lugosi. The film is heavy on mood and symbols, and some modern viewers find it a bit silly. Others regard it as one of the great classics of the fantastic cinema. A stylish 1979 remake *Nosferatu the Vampire*, was directed by Werner Herzog and starred Klaus Kinski.

Max Schreck as the horrifying Graf Orlok in *Nosferatu* (22).

Nothing Sacred (1937) USA, DIRECTOR – WILLIAM A WELLMAN

Hazel Flagg (Carole Lombard) is a young Vermont girl who thinks she is dying of radium poisoning. A slick city reporter (Fredric March) writes a series of heart wrenching stories about her suffering, and she becomes a national celebrity. Then she finds out that the diagnosis is wrong and she wants to come clean, but no one will let her. Ben Hecht wrote the bitingly cynical script for this classic, often called a screwball comedy, but more appropriately a black comedy. Lombard is wonderful in a performance that gathers steam as it goes along. Also in the cast are Charles Wininger, Walter Connolly, Sig Ruman, Frank Fay, Margaret Hamilton, Hedda Hopper, Monty Woolley and Hattie McDaniel.

Carole Lombard, Walter Connolly and Fredric March in *Nothing Sacred* (37).

Now, Voyager (1942) USA, DIRECTOR – IRVING RAPPER

The famous line of this monumental Hollywood tearjerker is Bette Davis': 'Oh Jerry, we have the stars. Let's not ask for the moon.' Davis plays a plump spinster on the way to a nervous breakdown because of the puritanical mother (Gladys Cooper). She is cured by kindly psychiatrist Claude Rains, and goes on an ocean voyage where she meets kindly but unhappily married Paul Henried. They fall in love but of course, they can't marry. Later she finds Henried's unhappy daughter at Rains' sanitarium, and becomes a second mother to her. Max Steiner's swelling music won an Oscar, and Davis received her sixth Best Actress nomination. In that less health conscious day Henried's act of lighting two cigarettes and giving Davis one become the supreme romantic gesture.

Paul Henried meets Bette Davis in *Now, Voyager* (42).

Occupe-Toi D'Amélie   (1949) FRANCE, DIRECTOR – CLAUDE AUTANT-LARA

Boulevard farces like those of Georges Feydeau are difficult to adapt for the screen. This one, known in English as *Keep an Eye on Amelia*, is one of the most successful and consistently hilarious efforts. The story around which all the mistakes, coincidences and narrow escapes are centered is that of a Parisian coquette who agrees to go through a mock marriage with her lover's best friend in order to fool his uncle. The ceremony, however, turns out to be real. The film features Danielle Darrieux, Jean Desally, Bourvil, Carette and Gregoire Aslan. The timing and editing are what make this film work so well.

Odd Man Out   (1947) GREAT BRITAIN, DIRECTOR – CAROL REED

While the politics are never made entirely clear, Johnny McQueen is obviously an IRA gunman in Belfast. Along with several accomplices he commits a robbery in which a man is accidentally killed and Johnny himself is seriously wounded. His companions abandon him and much of the film concerns Johnny's attempts to get back to his organization's headquarters, and the people who try to help or hinder him. Though director Reed may have had more in mind this film works best as a thriller. Johnny is played by James Mason at the height of his powers and popularity. The ending has impact and surprise.

Oh Mr Porter   (1937) GREAT BRITAIN, DIRECTOR – MARCEL VARNEL

Will Hay, who started as a musical hall comic and went on to become one of the most popular comedians in British films of the 1930s and 1940s was the standout star in this, one of the best British comedies of the era. A group of incompetent Irish gun-runners shipping weapons on a small Irish railroad disguised as ghosts, are caught by a railroad station-master. Director Varnel, who had started on the Paris stage, seemed to understand British humor perfectly for he came to London in 1933 and directed this film and a number of other excellent comedies.

Oliver!   (1968) GREAT BRITAIN, DIRECTOR – CAROL REED

A faithful adaptation of Lionel Bart's enormously popular stage musical *Oliver!*, based, of course, on Charles Dickens's novel *Oliver Twist* is one of the last of the successful, big-budget musicals. The film even won a Best Picture Oscar. Director Reed known mainly for his thrillers also put a lot of suspense into this, his first try at a musical, and won the Academy Award for Best Director. Ron Moody starred as a somewhat softened and sympathetic Fagin. Oliver Reed is appropriately brutal as Bill Sikes, and Shani Wallis as Nancy is both sympathetic and rousing when she sings. There are several well staged musical numbers, perhaps the best is Fagin's boys performing 'Consider Yourself.'

To the amazement of his fellow orphans, Oliver (Marc Lester) asks Mr Bumble (Harry Secombe) for more soup in *Oliver!* (68).

Mr Bumble (Francis L Sullivan) and Oliver (John Howard Davies) in *Oliver Twist* (48).

Oliver Twist (1948) GREAT BRITAIN, DIRECTOR – DAVID LEAN

The works of Charles Dickens have often been the basis for fine films, and this is one of the finest. The story of a London waif (actually of genteel birth) who is adopted by a gang of thieves and later rescued by his own family, stars Robert Newton as the brutal Bill Sikes. Kay Walsh gives an appealing and sympathetic performance as the tragic Nancy, and the scene where she is beaten to death by Sikes may make you turn away. The best remembered performance is that of Alec Guinness, a bearded, hook-nosed, soft spoken, but creepily evil Fagin. Some Jewish groups objected to the portrayal. Also in the large and excellent cast are Anthony Newley as the Artful Dodger, Francis L Sullivan, Diana Dors and Peter Bull. Oliver was played by John Howard Davies. There have been other films of *Oliver Twist*, none comes close to this one for showing the exploitive side of nineteenth century London which Dickens wished to expose.

Los Olvidados   (1950) MEXICO, DIRECTOR – LUIS BUÑUEL

A shocker when it was first released in the United States, this film, also known as *The Young and the Damned*, is a brutal, unsentimental and uncompromising look at young gang members in the Mexican slums. The central character is a good boy (Alfonso Mejia) who falls in with an older, hardened juvenile delinquent. The result is tragedy. The poverty in which the boys grow up dooms them, and often turns them into monsters. One of the most disturbing scenes is where young gang members attack and torment a legless man. There are no easy solutions in this film – indeed there are no solutions at all.

Alfonso Mejia in *Los Olvidados* (50).

Olympische Spiele   (1936) GERMANY, DIRECTOR – LENI RIEFENSTAHL

Though this film is a documentary on the 1936 Berlin Olympics there is very little reporting of the events. Often we don't know who the competitors are, or who won. Basically this is a beautifully photographed paean to the strength and beauty of the athletes. That is what has made this film controversial for director Riefenstahl's Nazi sympathies are well known, and the film appears to celebrate the Nazi superman ideal. Interestingly most of the shots we see of Jessie Owens breaking Olympic records also come from this film. The photography, editing, and music make this a stirring experience if you can forget what was happening and about to happen outside the Olympic stadium.

The Olympic Torch became a symbol for the Nazi ideology and supremacy of the Aryan superman in *Olympische Spiele* (36).

On Golden Pond (1981) USA, DIRECTOR – MARK RYDELL

Eighty-year-old Norman Thayer (Henry Fonda) and his wife (Katharine Hepburn) arrive at their lakeside cottage for what will probably be their last summer there. Their alienated daughter (played by Fonda's daughter Jane) her fiancé, and his son arrive. Thayer is cranky and bitter about growing old. His wife is devoted and cognizant. Ernest Thompson adapted the screenplay from his own Broadway play. It's sentimental and calculated, but it works primarily because Hepburn and Fonda are so wonderful they transcend their roles. The film has special poignancy because Fonda was known to be ill, and this was to be his last film, and because of his own sometimes estranged relationship with daughter Jane.

Henry Fonda gave his last performance in *On Golden Pond* (81). Katharine Hepburn played his loving wife.

On The Town (1949) USA, DIRECTORS – GENE KELLY, STANLEY DONEN

This musical about three sailors on leave in New York City was the first major musical to be shot on location. It was also Kelly and Donen's first full direction job; they went on to do *Singin' In The Rain*. But most of all this film based on the Betty Comden-Adolph Green-Leonard Bernstein Broadway musical is just plain fun. Kelly plays a happy-go-lucky sailor, Gabey, who falls in love with 'Miss Turnstiles'

(Vera-Ellen). He is aided by his two sailor buddies Frank Sinatra and Jules Munshin. Ann Miller and Betty Garrett play their girlfriends. And Alice Pearce is appealingly ugly as Lucy Shmeeler, Kelly's blind date. Some of Bernstein's Broadway songs were cut, because they were thought to be too avant-garde, but 'New York New York' ('It's a Wonderful Town') was kept.

On The Waterfront (1954) USA, DIRECTOR – ELIA KAZAN

'I could have been a contender' Terry Malloy (Marlon Brando), a not too bright ex-fighter tells his scheming gangster brother (Rod Steiger). Malloy who is a strong-arm man for the corrupt longshoreman's union is thinking about squealing to the crime commission. His brother, who has been betraying him for years, tries to talk Terry out of it. Brando is splendid as the punchy Malloy who slowly realizes what is happening to him, and he won an Oscar for the performance. Eva Maria Saint made her

screen debut as the sister of a man who was killed by union thugs, and she too won an Oscar. Lee J Cobb is truly nasty as the union leader, but Karl Malden is a bit too preachy as an honest waterfront priest. Leonard Bernstein composed his first movie score, and won an Oscar. It is somewhat ironic to consider that Kazan was one of those who 'named names' in the HUAC hearings of the early 1950s.

Terry Malloy (Marlon Brando) in *On the Waterfront* (54).

Jack Nicholson as Patrick McMurphy feigns madness in *One Flew Over the Cuckoo's Nest* (75).

One Flew Over The Cuckoo's Nest (1975) USA, DIRECTOR – MILOS FORMAN

Patrick McMurphy, (Jack Nicholson) is a drifter who pretends to be mentally ill in order to get out of work duty at prison. He is sent to a mental ward ruled by the tyrannical Nurse Ratched (Louise Fletcher) who regiments the lives of the patients without helping them. McMurphy who sees the absurdity of the situation becomes the patients' symbol of nonconformity and rebellion. Much of the film has a comic tone, but the results of McMurphy's actions are tragic. The film won five Oscars: Best Picture, Best Director, Best Script, Best Actor (Nicholson), Best Actress (Fletcher). Lawrence Hauben and Bo Goldman adapted the script from the novel by Ken Kesey.

Open City (1946) ITALY, DIRECTOR – ROBERTO ROSSELLINI

Even before the Germans had evacuated Rome, director Rossellini started making a film about the Italian resistance in Rome toward the end of World War II. Much of the power of the film comes from the fact that many of those involved with making it had themselves been part of the resistance. It was the first film of Italy's postwar 'neorealistic' movement, and it made an international star out of Anna Magnani. Sergio Amidei co-wrote the script with Federico Fellini. The gritty newsreel quality was provided by cinematographer Ubaldo Arata.

Ordinary People   (1980) USA, DIRECTOR – ROBERT REDFORD

Redford made his debut as a director, and won an Oscar, for this tense and painful look at the disintegration of an upper middle class family after the death of their eldest son. Mary Tyler Moore, was cast against type as the cold and unloving mother, and she received high praise. Timothy Hutton won a Best Supporting Actor Oscar for his performance as the troubled son (though he really was the film's star). Donald Sutherland was excellent as the loving but sometimes blind father, Judd Hirsch was also first rate as the psychiatrist. The Oscar-winning script by Alvin Sargent was adapted from a novel by Judith Guest.

Timothy Hutton and Donald Sutherland in *Ordinary People* (80).

Dorothy Gish (left) with Lillian Gish in *Orphans of the Storm* (21).

Orphans Of The Storm   (1921) USA, DIRECTOR – D W GRIFFITH

On the eve of the French Revolution Henriette (Lillian Gish) brings her blind adopted sister, Louise (Dorothy Gish) to Paris for an operation that will cure her. However, Henriette is kidnapped by a wicked baron for one of his orgies, but is rescued from the orgy by a kindly aristocrat (Joseph Schildkraut). They fall in love but his parents won't allow him to marry a commoner. Meanwhile Louise who happens to be the kindly aristocrat's illegitimate sister has been taken by a group of thieves and forced to beg in the streets. And this is just the beginning! *Orphans of the Storm* is visually exciting, as are all Griffith films. Lillian Gish was never better. It's old-fashioned, even silly, but it's grand entertainment.

Orphée   (1950) FRANCE, DIRECTOR – JEAN COCTEAU

Cocteau sets the myth of Orpheus in contemporary France. This is a deeply personal work, though more accessible than some of Cocteau's other films. There are his ideas about art and immorality, but what makes this film truly fascinating are the images. Jean Marais stars as the poet Orpheus, and it's not hard to see why the Princess of Death (Marie Casarès) falls in love with him. The scenes in which Marais enters the netherworld through a mirror and the netherworld itself, which looks like bombed out Europe, are striking and memorable.

The Ox-Bow Incident   (1943) USA, DIRECTOR – WILLIAM WELLMAN

This grim and uncompromising story of mob violence in the Old West is based on a Walter Van Tilburg Clark novel. In the Nevada town of Ox-Bow a rancher is murdered, and a mob catches, and ultimately lynches, three innocent strangers. Henry Fonda is the nominal star, but the film really is a fine ensemble acting job featuring Harry Morgan, Dana Andrews and Anthony Quinn, with Jane Darwell as a heartless leader of the mob. Producer Darryl Zanuck didn't want to do the film because it was too downbeat. It was a box-office disaster, but is now considered a classic.

Three innocent strangers are lynched in a tale of mob violence, *The Ox-Bow Incident* (43).

Paisàn   (1946) ITALY, DIRECTOR – ROBERTO ROSSELLINI

This is one of the first of the gritty realistic films to come out of Italy at the end of World War II. Six vignettes depict life in Italy between the years of 1943 and 1945. Many of the scenes are improvised by a largely nonprofessional cast and the film has a semi-documentary quality. To English speaking film audiences accustomed either to escapist fare, or superpatriotic war films this look at what life was like on the other side had a tremendous impact, and the success of the films like *Paisan* influenced filmmaking for years. Federico Fellini helped Rossellini write the script.

The Palm Beach Story   (1942) USA, DIRECTOR – PRESTON STURGES

There is the hard-of-hearing 'Weenie King', the gun-toting Ale & Quail club and an assortment of other loonies in this wild screwball comedy. The plot, which really doesn't make a lot of sense, deals with a young couple Claudette Colbert and Joel McCrea who split up because they have no money, and she runs off to Palm Beach. McCrea is less wooden than usual, and Colbert is extremely lively and sexy. There are lots of other delights such as Mary Astor as a nutty millionairess and Rudy Vallee as her bumbling brother. Also in the cast are Sig Arno, William Demarest, Franklin Pangborn and Jimmy Conlin. This is a fast-paced, consistently funny piece of Sturges madness.

Pandora's Box   (1929) GERMANY, DIRECTOR – G W PABST

Louise Brooks plays the film's leading character, Lulu (a title under which the film is often known) brilliantly. It is the role with which she was always identified. Because of its very frank treatment of sexual themes the film was banned for many years, and later was only available in severely cut versions. The full-length version, however, has now become available, and reveals the film to be both daring and masterful. Lulu is the mistress of a middle-aged newspaper editor, whom she finally induces to marry her. The consequences of the marriage are bizarre and ultimately tragic. Lulu is not the traditional vamp who ruins weaker men, she is in reality the victim of weak men. Pabst and cinematographer Gunther Krampf create a sensual and expressionistic atmosphere, but it is Brooks's performance that makes the film memorable.

Louise Brooks gave a remarkable performance as Lulu, heroine of the haunting tragedy *Pandora's Box* (29).

Les Parapluies De Cherbourg   (1964) FRANCE/GERMANY, DIRECTOR – JACQUES DEMY

It's hard to imagine how a very pretty, almost fairytale-like screen operetta about a bettersweet romance between a shopgirl and a gas station attendant would become popular in the 1960s. He is declared missing while on military service and she is forced to marry an older man although pregnant by her lover. It isn't isn't exactly an old-style Hollywood operetta because it does deal with such subjects as premarital sex, pregnancy and a hatred of war – and that may have had something to do with its appeal. The film has unexpected charm, beautiful color and a nice score by Michel Legrand. Catherine Deneuve, who played the young shopgirl, first became known for *Les Parapluies de Cherbourg/The Umbrellas of Cherbourg*.

Pather Panchali   (1955) INDIA, DIRECTOR – SATYAJIT RAY

Director Ray wrote as well as directed this extraordinary film, with a musical score by Ravi Shankar, and based on the novels of Bhibuti Bashan Bannerjee. *Pather Panchali* is the first film in the Apu Trilogy which includes *Aparajito* and *Apu Sansar/The World of Apu*. Set in a Bengal village the film is deliberately slow, capturing the grinding and tragic effects of poverty. Yet there is hope as well as sorrow in the Apu Trilogy and all three films are authentically simple and beautiful. Though made in the Bengali language and specifically Indian their meaning is universal.

Subir Banerji played Apu as a young boy in *Pather Panchali* (55).

Paths Of Glory   (1957) USA, DIRECTOR – STANLEY KUBRICK

During World War I a French general orders his men to make an insane and suicidal attack. When some men hesitate, the general orders the court-martial of one man from each platoon. Despite a vigorous defense at a military trial the innocent men are convicted and executed. While not quite an anti-war film *Paths of Glory* is a relentless and powerful attack on the military mind. Kirk Douglas is surprisingly effective as the defense attorney. Adolphe Menjou is near perfect as the self obsessed general. The three doomed men, Timothy Cary, Ralph Meeker and Joseph Turkel are all excellent. The success of the film, however, is primarily due to Kubrick. His direction, and handling of the actors is masterful, and he helped to write the script with Calder Willingham and Jim Thompson.

Kirk Douglas starred in *Paths of Glory* (57).

Patton (1970) USA, DIRECTOR, FRANKLIN J SCHAFFNER

George C Scott's bravura performance as George S Patton the flamboyant and odd World War II general, won him the Academy Award for Best Actor, which he refused to accept. Few pictures have a better opening than this one, Patton standing in front of a gigantic American flag delivers a cranky, yet stirring speech to his troops. The battle scenes are all wonderfully staged. Karl Malden is also excellent as General Omar N Bradley, Patton's superior officer and one of the few who understood the maverick warrior. Besides Scott's Oscar *Patton* won Awards for Best Picture, Schaffner won one for Best Director, Francis Ford Coppola and Edmund H North for Best Story and Screenplay.

General Patton and his troops welcome their British allies to an Italian town in *Patton* (70).

The Petrified Forest (1936) USA, DIRECTOR – ARCHIE MAYO

Humphrey Bogart had his first major screen role as Duke Mantee an escaped convict who holds a group of people captive in an isolated desert cafe. The film was a faithful adaptation of Robert E Sherwoods's play, and in fact, Bogart played Mantee on Broadway. Leslie Howard also reprised his Broadway role as the failed writer who is hitching his way across America. Bette Davis plays the cafe owner's daughter who wants to become something more than a cafe waitress. There are fine performances from Charlie Grapewin, Dick Foran, Genevieve Tobin and Porter Hall. The film is a bit too much like a play, and it's a bit talky, yet it remains surprisingly fresh and effective.

Bogart, Bette Davis and Leslie Howard in *The Petrified Forest* (36).

Lon Chaney was the eerie phantom in *The Phantom of the Opera* (25).

The Phantom Of The Opera (1925) USA, DIRECTOR – RUPERT JULIAN

Based on a novel by Gaston Leroux, this is a Gothic tale of a deformed madman who lives in the tunnels and chambers beneath the Paris Opera, falls in love with a young singer and kidnaps her. The silent version often seems to be a patchwork of barely connected scenes, hardly surprising since director Julian was replaced during shooting by a series of others, including star Lon Chaney. But the seams don't matter because Chaney's skull-like makeup is sensational and the scenes memorable, particularly the moment when the singer, played by Mary Philbin, unmasks the phantom Chaney.

The Philadelphia Story   (1940) USA, DIRECTOR – GEORGE CUKOR

Philip Barry wrote the Broadway play on which this film was based, specifically for Katharine Hepburn. She decided it was the perfect vehicle for her return to the screen. She hadn't made a film in two years and was regarded as box office 'poison'. The result is a classic screwball comedy. Hepburn plays socialite Tracy Lord who has dumped her drunken husband Cary Grant, and rejected her father John Halliday. She's about to marry a prig, when Grant, accompanied by a fast-talking reporter (James Stewart) and a photographer (Ruth Hussey) shows up. After a wild and eventful night all is resolved. The material may be dated, but the wonderful performances will never date. Stewart won a Best Actor Oscar. The film was later turned into a musical film *High Society* (1956).

Grant, Hepburn, Stewart and Hussey in *The Philadelphia Story* (40).

Picnic At Hanging Rock   (1975) AUSTRALIA, DIRECTOR – PETER WEIR

A superb example of the kind of movies made in Australia this exquisite gem is a mysterious, supernatural and haunting tale of a group of young ladies who go exploring during a school picnic in 1900 with mystical results. Several disappear, seemingly vanishing into thin air. The movie has overtones of repressed Victorian sexuality coming up against magical primitive forces. Highly atmospheric and beautifully photographed the movie stars Rachel Roberts, as the head mistress of the school who is ultimately destroyed herself by the disappearance. Based on a novel by Joan Lindsay, the screenplay was by Cliff Green. The cinematographer is Russell Boyd.

Rachel Roberts at the *Picnic at Hanging Rock* (75).

David Niven meets a second gorilla at costume ball in *The Pink Panther* (64).

The Pink Panther   (1964) USA, DIRECTOR – BLAKE EDWARDS

This is a light romantic caper film about a charming semi-retired international jewel thief played by David Niven who comes out of retirement to steal the famous ruby, known as the Pink Panther. The film introduced two truly memorable characters. The bumbling Inspector Clouseau was played by Peter Sellers. When he is on screen the film is hilarious, and his character proved so popular that it was used in a series of films, *A Shot in the Dark, The Pink Panther Strikes Again* and *Revenge of the Pink Panther*, that were even better than the original. The second memorable character is the cartoon figure the Pink Panther, seen only in the opening credits. The credits, indeed the whole film is helped immeasurably by a catchy score by Henry Mancini.

Pinocchio   (1940) USA, WALT DISNEY

The Disney studios turned Carlo Collodi's story of the wooden puppet who wanted to be a real boy into an animated masterpiece; only Disney's own *Snow White* even comes close to matching it. The characters include Pinocchio himself, his 'father' Geppetto, his conscience, Jiminy Cricket, foxy 'Honest John' even Figaro the cat and Cleo the goldfish. The musical score by Leigh Harline, Ned Washington and Paul J Smith introduced the songs: 'Hi Diddle Dee Dee', 'When You Wish Upon a Star', 'I've Got No Strings', 'Give a Little Whistle'. The film contains some of the most frightening scenes in the movies, Lampwick's transformation into a donkey, and the terrifying Monstro the whale. The characters and sets are drawn so well, that in a moment you forget they are drawings at all. As in all Disney productions the success was due to the work of a large and largely anonymous (except for Disney himself) team. The supervising directors were Ben Sharpsteen and Hamilton Luske.

The Plainsman   (1936) USA, DIRECTOR – CECIL B DeMILLE

DeMille didn't merely bend history he shattered it in this epic which somehow involves Wild Bill Hickok, Calamity Jane, Buffalo Bill, General George Armstrong Custer and Abraham Lincoln. The massive Indian siege was all filmed indoors and takes on a practically surrealistic quality as a result. It's all Hollywood hokum and DeMille schmaltz, and it's all great fun. Gary Cooper is appropriately rugged as Wild Bill, but he's barely a match for Jean Arthur's

Calamity Jane. The repartée between the two keeps the film moving. The cast includes Charles Bickford, James Ellison and Gabby Hayes and Anthony Quinn has a small role as an Indian brave. A very poor remake was released in 1966.

Wild Bill Hickok (Gary Cooper) organizes the defense of a western town besieged by indians in *The Plainsman* (36).

Les Portes De La Nuit   (1946) FRANCE, DIRECTOR – MARCEL CARNÉ

A very atmospheric postwar *film noir*, about a group of people in Paris who are drawn into a pattern woven by Destiny. Destiny appears in the shape of a melancholy tramp. The film stars Pierre Brasseur, Yves Montand, Nathalie Nattier, Serge Reggiani, Jean Vilar, Saturnin Fabre,

Mady Berry and Dany Robin. This was one of director Carné's last successful films. His type of highly technical filmmaking became the object of much criticism from New Wave filmmakers. But *Les Portes de la Nuit/The Gates Of Night* holds up better than many New Wave films.

Portrait Of Jennie   (1948) USA, DIRECTOR – WILLIAM DIETERLE

A romantic supernatural story stars Jennifer Jones, as the most appealing spirit you would ever want to meet, and Joseph Cotton as a penniless New York artist who meets a strange little girl while walking through Central Park. She seems to grow up with astonishing speed in subsequent meetings. There is some pretentious talk about art and the meaning of life, but the cast including Ethel Barrymore,

Lillian Gish, David Wayne and Henry Hull is splendid. The last reel, which includes the sea storm in which Jennie is killed, is tinted green, and the final shot which was originally shown in Technicolor, was enough to earn *Portrait of Jennie* an Oscar for special effects. But it's the mood, tone and romance that make this finely crafted David O Selznick film special.

The Postman Always Rings Twice (1946) USA, DIRECTOR – TAY GARNETT

Author James M Cain complained that too many changes had been made in his original story, but most of them were made in order to get the picture past the censors at the Hays Office. Director Garnett acknowledged it was a tough job but that he thought he got the sex across pretty well despite restrictions. Lana Turner, in her best role, starred with John Garfield as the pair of lovers who decide to murder her husband. Also appearing in this classic *film center*

noir are Cecil Kellaway, Hume Cronyn, Audrey Totter and Leon Ames. Somehow this film packs much more punch than a more explicit and violent 1981 remake which starred Jessica Lange and Jack Nicolson. There have also been French and Italian film versions of the story.

Lana Turner and John Garfield plot the murder of her husband in *The Postman Always Rings Twice* (46).

Potemkin   (1925) USSR, DIRECTOR – SERGEI M EISENSTEIN

In 1948 and again in 1958 panels of international film critics voted *Potemkin* the greatest film ever made. It is one of the first films shown in every introduction to film courses. The scene in which the Tsar's troops march down the 'Odessa Steps' killing men, women and children in their path is the most famous single scene in film history. But *Potemkin* is more than a historical monument, even today when film techniques have advanced light years beyond those available to Eisenstein, *Potemkin* remains an astonishing, breathtaking experience. The film was made to celebrate the 20th anniversary of a mutiny aboard the Russian battleship *Potemkin*, an event which marked the start of the 1905 revolution, and ultimately the downfall of the Tsarist regime. This is the seminal work of the man who is generally considered the most important director in film history.

Pride And Prejudice   (1940) USA, DIRECTOR – ROBERT LEONARD

When MGM decided to do a film based on Jane Austen's classic *Pride and Prejudice*, they wisely called on British talent to help. Aldous Huxley co-wrote the screenplay. Recently arrived Irish actress Greer Garson got the role of the spirited Elizabeth Bennett. Laurence Olivier played the elegant and arrogant Mr Darcy (though Clark Gable had originally been scheduled for the role). The cast does include some Americans, Mary Boland and Ann Rutherford, for example. The result is an extremely entertaining, intelligent and faithful adaptation of a classic. It is a civilized, romantic comedy of manners, with sensible ideas and support for solid values, and like the book on which it is based it has held up very well.

Frieda Inescourt, Laurence Olivier, Edward Ashley and Greer Garson in *Pride and Prejudice* (40).

The Pride Of The Yankees (1942) USA, DIRECTOR – SAM WOOD

This sentimentalized, yet superior biography of Yankee great Lou Gehrig, is still the finest baseball film ever made. Gehrig was the Yankee's iron man, the image of strength and health, he never missed a game until he finally succumbed to the terrible muscle disease which now bears his name. The final sequence where a dying Gehrig stands in Yankee Stadium as the crowd cheers and makes his moving farewell address still brings a lump to the throat. Gary Cooper gives an excellent performance as Gehrig, and Teresa Wright is equally good as his devoted wife. The cast also includes Walter Brennan, Dan Duryea and Babe Ruth, as himself.

Gary Cooper as Lou Gehrig in *The Pride of the Yankees* (42).

The Prisoner Of Zenda (1937) USA, DIRECTOR – JOHN CROMWELL

Of the many versions of Anthony Hope's swashbuckling novel about an Englishman who is forced to impersonate his kidnapped cousin the King of Ruritania, this lavish David O Selznick production is the best. Ronald Colman is elegant and dashing as the hero, Rudolph Rassendyll, and as the king. Madeline Carroll is beautiful as his love the Princess Flavia. Raymond Massey is appropriately nasty as the usurping Black Michael and Douglas Fairbanks Jr gives one of his best performances as the evil Rupert of Hentzau.

Mary Astor, C Aubrey Smith, David Niven, Montagu Love and Alexander D'Arcy costar. The sets and costumes are lavish, the sword fights energetic, the sepia-toned cinematography striking. *The Prisoner of Zenda* had previously been filmed in 1913 and 1922 and was filmed again with Stewart Granger and Deborah Kerr in 1952.

Douglas Fairbanks Jr and Ronald Colman duel in *The Prisoner of Zenda* (37).

The Private Life Of Henry VIII   (1933) GREAT BRITAIN, DIRECTOR - ALEXANDER KORDA

This was the film that made Charles Laughton a major star and won him a well-deserved Oscar for Best Actor. Most of the political and religious struggles in the life of the turbulent sixteenth century monarch are ignored or glossed over, and the film concentrates on his relationships with five of his six wives. Even here, while such things as the beheading of Anne Boleyn are not ignored they are softened, and the whole film is played more like a domestic drama/comedy. Laughton manages to make the character of Henry believable and sympathetic and he is supported by a fine cast of wives, Binnie Barnes, Merle Oberon, Wendy Barrie, Everley Gregg and his own real life wife Elsa Lanchester, as Anne of Cleves.

Charles Laughton as Henry VIII repudiates Elsa Lanchester as Anne of Cleves in *The Private Life of Henry VIII* (33).

Psycho   (1960) USA, DIRECTOR — ALFRED HITCHCOCK

Even today, when practically everyone knows what's going to happen *Psycho* can provide a shock. Back in 1960 when it was first released it literally scared people out of the shower for months. The murder of Janet Leigh in the shower of Room One of the Bates Motel is one of the most shocking and famous scenes in the history of films. Anthony Perkins's portrayal of the peculiar Norman Bates is so good that it has dogged his career. Bernard Herrmann's score is legendary. Hitchcock always insisted the film was black comedy, everybody else thought is was pure horror. *Psycho* was enormously successful, and has inspired a host of imitations and parodies. Two sequels with Perkins (but without Hitchcock, of course) were produced in the 1980s, both were disappointments.

Anthony Perkins discovers a body in the shower in *Psycho* (60).

Public Enemy   (1931) USA, DIRECTOR – WILLIAM WELLMAN

James Cagney stars as Tom Powers a boy who grew from simple delinquent to full fledged Prohibition-era gangster. The studio claimed that the film was meant to deglamorize gangsters, but by accident or design, Cagney is by far the most appealing character in the film – tough, charming, unafraid, and until he is killed, far more successful than his dour law-abiding brother who is a ticket puncher on a trolley car. Despite some dated sociology, the great performances make this film a winner even today. In addition to Cagney and Mae Clark, Jean Harlow, Eddie Woods, Beryl Mercer, Donald Cook and Joan Blondell are featured.

James Cagney and Mae Clark in *Public Enemy* (31).

Pygmalion   (1938) GREAT BRITAIN, DIRECTOR – ANTHONY ASQUITH

Most people know George Bernard Shaw's play about the professor of phonetics who turns a cockney flower seller into a lady who can pass as a duchess, from the musical adaptation *My Fair Lady*. But no one should miss this absolutely magnificent screen adaptation of the original play. Leslie Howard stars as Professor Henry Higgins, and one can not imagine a better Eliza than Wendy Hiller.

Wilfred Lawson is especially memorable as Eliza's father, the dustman Alfred Dolittle. Shaw himself wrote the screenplay and was insulted by winning an Academy Award. Howard, Hiller and the film all received nominations.

Left: Leslie Howard and Wendy Hiller in *Pygmalion* (38).

Les Quatre Cents Coups   (1958) FRANCE, DIRECTOR - FRANÇOIS TRUFFAUT

Antoine Doinel (Jean-Pierre Leaud) is a 12-year-old boy who is unwanted and unloved. He's basically good and sensitive but he keeps getting into trouble for petty offenses like playing hookey. Adults make some half-hearted attempts to help him, but he is really on his own. the famous last shot is a freeze frame of the runaway with no place to run. Antoine finds some happiness by romping through Paris streets and going to movies. *Les Quatre Cents Coups/The 400 Blows* was Truffaut's semi-autobiographical directorial debut and one of the early major films of France's New Wave. Truffaut used the character of Antoine Doinel in several later films.

Jean-Pierre Leaud in *Les Quatre Cents Coups* (58).

Queen Christina   (1934) USA, DIRECTOR – ROUBEN MAMOULIAN

Greta Garbo is generally considered to be at her absolute best in her portrayal of the strong-minded seventeenth century Swedish queen. The Queen is being badgered by her advisers to marry a Swedish prince who is a war hero and a bore. But she doesn't want a loveless marriage and has an affair with the Spanish ambassador (played by John Gilbert, Garbo's most famous co-star from silent films). In the end she is forced to choose between her love and her throne. For a romance of the time the film is exceptionally well written but what really makes the film memorable is Garbo herself. This is the role she seemed to enjoy most. And of course, she is beautiful. The long final shot of her face is an enduring image from film history.

Right: Greta Garbo starred as the seventeenth century Swedish monarch, *Queen Christina* (34).

The Quiet Man   (1952) USA, DIRECTOR – JOHN FORD

Ford and his favorite star John Wayne were known for their Westerns, but one of the best films they did together was set in County Galway, Ireland, the birthplace of the director's parents. Wayne plays Irish-born American boxer Sean Thornton, who returns to the village of his birth, where he sees, and after some complications, marries lovely spirited, red-haired Mary Kate Danaher (Maureen O'Hara). It's sort of an Irish village *Taming of the Shrew*. One of the complications is Kate's brawling brother Will (Victor McLaglen). The film's most memorable scene is a lengthy fight between Sean and Will. The photography is gorgeous, and there are rousing performances by the stars and supporting players like Barry Fitzgerald, Ward Bond, and Mildred Natwick. Ford won an Oscar for his direction as did cinematographers Winton Hoch and Archie Stout.

Raiders Of The Lost Ark   (1981) USA, DIRECTOR – STEVEN SPIELBERG

Indiana Jones (Harrison Ford) is a whip-and-gun-carrying archaeologist-adventurer. He's searching for the Ark of the Covenant, which held Moses's Ten Commandments, but so are the Nazis. The chase goes from Tibet where Indy picks up his spirited girlfriend Marion (Karen Allen) to Egypt where he runs afoul of a Nazi monkey to a mysterious island in the Mediterranean. From its opening moment to its slam-bang conclusion this is simply a marvelous film with some of the greatest adventure sequences ever. It's supposed to be a tribute to Saturday serials, but it's much better than they ever were. It gives even jaded viewers the feeling of being kids watching those serials again. George Lucas produced the film and wrote the story on which the script is based. The 1984 sequel *Indiana Jones and the Temple of Doom* with Harrison Ford and Kate Capshaw is not quite up to the original, but rousing nonetheless.

Left: Karen Allen and Harrison Ford look away from the ark when it is opened by Nazi officials in *Raiders of the Lost Ark* (81).

Rashomon   (1950) JAPAN, DIRECTOR – AKIRA KUROSAWA

This was the first Japanese film to receive widespread international recognition after World War II. A bandit (played with wild abandon by Toshiro Mifune) is on trial for raping a woman in a forest in front of her husband and then murdering the husband. The events are related by the three principals (the dead man speaks through a medium) and a woodcutter who witnessed the crime. All the versions contradict one another and all are equally convincing. The film is vivid, strange and has been extremely influential. A poor Hollywood remake with Paul Newman called *The Outrage* was released in 1964.

In one of the versions of the crime in *Rashomon* (50), the bandit Toshiro Mifune is seduced by the woman (Machiko Kyo).

Rear Window (1954) USA, DIRECTOR – ALFRED HITCHCOCK

James Stewart stars as a news photographer with a broken leg who is confined to a wheelchair in his Greenwich Village apartment. He passes the time by spying on his neighbors, sometimes through a telephoto lens. A man in an apartment across the back (Raymond Burr) is behaving oddly, and the photographer becomes convinced he has murdered his wife. At first the photographer's fiancée (Grace Kelly) is skeptical but evidence begins to pile up. The action is confined entirely to the apartment and the audience identifies entirely with the trapped photographer. Based on a Cornell Woolrich story, this excellent film costars Thelma Ritter and Wendell Corey.

Grace Kelly and James Stewart in *Rear Window* (54).

Rebecca (1940) USA, DIRECTOR – ALFRED HITCHCOCK

This was Hitchcock's first American film, but it's more British than his British films and much closer in spirit to the Daphne du Maurier Gothic romance on which it is based than to a typical Hitchcock work. And it's wonderfully entertaining. Joan Fontaine stars as the shy girl who marries Maxim de Winter (Laurence Olivier) a man with a big house and a terrible secret. The young wife is made more nervous by the housekeeper Mrs Danvers (Judith Anderson, at her menacing best) who is devoted to the memory of Max's first wife Rebecca. The supporting roles are played by some of the best character actors in Hollywood, Nigel Bruce, George Sanders, C Aubrey Smith and Reginald Denny. The film was very popular and won the Oscar for Best Film.

Judith Anderson taunts Joan Fontaine in *Rebecca* (40).

The Red Badge Of Courage (1951) USA, DIRECTOR – JOHN HUSTON

Stephen Crane's classic Civil War novel about a young man getting his first taste of battle was turned into a surprisingly fresh and poetic film. As in the book the attention is concentrated on the individuals rather than the spectacle of battle. The unusual casting featured Audie Murphy a war hero turned actor, as the youth and he was outstanding.

Wartime cartoonist Bill Mauldin also appeared. Among the more conventional actors were Andy Devine, Royal Dana and Arthur Hunnicutt. The many troubles encountered in making *The Red Badge of Courage* are chronicled in *Picture* a book by Lillian Ross. A 1974 made-for-TV movie version of the Crane novel was quite good.

Red Dust (1932) USA, DIRECTOR – VICTOR FLEMING

Clark Gable and Jean Harlow starred in this jungle romance. She played a wise cracking prostitute on the run from the police in Indochina and he was a rubber planter who has an affair with the well-bred Mary Astor. He is better off with Harlow. The film contains Harlow's famous nude bath in a rain barrel. Gene Raymond costars as Astor's husband, and veteran character actors Donald Crisp and Tully Marshall appear as Gable's partners. There

have been two remakes of *Red Dust*, including John Ford's *Mogambo*, in 1953, which also starred Gable. Harlow's part had been taken by Ava Gardner, Grace Kelly had the Astor role and the action had shifted to Africa. It's not bad, but the original really crackles.

Prostitute Jean Harlow is quite a match for Clark Gable, the rude but handsome rubber planter in *Red Dust* (32).

'The Red Shoes Ballet' starred Moira Shearer, Robert Helpmann and Leonid Massine – *The Red Shoes* (48).

The Red Shoes   (1948) GREAT BRITAIN, DIRECTOR – MICHAEL POWELL

One of the best ballet films ever made *The Red Shoes* is also one of the most beloved movies. A gifted young dancer played by Sadler's Wells Ballet star Moira Shearer is forced to chose between her career represented by impresario Boris Lermontov (Anton Walbrook) and love represented by composer Julian Craster (Marius Goring). A beautifully photographed film it's both a backstage musical and high art. The highlight of the film is the 14-minute 'Red Shoes Ballet' with Shearer dancing a version of the Hans Christian Anderson fairy tale, and her own dilemma. The stunning choreography is by Robert Helpmann who also appeared in the film. Both the score and the art direction won Academy Awards.

Richard III   (1955) GREAT BRITAIN, DIRECTOR – LAURENCE OLIVIER

Not as good as Olivier's *Henry V* or as famous as his *Hamlet*, this is nevertheless one of the great films made from a Shakespeare play. Olivier is absolutely riveting as the evil Richard, Duke of Gloucester who schemes to inherit the Kingdom of England and kills his elder brother and two nephews to achieve it. Olivier claimed he modeled the character on a well known director. There are splendid performances by Claire Bloom as Lady Anne, Ralph Richardson as the Duke of Buckingham, Cedric Hardwicke as Edward IV, Stanley Baker as Henry Tudor and Alec Clunes, John Gielgud, Mary Kerridge and a host of other fine Shakespearean actors. The play is responsible for the popular view of the last Plantagenet king, and can be viewed as a particularly strong piece of propaganda.

Right: Laurence Olivier as the conniving *Richard III* (55).

Rififi   (1955) FRANCE, DIRECTOR – JULES DASSIN

This movie is notable for one of the most inventive heist sequences in the history of film in the form of an exciting silent twenty-five minute robbery of a jewelry store. The movie's ending is based on the old adage that 'there is no honor among thieves' and the crooks turn on each other with explosive violence. The word 'rififi' is French underworld slang for trouble and the title set the tone for the movie which is distinctly crisp and chic. *Rififi* was heavily influenced by the (1950) film *The Asphalt Jungle* and in turn gave birth to numerous imitations such as *Topkapi* (1961) and *Gambit* (1966). Director Jules Dassin who fled America during the McCarthy era played the character Perlo Vita in the film.

Risky Business   (1983) USA, DIRECTOR – PAUL BRICKMAN

Here is a teenage-sex comedy everyone can enjoy. Through a series of highly improbable circumstances high school senior Tom Cruise hires Rebecca De Mornay a $300-a-night hooker, and is then forced to turn his parents' ritzy home into a brothel. As a result he gets into Princeton because of his business acumen, wins the respect of his parents and friends, and falls in love with De Mornay. There is also sharp dialogue also by Brickman, which is a biting satire of the free enterprise system. The film marked Brickman's impressive directorial debut, and catapulted Cruise to stardom.

Rebecca De Mornay and Tom Cruise in *Risky Business* (83).

The Road To Singapore   (1940) USA, DIRECTOR – VICTOR SCHERTZINGER

The first of the 'Road Series' set the pattern for all that followed. Bob Hope plays the wise cracking coward and Bing Crosby the conniving crooner who swear off women until they meet Dorothy Lamour, the object of their mutual affections, in Singapore, which looks just like a Paramount studio set. Actually *Singapore* is more of a light romantic comedy. The series got zanier and better as it went along.

The 'Road' ran to *Zanzibar* (1941), *Morocco* (1942), *Utopia* (1945), *Rio* (1947), and *Bali* (1952). Ten years later a British studio tried to revive the series with *Road to Hong Kong*, but the old spark was gone.

Bing Crosby, Bob Hope and Dorothy Lamour in *The Road To Singapore* (40).

Rocky   (1976) USA, DIRECTOR – JOHN G AVILDSEN

The original Rocky film was a low-budget sleeper written by its unknown star Sylvester Stallone. Stallone played Rocky Balboa, a part-time Philadelphia fighter and full-time loser, who falls in love with a good woman, Adrian (Talia Shire) and gets a chance to fight for the championship. Carl Weathers costarred as Rocky's opponent and Burgess Meredith played his trainer Mickey. The film was touching and enormously popular. It won Oscars for Best Picture and Best Director. Stallone became an instant superstar and working-class hero. The whole thing became more of a phenomenon than a film. Three sequels have followed so far. They range from the overtly sentimental to the absolutely embarrassing, but their popularity is unquestionable.

Right: Sylvester Stallone as Rocky Balboa in *Rocky* (76).

Roman Holiday (1953) USA, DIRECTOR — WILLIAM WYLER

Audrey Hepburn made her major screen debut (she had a few bit parts before) in this charming romantic film. A princess from a mythical middle-European country is on a state visit to Rome. Yearning for a normal life she slips away from the official party for a brief romantic (but thoroughly chaste) fling with an American reporter (Gregory Peck). Hepburn won a deserved Oscar for her performance as the princess. Eddie Albert, Hartley Power and Harcourt Williams costarred. Rome never looked lovelier, thanks to the photography of Franz F Planer, and Henri Alekan who had worked with Cocteau.

La Ronde (1950) FRANCE, DIRECTOR — MAX OPHULS

A charming and civilized look at the transitory nature of love, Ophuls adapted this film from the play by Arthur Schnitzler. Each episode has a different couple, but one of the couple is from a previous episode so a prostitute meets a soldier meets a housemaid meets the master of the house meets a married woman meets her husband and so on. Anton Walbrook is the narrator storyteller. Simone Signoret is especially appealing and beautiful as the prostitute. The film also features Danielle Darrieux, Jean-Louis Barrault, Simone Simon, and Gerard Philipe. In 1964 Roger Vadim attempted to remake the film with a script by Jean Anouilh, and featured his wife Jane Fonda.

Anton Walbrook and Simone Signoret in *La Ronde* (50).

Harold Lloyd hanging from the famous clock in *Safety Last* (23).

Safety Last   (1923) USA, DIRECTORS – FRED NEWMEYER, SAM TAYLOR

Harold Lloyd is considered one of the great comedians of the silent era with Charlie Chaplin and Buster Keaton, and this is his finest feature film. The bespectacled Lloyd plays a naive go-getter who is trying to impress his fiancée with his position at a department store. He becomes involved with a human-fly publicity stunt and winds up climbing up the outside of the store. The scene in which Lloyd clings to the hands of a giant clock is one of the best known in film history. The film also shows Lloyd as a master of less-frantic comedy.

San Francisco   (1936) USA, DIRECTOR – W S VAN DYKE

Set on the rowdy Barbary Coast in early 1906, this astonishingly popular MGM spectacular ends with the famous earthquake scene. Jeanette MacDonald, Hollywood's reigning operetta queen, plays a parson's daughter who wants to sing opera, but winds up singing in a dance hall owned by a tough but basically decent saloon proprietor Clark Gable. MacDonald has a couple of good musical numbers including a rousing rendition of the title song, 'Would You' and 'The One Love'. Spencer Tracy received the first of his many Oscar nominations for playing a priest. In the end the earthquake brings Gable and MacDonald together. The plot is improbable, but the spectacle is very entertaining.

Jack Holt, Gable and MacDonald in *San Francisco* (36).

Le Sang D'Un Poete   (1930) FRANCE, DIRECTOR – JEAN COCTEAU

A wealthy backer gave Cocteau the freedom to do whatever he wished with this, his first film, which is also known as *The Blood of a Poet*. The French man-of-all arts used that freedom to the fullest. The film has been described as indescribable. A highly personal work filled with strange and often striking images, the film centers around the poet's inner life, his fears, obsessions and particularly his preoccupation with death. Cocteau insisted that this is not a surrealist picture, but that is what most people label it. Appearing amid the images are Lee Miller, Pauline Carton and Odette Talazac.

Saturday Night And Sunday Morning   (1960) GREAT BRITAIN, DIRECTOR – KAREL REISZ

A strong performance by Albert Finney and a sharp realistic look at British working class life highlight this film which was enormously popular and influential when it first came out. Adapted by Alan Sillitoe from his own novel the film focuses on a Nottingham factory worker (Finney) who is deeply dissatisfied with his lot in life. There's lots of raw humor and frank sexuality. Unlike the workers of many earlier British films, Finney turns his nose up at authority. Finney's costar is Rachel Roberts as a married woman with whom he has an affair.

Finney and Roberts in *Saturday Night and Sunday Morning* (60)

Saturday Night Fever   (1977) USA, DIRECTOR – JOHN BADHAM

This film both capitalized on, and helped to create the disco craze, and propelled a little known TV actor John Travolta into movie stardom. Travolta plays Tony Manero, a 19-year-old Brooklyn boy with a dead end job. Most of the week he's a nobody but on Saturday night he's top dog at the local disco. He sees his chance to 'make it' across the bridge to Manhattan in the disco's upcoming dance contest. The Brooklyn scenes have a gritty reality, and the dance scenes are electrifying. The disco score featured songs by the then-popular Bee Gees. Sylvester Stallone directed Travolta in a sequel, *Staying Alive*, but the film was a disappointment.

The Scarlet Pimpernel   (1935) GREAT BRITAIN, DIRECTOR – HAROLD YOUNG

In France during the Terror, when aristocrats were being hauled off to the guillotine by the filthy rabble, some are being saved by the timely intervention of a mysterious Englishman known as the Scarlet Pimpernel (who uses the flower as his symbol). In reality the heroic Pimpernel is Sir Percy Blakeney who pretends to be a poetry-reading fop. Leslie Howard was perfect as Sir Percy and a stunning Merle Oberon played his French wife who doesn't know about his double life. The film is romantic adventure, and it works as entertainment. Raymond Massey plays the fiendish Frenchman Chauvelin and there are good supporting performances by Nigel Bruce, Joan Gardner, Walter Rilla and Melville Cooper. The screenplay by Robert Sherwood, Sam Berman, Arthur Wimperis and Lajos Biro was based on a popular novel by Baroness Orczy.

The Searchers   (1956) USA, DIRECTOR – JOHN FORD

Considered John Ford's masterpiece, this film is exciting, breathtakingly beautiful and psychologically complex. Ethan Edward (John Wayne) returns home to find that his brother's family has been massacred by Indians. One of the daughters has survived, and the film covers Edwards' five year search for the missing girl who he comes to feel he must kill because she has been 'defiled' by the Indians. John Wayne is wonderful as the isolated and embittered Edwards, and there are a flock of other outstanding performances. Young Natalie Wood is fine as the kidnapped girl. Great credit must be given to Winton C Hoch who did the cinematography, much of it in Monument Valley.

John Wayne and Martin Pawley pray at the Edwards' graves with Parson Ward Bond (center) in *The Searchers* (56).

Sergeant York   (1941) USA, DIRECTOR – HOWARD HAWKS

Alvin York, a Tennessee farm boy was a conscientious objector at the start of World War I. He served in the medical corps but after seeing an army buddy killed he abandoned pacificism and singlehandedly killed twenty five Germans and captured 132 more. He was America's greatest World War I hero, and as the United States was about to enter World War II his story was made into an enormously popular film. The film picked up eleven Academy Award nominations and Gary Cooper who was York's own choice for the part won the Best Actor Oscar for the title role.

Gary Cooper played the World War I hero *Sergeant York* (41).

The Servant   (1963) GREAT BRITAIN, DIRECTOR – JOSEPH LOSEY

Harold Pinter wrote the script for this absorbing and effective study of a man's descent into decadence. Dirk Bogarde gives one of his finest performances as a corrupt, lower-class manservant who slowly and insidiously becomes the master of his employer. James Fox does a remarkable job as the initially arrogant but basically weak master. His transformation is altogether believable. The decadence is hinted at rather than splashed across the screen, but the effect is even stronger. The film also features Sarah Miles, Wendy Craig, Catherine Lacy and Patrick Magee.

Sarah Miles and Dirk Bogarde in *The Servant* (63).

The famous 'Barn-Raising Ballet' in *Seven Brides for Seven Brothers* (54).

Seven Brides For Seven Brothers   (1954) USA, DIRECTOR – STANLEY DONEN

Choreographer Michael Kidd's exhuberant dance numbers are the best of many good things about this joyful musical set in Oregon in 1850. The plot concerns a family of six brothers who abduct the only available women in town to be their wives, at the instigation of their eldest sibling, who is married. Johnny Mercer and Gene DePaul's catchy tunes 'Bless Your Beautiful Hide', 'Goin' Courtin'' and 'Spring, Spring, Spring' are well sung by leads Howard Keel and Jane Powell. Also notable is director Donen's decision not to make the film on location, but keep it on a set that looks like a set so you can concentrate on the action not the scenery. The spectacular 'barn raising' number is a showstopper, and probably the best dancing scene of its kind.

Seven Samurai   (1954) JAPAN, DIRECTOR – AKIRA KUROSAWA

In sixteenth century Japan, a time of great unrest, a group of farmers fear that when they harvest their crops they will be robbed by brigands, so they hire a wise and aging samurai to defend them. He enlists the aid of six other fighters including an energetic, fearless and undisciplined farmer's son played beautifully by Toshiro Mifune. A climactic battle fought in driving rain has unparalleled action. *Shichi-Nin No Samurai* is Kurosawa's most celebrated 'eastern Western' and it was clearly influenced by John Ford and others. Enormously and deservedly popular, it was remade in 1960 as an American western, *The Magnificent Seven*.

The farmers fight the bandits in *Seven Samurai* (54).

The Seven Year Itch (1955) USA, DIRECTOR – BILLY WILDER

Tom Ewell has sent his wife and little boy away from the heat of the New York summer on vacation, and an actress-model, played by Marilyn Monroe, has just moved in upstairs. Ewell is torn between his desire to remain faithful to his absent wife and clumsy attempts to seduce his new neighbor. Marilyn is delightful and the film contains one of her best known scenes as she stands over a subway grating while the breeze blows her dress up. Ewell is suitably dopey and Oscar Homolka gives a wonderful performance as a psychiatrist. Wilder and George Axelrod, adapted Axelrod's funny, if farfetched, play for the screen.

The Seventh Seal (1956) SWEDEN, DIRECTOR – INGMAR BERGMAN

A Swedish knight (Max Von Sydow) who has been on the Crusades and has lost his faith returns home to a land beset by plague and panic. He meets Death (Bengt Ekerot) who offers him a short reprieve by playing a game of chess. This is a film about disillusionment, good vs evil, the existence or non-existence of God, and other questions. What makes it a masterpiece, however, are the strong performances and stunning photography. Many of the images, the chess match, the final Dance of Death, are among the most famous in the history of cinema. *The Seventh Seal/Det Sjunde Inseglet* helped gain Bergman international recognition. The cast also includes Gunnar Bjornstrand, Bibi Andersson and Gunnel Lindblom.

Death (Bengt Ekerot) invites the Swedish knight (Max Von Sydow) to play chess in Bergman's *The Seventh Seal* (56).

Shane (1953) USA, DIRECTOR – GEORGE STEVENS

A mysterious gunslinger (Alan Ladd) takes a job as a hand with a homesteader and his family (Van Heflin, Jean Arthur, Brandon de Wilde). He wants to give up his violent past, but is forced to defend his new friends from hired gunmen, and in the end rides off into the distance – alone. The plot may be agonizingly familiar, but it is handled with dignity and beauty by director Stevens. The film contains many memorable scenes. One of the best features Jack Palance, surely the worst of all Western villains, smilingly pulling on his gloves before the final confrontation.

Alan Ladd says goodbye to Brandon de Wilde in *Shane* (53).

Shanghai Express (1932) USA, DIRECTOR – JOSEF VON STERNBERG

Marlene Dietrich stars as 'Shanghai Lilly' the most infamous woman in China. Riding a train through the civil war-wracked land she meets an old flame, a British doctor (Clive Brook). When the train is captured by a cruel warlord (Warner Oland), he agrees to release the doctor if Shanghai Lilly will become his mistress. At the last moment Anna May Wong, playing a spunky partisan kills the cruel warlord and Dietrich is saved. It's all a bit dated and silly, but it's a great Dietrich vehicle. A 1951 remake starring Joseph Cotten and Corinne Calvet was retitled as *Peking Express*.

Marlene Dietrich as the infamous 'Shanghai Lilly' a woman confronted with a cruel choice in *Shanghai Express* (32).

She Done Him Wrong   (1932) USA, DIRECTOR – LOWELL SHERMAN

An adaptation of Mae West's often-banned stage hit *Diamond Lil*, this film was made before the Legion of Decency was established. In fact, *She Done Him Wrong* is widely regarded as the film that finally brought censorship to Hollywood. There are plenty of double entendres, and Mae is constant glorying in her own sexual prowess. Mae also performs her classic bawdy renditions of 'Frankie and Johnny' and 'Easy Rider'. Cary Grant in his first major screen appearance is a policeman posing as a Salvation Army worker. Mae invites him to 'come up and see me', and when he refuses Mae replies confidently 'you can be had'.

She Wore A Yellow Ribbon   (1949) USA, DIRECTOR – JOHN FORD

Of Ford's cavalry trilogy the second, made between *Fort Apache* and *Rio Grande* has proved to be the most popular and entertaining. The catchy title song certainly helps the film. John Wayne stars as Captain Nathan Brittles who is retiring from the cavalry and must hand over his command to younger officers. Before that he must prevent a full-scale Indian war following Custer's massacre at Little Big Horn. John Agar and Harry Carey Jr play young lieutenants competing for the hand of Joanne Dru. Wayne is excellent as are Victor McLaglen, Mildred Natwick and other Ford favorites. Cinematographer Winton C Hoch's Monument Valley scenes may be the real star of this film.

John Wayne in *She Wore a Yellow Ribbon* (49).

Shoeshine (1946) ITALY, DIRECTOR – VITTORIO DE SICA

The collaboration of director de Sica and screenwriter Cesare Zavattini flowered into greatness with the production of *Shoeshine* and *Bicycle Thieves* (1948), two extraordinary examples of Italian postwar neorealism. Both films explore the urban chaos of Rome in the aftermath of World War II simply and honestly, and both films wring fine performances from nonprofessional actors. Set in Nazi-occupied Rome two shoeshine boys (Franco Interlenghi and Rinaldo Smordoni) find themselves drawn into the web of the black market with tragic consequences. Despite the social implications of the movie *Shoeshine/Sciuscia* is a deeply personal emotional tale and the tenderness and humanity inherent in the relationship of the two shoeshine boys remains the pivotal focus of the film. Zavattini's script received an Oscar nomination.

Showboat (1936) USA, DIRECTOR – JAMES WHALE

Of the three filmed versions of the Jerome Kern-Oscar Hammerstein II musical, Whale's is the best. The script, based on the novel by Edna Ferber is sugary and the portrayal of blacks is stereotyped, but there is some wonderful music from the first rate cast. The best moments are Helen Morgan's soulful rendition of 'Bill' and Paul Robeson's magnificent 'Old Man River'. Irene Dunne does a more than credible job acting and singing the lead as Magnolia the daughter of the show boat owner who marries the handsome but worthless gambler Gaylord Ravenel (Allan Jones). *Showboat* was first filmed in 1929. The 1951 remake starring Kathryn Grayson, Howard Keel and Ava Gardner seemed empty and dated by comparison.

Charles Winniger as Captain Andy and Allan Jones as Gaylord Ravenel in *Showboat* (36).

Singin' In The Rain   (1952) USA, DIRECTORS — GENE KELLY, STANLEY DONEN

This film is *the* Hollywood musical. Not only was it made *in* Hollywood, it's *about* Hollywood. Set in the days when movies were changing from silents to sound, the negligible plot concerns the career of a silent film star (Gene Kelly) who is caught between his predatory leading lady (Jean Hagen), a beautiful star with an unbeautiful voice, and a rising starlet (Debbie Reynolds) who saves the film from disaster and dubs Hagen's voice. The film is packed with musical gems, including the title number, 'Make 'Em Laugh' with Donald O'Conner running up the walls, Kelly, O'Conner and Reynolds singing and dancing 'Good Morning' and Kelly's dreamlike ballet sequence with Cyd Charisse. The film was also made into a stage musical in 1985.

Left: Gene Kelly dancing and *Singin' in the Rain* (52).

One pair of lovers in Bergman's sophisticated farce *Smiles Of A Summer Night* (55).

Smiles Of A Summer Night   (1955) SWEDEN, DIRECTOR — INGMAR BERGMAN

Known primarily for his darker films Bergman showed himself to be the master of sophisticated bedroom farce with this wise, cynical and thoroughly hilarious film, *Sommarnattens Leende*. Set in the late nineteenth century at a weekend party on a country estate, the story centers on a middle-aged lawyer who is married to a 16-year-old girl, but is still in love with his ex-mistress, the beautiful actress Desirée Armfeldt. The cast including Gunnar Bjornstrand, Eva Dahlbeck, Harriet Andersson, Jarl Kulle, Naima Wifstrand and Ulla Jacobsson is uniformly excellent. The film was adapted by Stephen Sondheim into the musical *A Little Night Music*, which was also made into a film in 1977.

The Snake Pit   (1948) USA, DIRECTOR — ANATOLE LITVAK

A shocker when it was first released, this film deals intelligently and brutally with conditions in mental hospitals. Virginia Cunningham, (Olivia de Havilland) has had a nervous breakdown and finds herself in a mental hospital. Through therapy, including shock treatment, (which the film favors) she finally recovers. But before she does there are a series of memorable and terrifying scenes in the hospital. De Havilland gives an exceptionally strong performance. Leo Genn costars as a kindly, pipe-smoking psychiatrist. The film also features Celeste Holm, Glenn Langan, Leif Ericson, Beulah Bondi and Isabel Jewell.

Snow White And The Seven Dwarfs (1938) USA, WALT DISNEY

An adaptation of one of Grimm's fairy tales became Disney's first feature-length animated film and possibly his best. Snow White herself is too good to be true but the dwarfs are wonderful, every one of them. The Queen is one of the most frightening creations in the history of film and there are several scenes that are still frightening to small children. The animation is so lush that the viewer realizes how much has been lost to the age of minimal or computer-created animation. David Hand was supervising director. The score by Larry Morey and Frank Churchill features songs like 'Whistle While You Work', 'Some Day My Prince Will Come' and 'Heigh-Ho, Heigh-Ho'.

Snow White and her new found friends, the Seven Dwarfs (38).

Jack Lemmon and Tony Curtis in *Some Like It Hot* (59).

Some Like It Hot (1959) USA, DIRECTOR – BILLY WILDER

Tony Curtis and Jack Lemmon star as a couple of musicians in Chicago in 1929 who are witnesses to a gangland rubout. To escape the mob they dress up as women and join an all-girl jazz band going to Miami. The singer and ukulele player for the band is Marilyn Monroe, and they both fall in love with her. She, of course, thinks they are women. Marilyn was never more delectable. There are memorable performances by George Raft as gang leader Spats Columbo and Joe E Brown as millionaire Osgood Fielding, who has one of the great last lines in films. The script by Wilder and I A L Diamond is consistently funny. It's simply one of the best comedies ever made. It was later adapted as a modestly successful Broadway musical called *Sugar*.

Sons Of The Desert (1939) USA, DIRECTOR – WILLIAM A SEITER

Generally regarded as the definitive Laurel and Hardy film, *Sons of the Desert* contains all the elements that make the team so popular. Stan and Ollie want to go to a lodge convention in Chicago, but their wives won't let them. So Ollie fakes illness and they pretend they are going to Hawaii for a cure. Naturally their wives find out they are in Chicago living it up. Actually they are getting into trouble rather than enjoying themselves. Mae Busch and Dorothy Christy costar as Stan and Ollie's wives, and Charlie Chase plays an extremely obnoxious brother-in-law. Sons of the Desert is also the name of the international Laurel and Hardy fan club.

Sophie's Choice   (1982) USA, DIRECTOR – ALAN J PAKULA

Some critics believe that Meryl Streep's performance as Sophie, the Polish Catholic concentration camp survivor is one of the truly great screen characterizations. She easily won the Best Actress Oscar. Director Pakula also wrote the screenplay for this faithful adaptation of William Styron's moving, complex, but deeply flawed novel. Streep's co-stars, Kevin Kline, who plays Nathan her charming, intelligent, and increasingly insane lover, and Peter MacNicol as Stingo, the young Southern writer who becomes their neighbor, are both excellent. But it's Streep that makes the film worthwhile.

Meryl Streep as Sophie, survivor of a concentration camp, with her lover Nathan (Kevin Kline) in *Sophie's Choice* (82).

The Sorrow And The Pity   (1970) FRANCE-SWITZERLAND, DIRECTOR – MARCEL OPHULS

This revealing, indeed shocking, documentary describes the behavior of the citizens of the French city of Clermont-Ferrand during World War II, when they were under the control of the Nazi-oriented Vichy government. What director Ophuls demonstrates so dramatically is that many French people welcomed the new regime and supported it actively. The film does not merely condemn the known collaborators, but it questions the reaction to the French nation in general. This film, *Le Chagrin Et La Pitie*, is powerful, moving, consistently interesting though it runs over four hours, and is profoundly depressing.

The liberation of Paris in *The Sorrow and the Pity* (70).

Sorry Wrong Number   (1948) USA, DIRECTOR – ANATOLE LITVAK

Barbara Stanwyck stars as a neurotic, bedridden woman who overhears a telephone conversation in which a murder is being plotted. It's her murder, and her attempts to get help on the phone are the core of this tense film. Stanwyck delivers a bravura performance which won her an Oscar nomination. Also in the cast are Burt Lancaster, Ann Richards, Wendell Corey, Ed Begley, Leif Ericson and William Conrad. The film was adapted by Lucile Fletcher from her own radio drama, which was even better, for the essence of the suspense is vocal, not visual.

Stagecoach   (1939) USA, DIRECTOR – JOHN FORD

A group of disparate passengers are traveling by stagecoach through hostile territory, and are attacked by Indians. This is the simple basic premise of this seminal Western. The film transformed the Western from a Saturday afternoon entertainment for kids, into a mature art form. It also made John Wayne, who had appeared in many of those quickie Westerns, a major star. There are so many fine things about this film it's hard to chose a few. There are the performances by Claire Trevor, John Carradine and Thomas Mitchell (who won an Oscar). There is the spectacular Monument Valley scenery, and there is the unbelievable stunt work of Yakima Canutt.

The passengers of *Stagecoach* (39) included John Carradine, Donald Meek, Louise Platt, Claire Trevor and John Wayne.

A Star Is Born   (1954) USA, DIRECTOR – GEORGE CUKOR

The story of Esther Blodgett, the small-time performer who is transformed into star Vicki Lester with the help of her husband the fading star Norman Maine, has been filmed several times. The plot is said to have been inspired by the lives of silent screen stars John Bowers and Marguerite de le Motte. The most famous is Cukor's 1954 semi-musical version with Judy Garland as Esther/Vicki and James Mason as Maine. Garland has some excellent songs including 'Born In A Trunk' and 'The Man That Got Away', and there is a cynical yet compassionate script by Moss Hart. A 1937 version with Janet Gaynor and Frederic March, and written by Dorothy Parker among others is also excellent. The 1976 version was a vehicle for Barbra Streisand and is bearable only when she sings.

Judy Garland's rise to fame as singer Vicki Lester threatens her marriage and the life of her husband James Mason in *A Star Is Born* (54).

Star Wars (1977) USA, DIRECTOR – GEORGE LUCAS

A hit of monumental proportions; the film is basically a space opera in which young Luke Skywalker (Mark Hamill) becomes involved in the rebellion against the evil Empire. He is aided by a princess (Carrie Fisher), a wise old warrior (Alec Guinness), a tough mercenary pilot with a heart of gold (Harrison Ford) and a couple of cute robots. The plot creaks, but the action is so fast, the special effects so stunning that millions were swept up in the excitement. Originally intended as part four of a nine part series, only two other *Star Wars* films have been made – *The Empire Strikes Back* (1980) and *The Return of the Jedi* (1982). Though both of these films are nearly as good as the original, Lucas seems to have lost interest in the cycle.

The evil lord of the dark side, Darth Vader was played by David Prowse in *Star Wars* (77).

The Stars Look Down (1939) GREAT BRITAIN, DIRECTOR – CAROL REED

A J Cronin's novel about Welsh coal miners struggling against unhealthy and dangerous working conditions was effectively adapted for the screen with the aid of Cronin himself. Though the film was produced on a very modest budget the backgrounds are authentic and the cast is excellent. Michael Redgrave stars as a miner who tries to do something about the miners' plight by running for Parliament. Also in the cast are Margaret Lockwood, Edward Rigby, Emlyn Williams, Nancy Price, Cecil Parker and Linden Travers.

Paul Newman and Robert Redford set up mobster Robert Shaw in *The Sting* (73).

The Sting (1973) USA, DIRECTOR – GEORGE ROY HILL

Paul Newman and Robert Redford star in this highly entertaining yarn about a couple of con men, in Depression-era Chicago. Redford and Newman develop an elaborate scheme to cheat mobster Robert Shaw for revenge. A good part of the picture's charm comes from Marvin Hamlisch's adaptation of ragtime-era composer Scott Joplin's melodies. The film received Oscars including Best Picture, Best Director and Best Screenplay. In a male-dominated cast Eileen Brennan, as the brothel keeper with the heart of gold stands out. Charles Durning, Ray Walston and Harold J Gould costar.

The Story Of Gösta Berling (1923) SWEDEN, DIRECTOR – MAURITZ STILLER

This four-hour long film, known under a variety of titles, relates the tale of a drunken and defrocked pastor, who after a number of love affairs and much suffering manages to find his way to a happy ending. The complicated narrative is sometimes uneven, but there are many lovely sequences in the film. Based on a popular Swedish novel by Selma Lagerlof, *The Story of Gösta Berling* was the film which led directly to Greta Garbo's international stardom. Stiller was looking for a young actress to play the second lead in the film. He found Garbo at the training school of Stockholm's Royal Dramatic Theater, and became her mentor, teacher and inseparable companion.

La Strada (1954) ITALY, DIRECTOR – FEDERICO FELLINI

With this film, Fellini became known to US audiences. Indeed two of the stars were American. Anthony Quinn played the brutish strongman and Richard Basehart, the gentle clown 'Fool'. The third star is Fellini's wife Giulietta Masina who plays the poor simpleton whose mother sells her services to the traveling strongman. She is later driven mad when the strongman kills the fool in a mindless rage. It is her performance which evoked memories of Charlie Chaplin that truly makes this film. There are inconsistencies in the film, but there are also memorable and touching scenes. *La Strada* won, and deserved, the Academy Award for Best Foreign Film in 1956.

Giulietta Masina, Anthony Quinn and Richard Basehart in *La Strada* (54).

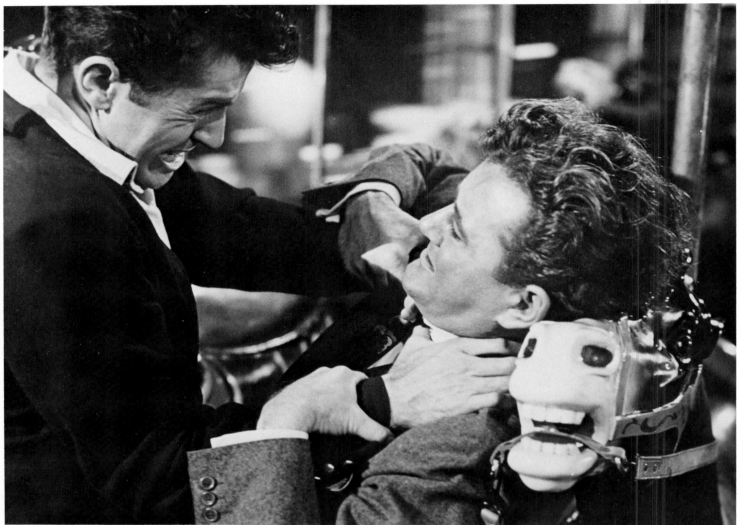

Farley Granger tries to kill Robert Walker in *Strangers on a Train* (51).

Strangers On A Train   (1951) USA, DIRECTOR – ALFRED HITCHCOCK

Tennis champ Guy Haines (Farley Granger) meets playboy Bruno Anthony (Robert Walker) on a train. Their idle conversation turns to the subject of murder. Guy would like to get rid of his estranged wife, Bruno wants someone to murder his father. Guy is just kidding, but Bruno is not and murders Guy's wife. He then shadows Guy trying to force him to fulfil his side of the agreement. Not one of Hitchcock's masterpieces, *Strangers on a Train* is nonetheless a gripping film with a standout performance by Walker as the deranged Bruno, and a climatic carousel scene that leaves audiences gasping.

A Streetcar Named Desire   (1951) USA, DIRECTOR – ELIA KAZAN

Streetcar is the most successful adaptation of a Tennessee Williams play to the screen. Fragile Blanche Dubois comes to New Orleans to stay with her younger sister, Stella and Stella's brutish husband Stanley Kowalski. Blanche's world of make-believe is shattered by Stanley and his revelations about her. All the performances are near perfect, and Vivien Leigh as Blanche is absolutely brilliant. Leigh, Kim Stanley who played Stella and Karl Malden who played Blanche's suitor all won Oscars. Marlon Brando who left an indelible impression as Stanley was nominated, as were the picture, the script, which had been adapted by Williams and Kazan's direction. A 1984 TV movie version of *Streetcar* starring Ann-Margret and Treat Williams was surprisingly good.

Stanley Kowalski (Marlon Brando) threatens the fragile Blanche Dubois (Vivien Leigh) in *A Streetcar Named Desire* (51).

Strike (1924) USSR, DIRECTOR – SERGEI M EISENSTEIN

The great Soviet director's first film was this account of a 1912 strike of factory workers that was brutally put down by the Tsarist authorities. The novice director was very fortunate to have a talented and experienced cameraman, Edward Tissé, working with him. Their association lasted throughout most of Eisenstein's career. Many of the effects which Eisenstein was to use so well in later films are first tried out in *Strike*. Some Soviet critics found the film, though a brilliant piece of propaganda, too unorthodox and the public did not react well to the experimental techniques, but *Strike* did attract attention in film circles beyond the Soviet Union, and Eisenstein was then commissioned by the Central Committee to direct more ambitious works.

Die Student Von Prag (1926) GERMANY, DIRECTOR – HENRIK GALEEN

A student named Baldwin, in love with a highborn lady sells his mirrored image, or his soul, to a Mephistophelean character named Scapinelli, in return for riches and power. Inevitably all turns out badly for Baldwin. The story was first made into a film in 1913 and is regarded as one of the best early German films. It was remade in high romantic style in 1926, with the gaunt and tense Conrad Veidt as Baldwin. Veidt's powerful performance and fine innovative camerawork, make this version the most memorable. Another version of the film was made in Austria in the mid-1930s. Sound and some musical scenes were added, but the brooding atmosphere was lost.

Sullivan's Travels (1941) USA, DIRECTOR – PRESTON STURGES

Successful Hollywood director John L Sullivan (Joel McCrea) tires of making light comedies during the Depression; he wants to make a serious film about the harsh realities of life. With an aspiring actress called only 'The Girl' (Veronica Lake) he sets off across the underside of America. At one point he's mugged and gets tossed into a Southern prison on a murder charge. It's there he learns that laughter is all some people have, and he returns to Hollywood with a renewed desire to make comedies. This film, considered a landmark in Hollywood history, is a unique blend of slapstick and seriousness. There are outrageous Keystone Kops-like chase scenes, and deeply moving scenes of poverty in America. Somehow the blend works. Also in the cast were other Sturges regulars like Robert Warwick, William Demarest, Franklin Pangborn, Eric Blore and Margaret Hayes.

Sunset Boulevard (1950) USA, DIRECTOR – BILLY WILDER

Aging silent-screen legend Gloria Swanson returned to the screen to play an aging silent screen legend, Norma Desmond, who is planning a return to the screen in this classic. Desmond lives in a crumbling Hollywood mansion with her butler/chauffeur Erich von Stroheim who was once a famous director. A hack writer (William Holden), running from bill collectors takes refuge there and Desmond asks him to polish a script for her comeback.

Anyone can enjoy this film, but it is a particular treat for lovers of film because it abounds with movie references and images. There are also brief appearances by Cecil B De Mille, Hedda Hopper, H B Warner and Buster Keaton. Most of all *Sunset Boulevard* is a triumph for Swanson.

Gloria Swanson as Norma Desmond fantasizes her return to the screen when she is arrested in *Sunset Boulevard* (50).

Superman (1978) USA, DIRECTOR – RICHARD DONNER

The celebrated comic book was made into a glorious comic book of a movie. After a slow beginning in which Marlon Brando and Susannah York play the Man of Steel's parents, the action picks up. A handsome but unknown actor named Christopher Reeve was given the title role and played it to perfection, with deadpan humor, and romantic charisma. Margot Kidder's Lois Lane is spirited, quirky and sexy. Gene Hackman costars as the villainous Lex Luthor whose sidekicks are played by Ned Beatty and Valerie Perrine. The special effects are impressive, even stirring, as is the score by John Williams. *Superman II* released in 1980 is every bit as good as the original. By *Superman III*, however, the formula was wearing thin.

Christopher Reeve played the Man of Steel in *Superman* (78). The special effects in the film were very convincing.

Suspicion (1941) USA, DIRECTOR – ALFRED HITCHCOCK

This could have been another Hitchcock masterpiece but David O Selznick could not bear to have Cary Grant turn out to be a cad and a murderer, so the studio tacked on an idiotic ending which violates the entire spirit of the film. It could have been worse, at one point the studio tried to cut every indication that Grant was a bad guy, but the film was then too short. Still there is plenty that is worthwhile in this film. Joan Fontaine won an Academy Award for her part as spinsterish Lina MacKinlaw. Grant is charming (as always) and truly sinister as Johnny Aysgarth the cad she marries. The suspense builds as Lina begins to suspect that Johnny has killed before and will kill her too.

Right: Joan Fontaine suspects Cary Grant in *Suspicion* (41).

Sweet Smell Of Success (1957) USA, DIRECTOR – ALEXANDER MACKENDRICK

The most startling thing about this film is the performance of Tony Curtis. Long regarded as an actor of limited ability Curtis is completely convincing as Sidney Falco, a two-bit New York City press agent who is willing to sell out anybody to win favors from powerful but paranoid Broadway columnist J J Hunsecker (Burt Lancaster). Hunsecker wants Falco to frame the musician boyfriend (Martin Milner) of his sister (Susan Harrison). As the only decent people in a swarm of sharks Milner and Harrison seem out of place. James Wong Howe's *film noir* photography captures the seedy show business scene perfectly, and there is a fine jazz score by Elmer Bernstein. Clifford Odets and Ernest Lehman wrote the savage screenplay based on Lehman's story.

Ginger Rogers and Fred Astaire in *Swing Time* (36).

Swing Time (1936) USA, DIRECTOR – GEORGE STEVENS

Many consider this the finest of the Fred Astaire-Ginger Rogers musicals. The screenplay by Howard Lindsay and Allan Scott which involves a romantic triangle is witty and a little less farfetched than some others, but no one remembers an Astaire-Rogers film for the plot. The score by Jerome Kern and Dorothy Fields includes such classic numbers as 'Pick Yourself Up', 'Bojangles of Harlem', 'Never Gonna Dance', a fine duet in the snow for 'A Fine Romance' and the Oscar winning 'The Way You Look Tonight.' The supporting cast includes Betty Furness, George Metaxa, Victor Moore, Helen Broderick, Eric Blore and Frank Jenks.

La Symphonie Pastorale (1946) FRANCE, DIRECTOR – JEAN DELANNOY

Director Delannoy and Jean Aurenche adapted this tragic story from a novel by André Gide. A Swiss pastor adopts an orphan who grows into a beautiful girl. Through no fault of her own she causes tremendous jealousy between the pastor and his son. The film stars Pierre Blanchar and the stunning Michele Morgan, who won a Best Actress Award at Cannes for her performance. *La Symphonie Pastorale* itself took the Grand Prix at Cannes. Widely hailed by critics at the time the film has lost some of its lustre today, but it remains a strikingly visual work with its symbolic use of snow and water.

A Tale Of Two Cities   (1935) USA, DIRECTOR – JACK CONWAY

A real Hollywood epic ('cast of thousands') adaptation of Charles Dickens' sweeping novel of the French Revolution. Ronald Colman has the plum part of Sydney Carton, the worthless English lawyer who finally goes to the guillotine for the love of Lucy Manette (Elizabeth Allen) in place of her husband Charles Darnay (Donald Woods). Colman's speech 'It's a far, far better thing I do ...' is the most famous part of the film. Blanche Yurka, as the vengeful Madame Defarge, and Edna Mae Oliver as Miss Pross costar. There was a silent version of *A Tale of Two Cities* made in 1917 and a number of later sound ones. The 1958 British film with Dirk Bogarde is excellent.

Sydney Carton (Ronald Colman) bribes the jailor (Walter Kingsford) and takes the place of Charles Darnay (Donald Woods) in *A Tale of Two Cities* (35).

Tarzan, The Ape Man (1932) USA, DIRECTOR – W S VAN DYKE

There had been eight silent films based on the Edgar Rice Burroughs tale of the 'lord of the jungle' but *Tarzan, The Ape Man* was the first talkie, and it introduced the most famous Tarzan, Olympic swimming champion Johnny Weissmuller and the most famous Jane, Maureen O'Sullivan. The picture opens with Jane, her fiancée (Neil Hamilton) and her father (C Aubrey Smith) making their way through the jungle. She is rescued by Tarzan and the rest is history. There were five more Weissmuller-O'Sullivan films, and many many others have played the parts of Tarzan and Jane, but no one was better.

Jane (Maureen O'Sullivan) is rescued by Tarzan (Johnny Weissmuller) and Cheetah in *Tarzan, the Ape Man* (32).

Shirley MacLaine and Jack Nicholson in *Terms of Endearment* (83).

Terms Of Endearment   (1983) USA, DIRECTOR – JAMES L BROOKS

Part comedy, part tearjerker, this film was enormously popular and won a number of Oscars including Best Picture, Best Director and a Best Actress Award for star Shirley MacLaine. She plays Aurora Greenway and the film traces the thirty-year relationship between Greenway and her daughter, played by Debra Winger. Jack Nicholson won a Best Supporting Actor Oscar for his portrayal of Garrett Breedlove, an aging womanizing ex-astronaut. Excellent performances are also turned in by John Lithgow, Jeff Daniels and Danny De Vito.

The Testament Of Dr Mabuse   (1932) GERMANY, DIRECTOR – FRITZ LANG

In 1922 Lang created the character of Dr Mabuse in a silent classic *Dr Mabuse, The Gambler*. Mabuse is a diabolical villain who uses a form of mind control to dominate and destroy his victims. A decade later director Lang returned to the character in *The Testament of Dr Mabuse*. Mabuse is in an insane asylum, but is still able to control the activities of a criminal gang who have never actually seen their boss. Both films are highly stylized and even contain supernatural elements. Some thought that Lang was drawing parallels between the evil Mabuse and Hitler, and Lang fled Germany. Lang used the character once again in *The Thousand Eyes of Dr Mabuse* (1960).

The Thin Man   (1934) USA, DIRECTOR – W S VAN DYKE

The 'thin man' was not William Powell but a character played by Edward Ellis who appears briefly in the film and is murdered. However, the blend of mystery and screwball comedy was so wildly and deservedly popular that it inspired a series of five additional 'thin man' films. Though none of the follow ups is quite as classy as the original, they represent what is probably the best series ever to come out of Hollywood. Powell stars as Nick Charles, a semi-retired detective, and full-time drinker, and Myrna Loy is Nora his rich, wise-cracking, hard-drinking wife. Their dog Asta, who accompanies them everywhere is not quite housebroken. Director Van Dyke, whose nickname was 'One-shot Woody', filmed the original *Thin Man* in twelve days.

Things To Come   (1936) GREAT BRITAIN, DIRECTOR – WILLIAM CAMERON MENZIES

The 70-year-old H G Wells adapted his own novel *The Shape of Things to Come*, for the screen. His script was greatly revised and he hated the final result. Much of the film now sounds dated, even ridiculous, but *Things to Come* remains an extraordinarily fascinating work. The film envisions much of the world being reduced to barbarism by war, but ultimately being saved by the apostles of technology. Producer Alexander Korda spent a fortune on the bizarre sets and innovative special effects. Ralph Richardson is outstanding as the barbarous Boss. The film also stars Raymond Massey and Cedric Hardwicke.

The sets for *Things to Come* (36) were extraordinary.

216

The Third Man (1949) GREAT BRITAIN, DIRECTOR – CAROL REED

Graham Greene adapted this masterful thriller from his own novel. The time is shortly after World War II, and Vienna is a city occupied by the Allied forces. An American, Holly Martins, (Joseph Cotton) is in Vienna looking for his old friend Harry Lime. He first hears Lime is dead, and then discovers his buddy is alive, and mixed up in some very illegal smuggling. Lime is played by Orson Welles, and his presence is so dominating that it's hard to believe he appears for only a few minutes. Anton Karas's zither music helps make the film memorable.

Orson Welles on the run as Harry Lime in *The Third Man* (49).

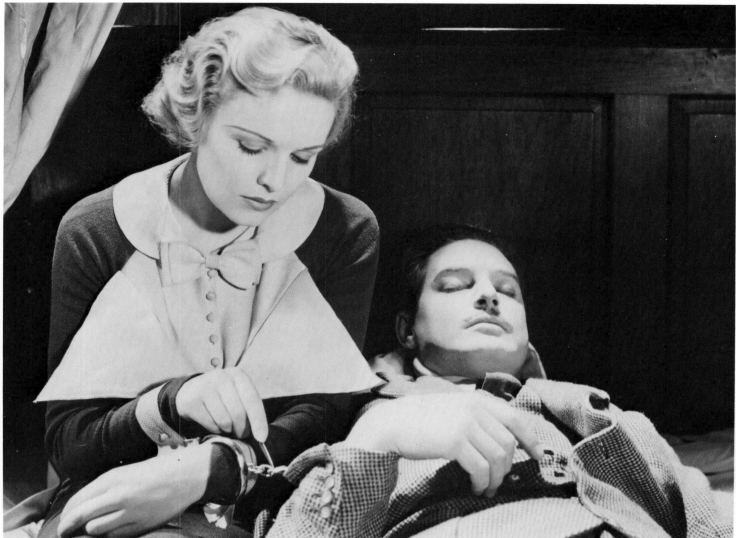

Madeleine Carroll is handcuffed to Robert Donat in *The 39 Steps* (35).

The 39 Steps (1935) GREAT BRITAIN, DIRECTOR – ALFRED HITCHCOCK

Hitchcock always rated this film based loosely on the novel by John Buchan as one of his best. It was the first time he used a favorite theme, an innocent man framed by circumstances must flee from his enemies and the police. Richard Hannay, splendidly played by Robert Donat, is on the run after a mysterious woman is murdered in his London flat. He meets up with Pamela (Madeleine Carroll) who is dragged into the chase. The whole thing ends with the shooting of the enigmatic Mr Memory. The film is full of great characters, great suspense, and great humor. Some Hitchcock films may equal this early masterpiece, none surpass it. Kenneth More played Hannay in the 1960 remake, and Robert Powell starred in the 1978 version which is somewhat closer to Buchan's original story.

This Happy Breed (1944) GREAT BRITAIN, DIRECTOR – DAVID LEAN

Based on a Noel Coward play this film is an outrageous piece of homefront propaganda, designed to encourage the average Englishman during the dark days of World War II. The saga of an average suburban London family and their neighbors in the years between World War I and World War II, their trials, tribulations and triumphs. It was comforting, very popular, and it succeeds primarily because of the splendid work of the cast of Robert Newton, Celia Johnson, John Mills, Kay Walsh and Stanley Holloway, and settings that the audience could recognize and identify with.

Throne Of Blood (1957) JAPAN, DIRECTOR – AKIRA KUROSAWA

Throne of Blood/Kumonosu Jo is the samurai *Macbeth*, with a warrior spurred on by his wife and a witch to murder his lord. Feudal Scotland and feudal Japan don't seem all that different, so the change of scene and culture works surprisingly well. As is usual for a Kurosawa film, this one is a treat to look at. The Macbeth character Taketoki Washizu, is masterfully played by Toshiro Mifune. The final sequence in which he is shot to death with arrows is absolutely horrifying.

Thunder Rock (1942) GREAT BRITAIN, DIRECTOR – ROY BOULTING

The *Manchester Guardian* called this rarely seen film 'More interesting technically than anything since *Citizen Kane*.' Adapted from a Robert Ardrey play it is the story of a disillusioned journalist who retires to a lighthouse on Lake Michigan. His faith in humanity is restored by visions of ghosts of immigrants drowned a century before. The impressive cast includes Michael Redgrave, Lilli Palmer, and James Mason. The topical wartime message of the film (and the play) was anti-isolationism.

Tiger Bay (1959) GREAT BRITAIN, DIRECTOR – J LEE-THOMPSON

Young Hayley Mills made an impressive screen debut in this very popular police-chase melodrama. A Polish seaman in Cardiff, Wales kills his unfaithful girlfriend and is on the run from the police. He kidnaps a young girl (Mills) who has witnessed the crime. The film is a sensitive character study, rather than a 'child in danger' thriller. Hayley's father, actor John Mills, is also excellent in the film as is Horst Bucholtz as the seaman.

To Be Or Not To Be (1942) USA, DIRECTOR – ERNST LUBITSCH

A comedy about the Nazi invasion of Poland, starring Jack Benny and released shortly after the United States entered the war is an improbable project. The film was widely criticized for making jokes about a serious subject, but Edwin Justus Mayer's script is brilliant black comedy, and an early debunking of the Nazi myth. Benny was wonderful as the ham actor Joseph Tura, and Carole Lombard in her last role, as his wife was never better. The film was released after her death. There are many other great performances including Sig Ruman's 'So they call me 'Concentration Camp Erhardt!'. Mel Brooks' 1983 remake was also funny but never had much of an audience.

Carole Lombard was the wife of Joseph Tura, played brilliantly by Jack Benny in black comedy *To Be or Not To Be* (42).

To Catch A Thief   (1955) USA, DIRECTOR – ALFRED HITCHCOCK

Legend has it that Grace Kelly met Prince Rainier while making this film in Monaco. In truth she met him when she attended the Cannes Film Festival. But *To Catch a Thief* was made in Monaco the year before Kelly married the Prince. It's not one of Hitchcock's best efforts, but it stars a cool Kelly, a very handsome Cary Grant as ex-jewel thief John Robie, some nice Hitchcock touches and all that mouthwatering French Riviera scenery.

Grace Kelly and Cary Grant on a picnic in *To Catch a Thief* (55).

To Kill A Mockingbird
(1962) USA, DIRECTOR – ROBERT MULLIGAN

Based on Harper Lee's novel about the still-sensitive subject of race relations in the South, Gregory Peck won an Oscar for this film. He plays Atticus Finch, an Alabama lawyer, who defends a black man falsely accused of raping a white woman. Robert Duvall made a striking, if silent, screen debut as a recluse. The three children in the film, Philip Alford as Jem, Mary Badham as Scout, and John Megna as Dill are exceptional. Horton Foote's Oscar-winning screenplay is intelligent and the setting creates just the right atmosphere of a small town in the Depression South.

Gregory Peck as Alabama lawyer Atticus Finch visits the family of his client, a black man wrongly accused of raping a white woman in *To Kill a Mockingbird* (62).

Tom Jones (1963) GREAT BRITAIN, DIRECTOR – TONY RICHARDSON

This romping bawdy adaptation of Henry Fielding's picaresque novel of the eighteenth-century was an enormous hit, and won a number of Oscars including Best Picture. Albert Finney stars as the young man who travels to London to seek his fortune. Finney's brilliant costars include Hugh Griffith as the roistering Squire Western, Susannah York as his daughter, and Tom's true love Sophie, Edith Evans as Sophie's prudish aunt, not to mention Diane Cilento as the sluttish Molly Seagrim, Joyce Redman as 'that trull Mrs Waters' and Joan Greenwood as 'the notorious Lady Bellaston', just three of the women

Tom becomes involved with. John Osborne's witty script is brilliantly aided by the score by John Addison and Richardson's direction which makes ample use of several venerable film techniques – a split second freeze, a wipe across the screen and even actors addressing the audience directly.

Tom Jones (Albert Finney) casts a flirtatious glance at Sophie Western, played by Susannah York in Oscar-winning *Tom Jones* (63).

Dustin Hoffman finds a job as Dorothy Michaels in *Tootsie* (82).

Tootsie (1982) USA, DIRECTOR – SYDNEY POLLACK

Dustin Hoffman plays actor Michael Dorsey who can't get a job. In desperation he disguises himself as a woman, Dorothy Michaels, and gets a part on a soap opera. He discovers he's a better person as a woman and becomes an inspiration for women all across America. It's an unlikely premise that works perfectly and hilariously. Hoffman is marvelous as Dorsey and Michaels who have different personalities. Bill Murray is winning as his friend, Teri Garr is fine as his downtrodden girlfriend and director Pollack is extremely convincing as Michael's agent. However, it was Jessica Lange who won the Best Supporting Actress Oscar, as the young actress Michael falls in love with.

Top Hat   (1935) USA, DIRECTOR – MARK SANDRICH

This is a great Fred Astaire-Ginger Rogers musical. The Irving Berlin score has numbers like 'Top Hat, White Tie and Tails', 'No Strings' with Astaire dancing around a hotel room kicking over the props, and the 'Cheek to Cheek' duet. Once again based on the play, *The Gay Divorce*, the plot concerns mistaken identity. The screenplay by Dwight Taylor and Allen Scott has plenty of laughs however, for Edward Everett Horton, Eric Blore, Helen Broderick and Erik Rhodes. Hermes Pan did the choreography and Van Nest Polglase and Carroll Clark designed the stylish Art Deco sets.

Left: The legendary Fred Astaire heads a sea of top hats, white ties and tails in the musical *Top Hat* (35).

Topper   (1937) USA, DIRECTOR – NORMAN V McLEOD

The wealthy and fun loving Kerbys (Cary Grant and Constance Bennett) are killed in an auto crash and return as ghosts. Before they can get to heaven they must perform a good deed, and that is to bring a little fun into the life of banker Cosmo Topper (Roland Young). The film also boasts a fine supporting cast with such standouts as Billie Burke and Alan Mowbray. Dialogue is snappy, and the special effects while predictable are entertaining. The film was based on a novel by Thorne Smith. There were two *Topper* sequels and a TV series in the 1950s. *Topper* was also the first black-and-white film to undergo colorization in 1985.

Cary Grant, Constance Bennett and Roland Young in *Topper* (37).

The Treasure Of The Sierra Madre (1948) USA, DIRECTOR – JOHN HUSTON

John Huston won an Oscar for directing, this film, and for his screenplay, adapted from B Traven's novel of gold, greed and human nature. His father Walter Huston won an Oscar for best supporting actor as the old prospector, Howard. Humphrey Bogart didn't win an Oscar for his masterful portrayal of the increasingly paranoid Fred C Dobbs. Tim Holt plays the third prospector Curtin, and

Alfonso Bedoya as 'Gold Hat' is one of the great movie villains. The film was extremely famous when it was released, but is not shown as often as it should be, though it is among Bogart's best.

Walter Huston, Humphrey Bogart and Tim Holt in *The Treasure of The Sierra Madre* (48).

Triumph Of The Will (1935) GERMANY, DIRECTOR – LENI RIEFENSTAHL

Riefenstahl was commissioned by the Nazi Party to produce a documentary on the Party's 1934 Congress in Nuremberg. Later Riefenstahl was to claim that the film was art not propaganda. The claim is nonsense; the film is brilliantly made, but it is most certainly propaganda, from

the beginning when the clouds seem to part as Hitler's plane arrives through the processions and speeches. The footage has been widely used in films about the Nazis.

Right: Hitler Youth parade in *Triumph of the Will* (35).

Trouble In Paradise (1932) USA, DIRECTOR – ERNST LUBITSCH

This absolute gem of a film by the master of wit and sophistication just slipped in before the Hays Office really cracked down. Nothing is explicit, but the sexual innuendoes crackle in the dialogue between a couple of international thieves, Herbert Marshall and Miriam

Hopkins. Ultimately Marshall is forced to choose between becoming a hypocrite and remaining a thief, where being dishonest is only a job, not a way of life. The excellent supporting cast includes Kay Francis, Charles Ruggles, Edward Everett Horton and C Aubrey Smith.

The True Glory (1945) GREAT BRITAIN/USA, DIRECTORS – CAROL REED, GARSON KANIN

If you want to know what the final year of World War II felt like, this is the film to see. Compiled jointly for the British Ministry of Information and the US Office of War Information this compilation of newsreels covering the time from D-Day to the Fall of Berlin still provides an

exhilarating experience for a viewer. The film is energetically and intelligently edited. The commentary which strives for Shakespearean eloquence seems a bit overblown, but you can't beat the shots or the storyline.

True Grit (1969) USA, DIRECTOR – HENRY HATHAWAY

After forty years in films John Wayne finally won an Academy Award for Best Actor for his portrayal of Rooster Cogburn, a fat, over-the-hill, one-eyed, drunken marshal. Based on a novel by Charles Portis, the film is supposed to be a story about a fourteen-year-old girl (Kim Darby) who hires a lawman to find her father's killer. In reality this is a picture about John Wayne, and it's a delight. Glen Campbell and Robert Duvall costar. Wayne assumed the character of the one-eyed marshal again in *Rooster Cogburn* (1975) with Katharine Hepburn.

John Wayne, Kim Darby and Glen Campbell in *True Grit* (69).

Tunes Of Glory (1960) GREAT BRITAIN, DIRECTOR – RONALD NEAME

A rough, up-from-the-ranks, colonel, (Alec Guinness) is replaced at the head of a Scottish regiment by a proper, disciplinarian with family connections (John Mills). There is a sub plot concerning the colonel's daughter (Susannah York) and a young piper. The contrast of the two officers' characters which threatens to divide the regiment is beautifully portrayed and the film costars Dennis Price, Kay Walsh, Duncan MaCrae and Gordon Jackson.

Twelve Angry Men (1957) USA, DIRECTOR – SYDNEY LUMET

A young Puerto Rican is on trial for murder, and eleven of the jurors are ready to pronounce him guilty. Only one of the jurors (Henry Fonda) stands against a rush to judgment. As this tense jury room drama unfolds Fonda manages to get his fellow jurors to change their minds. This is Fonda at his most heroic. The rest of the jury, made up of Lee J Cobb, Ed Begley, Joseph Sweeney, E G Marshall, Jack Warden, Martin Balsam, Edward Binns, John Fielder, Robert Webber, George Voskovec and Jack Klugman are also outstanding. The film marks Lumet's impressive directorial debut. The film is also notable because Reginald Rose adapted the script from his own television play, and many of the actors were television not film actors.

Twelve O'Clock High (1949) USA, DIRECTOR – HENRY KING

Gregory Peck gave one of his finest performances in one of the all-time great World War II films. Peck plays a young general given command of a bomber squadron in England after the previous commander (Gary Merrill) has a breakdown. Subtly the same pressures, particularly the agony of sending men on dangerous missions, begins to drive him to the same sort of breakdown. Peck and the film received Oscar nominations. Dean Jagger who played the general's adjutant won the Academy Award for Best Supporting Actor. The film was also the basis for a TV series.

Twentieth Century   (1934) USA, DIRECTOR – HOWARD HAWKS

Carole Lombard and John Barrymore star in this wonderful screwball comedy, which Ben Hecht and Charles MacArthur adapted from their own play. Barrymore is Oscar Jaffe, an egomanical director. Lombard is Mildred Plotka who Jaffe has transformed into Lily Garland, the theater's biggest star. Now he is down and she is up and they both meet on a cross country train - the Twentieth Century Limited. The film was later turned into a Broadway musical *On the Twentieth Century*.

2001: A Space Odyssey   (1968) GREAT BRITAIN, DIRECTOR – STANLEY KUBRICK

Though now considered a classic and possibly the greatest science-fiction film ever made *2001* opened to generally hostile reviews. But it gained an audience, particularly a young audience, and the critics were forced to revise their opinions, though there is still considerable argument over the meaning of the film which concerns in part, a space probe to Jupiter. Most memorable scenes are the computer HAL sadly crooning 'Daisy, Daisy, Give Me Your Answer Do' as he is being dismantled, and the Star Gate, a psychedelic light show. The Oscar-winning special effects were remarkable for their time. The film was based on an Arthur C Clarke story, but the vision is the director's. A muddled sequel *2010* (1984) which tried to explain the mysteries of *2001* was not directed by Kubrick.

The futuristic shuttle interior in *2001: A Space Odyssey* (68).

Two Women   (1961) ITALY, DIRECTOR – VITTORIO DE SICA

Based on a novel by Alberto Moravia, *Two Women* was an attempt by De Sica to recapture the powerful naturalistic style of some of his earlier post-World War II films like *Shoeshine*. The film is notable for the Award-winning performance of its star Sophia Loren. Known as one of the most beautiful women in films in *Two Women*, she proved she could act as well. It is the story of an Italian mother and her young daughter Eleanora Brown and their survival during the Allied invasion of Italy. Jean-Paul Belmondo and Raf Vallone costar.

Sophia Loren breaks down after her daughter and she are brutally raped by Moroccan troops in *Two Women* (61).

Ugetsu (1953) JAPAN, DIRECTOR – KENJI MIZOGUCHI

In sixteenth century Japan two peasants go to the city to sell their wares. One becomes the lover of what he believes to be a beautiful woman, though she is in fact, a ghost. The other buys a spear and armor and becomes a samurai. Their wives who are left behind are attacked by roving bands of samurai, one is killed, the other becomes a prostitute. It is the film's blend of the brutal and the lyrical, the real and supernatural, that have made *Ugetsu/Ugetsu Monogatari* one of the Japanese films most respected by Western audiences.

Umberto D (1955) ITALY, DIRECTOR – VITTORIO DE SICA

Umberto (Carlo Battista) an elderly and now retired government worker living on an inadequate pension in postwar Rome, is threatened with eviction unless he pays his back rent. Umberto is no lovable old man, but he does care deeply about his dog Flike, and about a pregnant and unmarried young maid (Maria Pia Casilio) who also faces eviction. This is a realistic, and deeply moving social drama, and one of director De Sica's best.

The Uninvited (1944) USA, DIRECTOR – LEWIS ALLEN

This classic ghost story stars Ray Milland and Ruth Hussey as a brother and sister who buy a large country house that turns out to be haunted. Their new neighbor Gail Russell, who lived in the house as a baby, seems to be the object of focus for the ghost. The film relies on atmosphere, suspense and a well-crafted plot rather than blood and shock to hold its audience. Milland is at his romantic best. The film also introduced the melody 'Stella by Starlight'. Donald Crisp and Cornelia Otis Skinner costar.

Ruth Hussey, Alan Napier, and Ray Milland visit their neighbor Cornelia Otis Skinner in *The Uninvited* (44).

Union Pacific   (1939) USA, DIRECTOR – CECIL B DeMILLE

If you like train wrecks, this is the film for you, because it has one filmed in the spectacular DeMille fashion. There are lots of other train scenes as well in this saga about the building of the first transcontinental railroad. The action centers on a struggle between hero Joel McCrea and villain Brian Donlevy, with Barbara Stanwyck (spouting an Irish brogue) in the middle. Even better than the leads are some of the supporting players like Akim Tamiroff, Robert Preston, Anthony Quinn and Evelyn Keyes.

Joel McCrea, Barbara Stanwyck, Lynn Overmann and Akim Tamiroff aboard the *Union Pacific* (39).

The Virgin Spring   (1959) SWEDEN, DIRECTOR – INGMAR BERGMAN

Set in medieval Sweden, this is a stark and brutal fable about an innocent young girl who is raped and murdered. When the murderers are finally tracked down and killed by her father a spring bubbles up from the spot where she died. The rape scene was considered shockingly violent when the film was first released in America. As usual Bergman gets wonderful performances from all his actors particularly Max Von Sydow as the father. *The Virgin Spring/Jungfraukällan* won an Academy Award for Best Foreign Film.

Les Visiteurs Du Soir   (1942) FRANCE, DIRECTOR – MARCEL CARNÉ

This is an unusual film, made in France during the German occupation. On the surface it is a stately medieval fable in which the Devil sends messengers to Earth to corrupt two lovers. The mission is a failure, so the Devil turns the lovers to stone, however, their hearts still beat. The film is beautifully photographed and filled with hidden, and not so hidden meanings. The Devil is Hitler, and the lovers France, the fact that their hearts are still beating indicated that France is not dead. The stars are Arletty, Jules Berry, Marie Déa, Alain Cuny and Fernand Ledoux. Next to *Les Enfants du Paradis*, this may be Carné's best film.

Wages Of Fear (1953) FRANCE/ITALY, DIRECTOR – HENRI-GEORGES CLOUZOT

Four Europeans played by Yves Montand, Charles Vanel, Peter Van Eyck and Folco Lolli, stranded and broke in a desolate South American country, take a job of driving two truckloads of nitro-glycerine over hundreds of miles of mountain roads. The roads are horrible and the trucks may blow up at any moment. The result is a classic of almost unbearable suspense. The film originally titled *La Salaire de la Peur* is also an angry denunciation of the exploitation of workers, and an exploration of the relationships between four men, none of whom can remotely be considered a hero. A disappointing American remake, *Sorcerer* was released in 1977.

Yves Montand rescues his companion in *Wages of Fear* (53).

A Walk In The Sun (1945) USA, DIRECTOR – LEWIS MILESTONE

Fifteen years after directing the anti-war classic *All Quiet on the Western Front* Milestone tackled a different kind of war. An American platoon lands in Salerno, Italy in 1943 and is ordered to march across hostile territory. Though it came out just at the end of World War II, this is no flag-waving, glory of war film. The conclusion is that war is a terrifying necessity. The film concentrates on the individual soldiers, and there is fine ensemble acting from Dana Andrews, Richard Conte, Sterling Holloway, Lloyd Bridges, John Ireland and others. A box office failure when released, the film is now considered a classic.

Walkabout   (1970) AUSTRALIA, DIRECTOR – NICOLAS ROEG

Lost in the Australian outback two English children meet a young aborigine who is off on his own to prove his manhood. The aborigine guides the English boy and girl back to civilization. The film is about a clash of cultures. There is a strong sexual attraction between the English girl played by Jenny Agutter, and the aborigine, David Gulpilil. She resists, treating him as a servant rather than a prospective lover. The eerie quality of film is intensified by Roeg's gorgeous photography of the outback.

War And Peace   (1968) USSR, DIRECTOR – SERGEI BONDARCHUK

Though this film can run up to eight hours (several different versions have been released) it's worth it. This is surely the preeminent film adaptation of Russia's preeminent novel, Leo Tolstoy's *War and Peace*. Produced in Moscow on a Hollywood style budget *War and Peace*, starring the director as Pierre, Luydmila Savelyeva as Natasha and Vyacheslav Tikhonov as Prince Andrei, contains some of the most spectacular battle scenes ever filmed, but also bring the lives of the characters and the times they lived in into focus, following the long and complex novel closely and respectfully. A 1956 US version with Henry Fonda, Audrey Hepburn and Mel Ferrer is nowhere near as long or as good.

The Russian troops are blessed before the Battle of Borodino – *War and Peace* (68).

Way Down East   (1920) USA, DIRECTOR – D W GRIFFITH

Director Griffith was hospitalized because of injuries suffered in an explosion while filming the final ice rescue sequence. Star Lillian Gish permanently injured her hand in the icy water during the scene. But somehow the picture was made and it turned out to be Griffith's biggest commercial success after *The Birth of a Nation*. It's the ultimate screen melodrama with a city slicker despoiling the virtuous heroine (Gish). When her pregnancy is revealed, the conservative farmer she works for throws her out. She is rescued from certain death in an icy river by the farmer's son, who has always loved her (Richard Barthelmess).

The Way We Were   (1973) USA, DIRECTOR – SYDNEY POLLACK

Robert Redford and Barbra Streisand have never been better than they are in this funny, tearful and thoroughly wonderful romance. Katie Morosky (Streisand) is a plain left-wing campus radical during the 1930s. Hubbell Gardiner (Redford) is a handsome apolitical WASP athlete who is also a writer. Improbably they fall in love and marry, but he sells out his writing talents to Hollywood, and she is willing to sacrifice everything, including Hubbell for her political convictions. Streisand also performs Marvin Hamlisch's Oscar winning title song.

West Side Story   (1961) USA, DIRECTORS – ROBERT WISE, JEROME ROBBINS

This energetic screen adaptation of the Leonard Bernstein-Stephen Sondheim Broadway classic, recalls the story of *Romeo and Juliet* set among New York street gangs of the 1950s. Natalie Wood and Richard Beymer are rather miscast as the leads, but everyone else is great, particularly Rita Moreno and George Chakiris, both of whom won Oscars for Best Supporting Actress and Actor respectively. Robbins earned a special award for his choreography, which is the best feature of the film. The score, changed little from the Broadway original, is wonderful.

Tony (Richard Beymer) recognizes the bodies of Riff (Russ Tamblyn) and Bernardo (George Chakiris) in *West Side Story* (61).

Whiskey Galore/*Tight Little Island*   (1949) GREAT BRITAIN, DIRECTOR – ALEXANDER MACKENDRICK

World War II has created a whiskey shortage among the hard drinking residents of a little Scottish island. Then a ship with a large cargo of whiskey sinks off the coast. The action of this thoroughly delightful comedy centers on the islanders largely successful attempts to recover the booze and hide it from a stuffy commander of the home guard. There are first rate performances from Basil Radford, Joan Greenwood, James Robertson Justice, Gordon Jackson, Jean Cadel and everyone else. The film was a big hit in the United States as well as Britain.

White Heat   (1949) USA, DIRECTOR – RAOUL WALSH

'Made it, Ma. Top of the world!' shouts gangster Cody Jarrett just before he is blown to bits at the end of this superb gangster film. After ten years away from gangster roles James Cagney returned to play Cody, a violent, mother-obsessed, madman. It's one of his best performances. Margaret Wycherly is also outstanding as the shrewd, amoral Ma. At the time critics warned that the film was excessively violent, though it does not seem so by today's standards. Walsh's fast pacing and brilliant editing contribute much to the success of *White Heat*.

James Cagney and Edmund O'Brien in *White Heat* (49).

Who's Afraid Of Virginia Woolf? (1966) USA, DIRECTOR – MIKE NICHOLS

When director Nichols decided to cast Elizabeth Taylor and Richard Burton as the leads in this adaptation of Edward Albee's searing play about an embittered couple, many doubted his wisdom. Taylor and Burton were known to be troublesome, and Taylor's acting ability was suspect. But the gamble paid off brilliantly. Burton was perfect as the boozy, resentful professor and Taylor was never better than as his bitchy but ultimately pathetic wife. George Segal and Sandy Dennis were also at the top of their form as the young couple who drop over for a few drinks. The film shattered some Hollywood taboos and Taylor and Dennis both won Academy Awards.

Taylor and Burton in *Who's Afraid of Virginia Woolf?* (66).

Why We Fight (1942-45) USA, PRODUCED BY THE US WAR OFFICE

Throughout World War II a series of documentaries, each about an hour in length, were prepared by the United States Government mainly for the armed forces. However, the series, which was made under the general direction of Frank Capra, was so powerful that it found a large audience among the general public. All the films had been edited by William Hornbeck, with music by Dimitri Tiomkin and a commentary spoken by Walter Huston. The films were: *Prelude to War, The Nazis Strike, Divide and Conquer, The Battle of Britain, The Battle of Russia, The Battle of China* and *War Comes to America*.

The Wild One (1954) USA, DIRECTOR – LASLO BENEDEK

This is the original motorcycle gang film, and far and away the best. It's based on a true story in which members of a motorcycle club terrorize a small California town. What makes this film is Marlon Brando's performance as the moody, mumbling leather jacketed leader of the 'Black Rebels.' Underneath Brando's tough guy act, he's basically decent, and he falls for the sheriff's daughter, Mary Murphy. Rival gang leader Lee Marvin is just plain mean, and the final clash between the two is fun to watch. The film is thought to have started the popular craze for leather jackets.

Right: Marlon Brando as the leader of the 'Black Rebels' in *The Wild One* (54).

Wild Strawberries (1957) SWEDEN, DIRECTOR – INGMAR BERGMAN

An elderly Swedish professor (played by Victor Sjostrom, a famed director from the silent era) drives back to his home town to receive an honorary degree. His past life is revealed through dreams and a series of flashbacks. *Wild Strawberries/Smultronstället* is one of the most influential films in history and is still studied by filmmakers everywhere. It's wonderfully touching to watch, and complex enough to be worth discussion afterwards. Max von Sydow, Gunnar Bjornstrand, Bibi Andersson, Ingrid Thulin and other Bergman favorites make up the cast.

The Wind (1927) USA, DIRECTOR – VICTOR SJOSTROM

The great Swedish director Victor Sjostrom came to Hollywood in the 1920s (in the US his name was spelled Seastrom). He directed a number of important silent films but his undoubted American triumph was *The Wind*, a powerful melodrama of disintegration and madness in an alien environment. The film is also probably Lillian Gish's finest hour as the woman who battles the elements of a barren dustbowl town and finally shoots the brute who raped her. The final desert storm sequence is a classic. The film itself is one of the last great silents.

Letty Mason (Lillian Gish) shoots a rapist in *The Wind* (27).

Wings (1927) USA, DIRECTOR – WILLIAM WELLMAN

The first Best Picture Oscar was given to the epic of two young Americans whose passion for flying leads them to join the American Expeditionary Forces in Europe in World War I. What makes this film memorable are the spectacular aerial dogfight sequences. Director Wellman, himself a pilot, drew on his own experience for the aerial photography and stunt work. Leads Charles 'Buddy' Rogers and Richard Arlen are rather flat but Clara Bow as 'the girl next door' is dandy and there is a brief appearance by a then-unknown young actor named Gary Cooper.

The Winslow Boy (1950) GREAT BRITAIN, DIRECTOR – ANTHONY ASQUITH

Terence Rattigan adapted his own play, based on an actual case of a naval cadet who was accused of a petty school theft and expelled. Though the incident seems a minor one the result is a superior courtroom melodrama. The settings are just right, and the performances, particularly that of Robert Donat as the barrister who defends the boy, are on target. Also in the cast are Cedric Hardwicke, Margaret Leighton, Frank Lawton, Francis L Sullivan, Wilfrid Hyde White and Ernest Thesiger.

Robert Donat (right) as the lawyer for the defense faces Francis L Sullivan, the prosecuting counsel in *The Winslow Boy* (50).

Witness For The Prosecution (1958) USA, DIRECTOR – BILLY WILDER

This adaptation of an Agatha Christie play is one of the most enjoyable courtroom dramas ever filmed. There are strong performances from Charles Laughton, as an aged and ailing London barrister, Tyrone Power as the boyish, but possibly murderous defendant and Marlene Dietrich as Power's cold and mysterious German wife. Elsa Lanchester appears in the minor role of Laughton's stern but doting nurse. As you might expect in a Christie story there are all sorts of twists and turns, and the ending comes as a real surprise.

The Wizard Of Oz

(1939) USA, DIRECTOR – VICTOR FLEMING

This tale of the little girl who is whirled away from home by a tornado, and manages to get back with the aid of three friends after a quest is one of the three or four greatest films ever made. We've all seen it, probably a dozen times, we know all the scenes and the songs; the characters are as familiar to us as the kids we grew up with: Judy Garland as Dorothy; Bert Lahr as the cowardly lion; Ray Bolger as the scarecrow; Jack Haley, the tin man; the showy wizard Frank Morgan, and that most wonderful of all villains Margaret Hamilton, the wicked witch of the west. There are the flying monkeys, the midget Munchkins, wonderful special effects and a terrific score by Harold Arlen and E Y Harburg. There was a 1925 version of L Frank Baum's classic but all attempts to remake or make sequels to the 1939 version seem sacrilegious.

Dorothy (Judy Garland), the Tin Woodman (Jack Haley), the Cowardly Lion (Bert Lahr) and Scarecrow (Ray Bolger) in *The Wizard of Oz* (39).

The Wolf Man

(1941) USA, DIRECTOR – GEORGE WAGGNER

Of all the werewolf films ever made, this is the classic. Lawrence Talbot, a skeptical young man is bitten by a werewolf. As a result, when the moon is full he turns into something that is not quite a wolf but a very savage and hairy two-legged monster. Lon Chaney Jr, normally a limited actor is superb as the tormented Talbot. The supporting cast including Claude Rains, Warren William and Maria Ouspenskaya is also unusually fine. Though the wolf man character has been recycled and satirized so many times it can't be taken seriously anymore, this film has a literate script, wonderfully atmospheric photography, and music so good it was used in many other chillers. Much credit goes to Jack Pierce who created the wolf man makeup.

Maria Ouspenskaya and Lon Chaney Jr in *The Wolf Man* (41).

Woman Of The Year (1942) USA, DIRECTOR – GEORGE STEVENS

This is the first of the nine Spencer Tracy-Katharine Hepburn films, and it was the beginning of a beautiful screen and personal partnership. She plays Tess Harding a famous political commentator and he's Sam Craig, a sports reporter. They marry but find it difficult to reconcile their lives. The film, with an Oscar-winning screenplay by Ring Lardner Jr and Michael Kanin, is a delightful battle of wits. It was the basis for a hit Broadway musical and was remade for TV in 1976.

Spencer Tracy and Katharine Hepburn in *Woman of the Year* (42), the first of the nine films in which they costarred.

The Women (1939) USA, DIRECTOR – GEORGE CUKOR

Anita Loos adapted Clare Boothe's funny, bitchy play for the screen, softening the characters. A group of mostly idle, rich women gossip, backstab, snoop, and brag, but are also shown as resilient, and capable of genuine camaraderie as they experience divorce and remarriage. The film also boasts the absolute best all-female cast ever assembled in Hollywood: Joan Crawford as the revolting Crystal Allen, Norma Shearer as the put-upon Mary Haines and Rosalind Russell as the bitchy, Sylvia Fowler, Paulette Goddard, Joan Fontaine, Mary Boland, Majorie Main, Hedda Hopper, Virginia Grey and Virginia Weidler costar. They're all good, but no one got even an Oscar nomination. A Technicolor fashion show sequence was tacked on at the end by MGM, just to show they could use the process.

Woodstock (1970) USA, DIRECTOR – MICHAEL WADLEIGH

The 1969 outdoor rock concert called Woodstock (though it was actually held on a dairy farm at nearby Bethel, New York) gave its' name to a generation, and came to symbolize the peace and love movement of the 1960s. Over 500,000 fans overwhelmed the facilities, and when the rains came the area was turned into a sea of mud. Yet there was no violence, and enormous good will during the three day event. This Oscar-winning documentary did as much as the concert itself to spread the legend of Woodstock. Some of the acts include Joan Baez, Jefferson Airplance, Jimi Hendrix, Arlo Guthrie and The Who. The real stars however are the vast audience. Scenes of nudity earned this film an undeserved X rating.

Roger Daltrey of The Who was featured at the legendary rock concert in New York State – *Woodstock* (70).

The World Of Apu (1959) INDIA, DIRECTOR – SATYAJIT RAY

Apu Sansar/The World of Apu is the final film in the Apu trilogy which also includes *Pather Panchali* and *Aparajito*. In it, the child first seen in *Pather Panchali*, who grew up to attend Calcutta University in *Aparajito*, becomes a teacher, a factory worker and marries, only to lose his wife in childbirth. Authentic, simple, and beautiful the Apu trilogy is one of the finest achievements in the art of cinema, winning director Ray a permanent place in the pantheon of great film directors. Ray wrote the script of *Apu Sansar/The World of Apu* and like other films in the series it is in the Bengali language but though specifically Indian it is universal in meaning.

The Wrong Box (1966) GREAT BRITAIN, DIRECTOR – BRYAN FORBES

A black comedy with a Victorian setting in which one aging brother tries to do in another to gain an inheritance, the film is rife with plots, counterplots, mixups, and a wild chase, all based on a story by Robert Lewis Stevenson and his stepson Lloyd Osborne. The murderously inclined brothers are Ralph Richardson and John Mills. Peter Cook and Dudley Moore play a couple of greedy cousins, and Peter Sellers makes a brief but memorable appearance as an oddball doctor. Michael Caine, Nanette Newman, Wilfrid Lawson and Tony Hancock are also in the cast.

Peter Cook and Dudley Moore sit on *The Wrong Box* (66).

Wuthering Heights   (1939) USA, DIRECTOR – WILLIAM WYLER

Scriptwriters Ben Hecht and Charles MacArthur simplified and shortened Emily Bronte's brooding and violent love story. Producer Sam Goldwyn rebuilt the bleak Yorkshire moors in Southern California. Young and handsome Laurence Olivier played Heathcliff, and young and beautiful Merle Oberon, Cathy. The result is a lush romantic drama that didn't please Bronte purists, but certainly pleased the movie going public. The New York

Film Critics named *Wuthering Heights* the best film of the year over *Gone With The Wind.* The excellent cast includes Flora Robson as the housekeeper, Hugh Williams as the brutal Hindley and David Niven as Edgar.

Laurence Olivier and Geraldine Fitzgerald in *Wuthering Heights* (39).

Yankee Doodle Dandy
(1942) USA, DIRECTOR – MICHAEL CURTIZ

This is supposed to be a biography of actor-playwright-songwriter George M Cohan. It is in reality a sentimental, superpatriotic, flag-waving musical vehicle for James Cagney. Cagney is absolutely magnificent as a hoofer, a singer and an actor, and won an Oscar for his performance. The songs by Cohan include 'Over There', 'Grand Old Flag', 'Give My Regards to Broadway' and the title song. Also in the cast are Joan Leslie, Walter Huston, Rosemary DeCamp, Jeanne Cagney, Frances Langford and Eddie Foy Jr playing his own father.

James Cagney as George M Cohan in *Yankee Doodle Dandy* (42).

The Year Of Living Dangerously
(1983) AUSTRALIA, DIRECTOR – PETER WEIR

Indonesia just before the fall of the Sukarno regime is the setting for this fascinating and gripping thriller-romance. Mel Gibson is the ambitious Australian correspondent who has an affair with a beautiful British attaché played by Sigourney Weaver. But the film is stolen by diminuitive Linda Hunt who plays Billy Kwan a half-Oriental, half-European dwarf photographer. Hunt deservedly won an Oscar for this, her first film appearance. The story is a bit weak but the mood, atmosphere and Hunt's performance are totally convincing.

Mel Gibson with Linda Hunt in *The Year of Living Dangerously* (83).

You Can't Take It With You (1938) USA, DIRECTOR – FRANK CAPRA

George S Kaufman and Moss Hart's play about a wacky family and the true meaning of happiness was a huge Broadway success and has been revived many times. Capra's adaptation had an all-star cast with James Stewart, Jean Arthur, Edward Arnold, Lionel Barrymore, Mischa Auer, Ann Miller (deliberately dancing badly), Spring Byington and Eddie 'Rochester' Anderson. The material seems perfect for the Capra mix of idealism and sentimentality, but somehow the film never quite works as well as it should. Still it's entertaining, and was hugely popular when it came out winning both Best Picture and Best Director Oscars.

Stewart and Arnold in *You Can't Take It With You* (38).

Young Frankenstein (1974) USA, DIRECTOR – MEL BROOKS

This is the most restrained, and, therefore, finest of Mel Brooks' films. It is also quite possibly the best spoof of horror films ever made. Gene Wilder stars as the wild haired descendant of the original doctor, with goggle-eyed comic Marty Feldman as the inevitable hunchbacked assistant, Teri Garr is astonishingly sexy as the lab assistant and Peter Boyle is the best monster since Karloff. Cloris Leachman, Madeline Kahn, Gene Hackman and everyone else in the cast is near perfect. The film features Wilder and Boyle performing 'Puttin' on the Ritz,' as well as the laboratory equipment from the original *Frankenstein*..

Right: Dr Frankenstein (Gene Wilder) in the electrical storm that will breathe life into his monster in *Young Frankenstein* (74).

The 1963 murder of a left-wing Greek leader by right-wing terrorists and the subsequent attempt to cover up the truth is the inspiration for this political thriller. Yves Montand plays the Greek leader and Jean-Louis Trintignant is the conservative but honest magistrate who slowly uncovers the widespread conspiracy. The film can be enjoyed simply as a spellbinding suspense film, but several right-wing governments banned it. Some leftists also criticized Costa-Gavras for making *Z* more of a moral than an ideological story. The picture was enormously popular throughout the world and won an Oscar for Best Foreign Film.

Yves Montand (right) is murdered by terrorists in *Z* (69).

Zero De Conduite (1933) FRANCE, DIRECTOR – JEAN VIGO

One of the most famous surrealist films of all time *Zero De Conduite/Zero for Conduct* set in a boy's boarding school is basically a parable of freedom versus authority. The headmaster of the school is a nasty dwarf and the school's staff is vicious. The result is revolution. The movie, removed from theaters at the urging of various civic organizations, was branded anti-French by the censors and was not released in France again until 1954. Despite its theme the movie is very funny and like Vigo's other major triumph *L'Atalante*, reflects a cynical anarchistic view of life.

Lt Gonville Bromhead (Michael Caine) fights off the Zulus in *Zulu* (64).

Zulu (1964) GREAT BRITAIN, DIRECTOR – CY ENDFIELD

Based on the true story of the defense of a mission station and hospital called Rorke's Drift, by a small British force of 100 facing a huge army of Zulus, during the Zulu War of 1879, this could have been a standard 'defense of Empire' film. But it's a good deal more than that. The performances by Jack Hawkins, Stanley Baker, Michael Caine, and Nigel Green are outstanding. The massive battle which takes up nearly half the film is spectacularly filmed. The narration by Richard Burton was done as a favor to Stanley Baker who co-produced the film, a tribute to the defenders of Rorke's Drift, members of the regiment of the South Wales Borderers.

Abbott, John 84, 112, 140
Abel, Walter 20
Abraham, F Murray 14
Adair, Jean *21*, 21
Adam, Alfred 119
Adler, Luther 59
Adorée, Renée 30, *30-31*
Agar, John 196
Agutter, Jenny 233
Aimée, Anouk 68
Albert, Eddie 188
Alerme, André 119
Alexander, Jane 14, 124
Alexander, John 21
Alford, Philip 221
Allan, Elizabeth 213
Allen, Karen 150, *180*, 181
Allen, Woody *19*, 19, 96
Allgood, Sara 101
Allwin, Pernilla *70*, 70
Allyson, June 110, 134, 149
Altman, Robert 140
Ameche, Don 12, 97, 99
Anderson, Broncho Billy 94
Anderson, Eddie 'Rochester' 42, 248
Anderson, Judith 17, *127*, 127, *182*, 182
Anderson, Lindsay 105
Anderson, Michael 20
Andersson, Bibi 194, 238
Andersson, Harriet 199
André, Marcel 27
Andress, Ursula 62
Andrews, Dana 28, 127, 163, 232
Andrews, Julie 148, *203*, 203
Annabella *144*, 144
Apted, Michael 51
Arden, Eve 144
Arlen, Richard 74, 239
Arletty 69, 115, 231
Armstrong, Louis 42
Armstrong, Robert 122
Arnold, Edward 13, 105, 145, *248*, 248
Arthur, Jean *145*, 145, 170, 194, 248
Asherson, Renée *98*, 98
Ashley, Edward *172*, 172
Asquith, Anthony 106, 177, 239
Asta 39, 215
Astaire, Fred *25*, 25, 68, *72*, 72, 82, *211*, 212, *224*, 224
Astor, Mary 134, *137*, 164, 173, 183
Attenborough, Richard 80, 92, 106, 129
Atwill, Lionel 42, 101, 149
Auclair, Michel 27
Audran, Stephane 61
Auer, Mischa 17, 149, 248
Aumont, Jean-Pierre 55
Autant-Lara Claude 59, 156
Avildsen, John G 186
Aykroyd, Dan *83*, 83
Aylmer, Felix 96
Ayres, Lew *13*, 13, 100, 115

Bacall, Lauren 30, *120*, 121
Baclanova, Olga *77*, 77
Backlinie, Susan *112*, 112
Bacon, Kevin 150
Bacon, Lloyd 73, 74
Badham, John 191

Badham, Mary 221
Badie, Laurence 113
Bainter, Fay 114
Baker, Stanley 52, 184, 251
Balsam, Martin 228
Bancroft, Anne *91*, 91
Banerji, Subir *165*, 165
Banks, Leslie 98, *139*, 139
Barnes, Binnie 174
Barnes, George 94
Barrault, Jean-Louis *69*, 69, 188
Barrie, Wendy 56, 101, 174
Barrymore, Drew 66
Barrymore, Ethel 170
Barrymore, John 30, 60, 91, 229
Barrymore, Lionel 42, 43, 54, 60, 64, *91*, 91, 110, 121, 133, 248
Barthelmess, Richard *39*, 39, *55*, 233
Bartholomew, Freddie *43*, 43, 54
Basehart, Richard *207*, 207
Bass, Alfie 128
Bates, Alan 123
Bates, Florence 140
Battista, Carlo 230
Baxter, Anne *13*, 13, 72
Baxter, Warner *74*, 74
Beatles, The *96*, 96
Beatty, Ned 210
Beatty, Warren *36*, 36, 97, 99
Becker, Jacques 44
Bedoya, Alfonso 226
Beery, Noah 26
Beery, Wallace 46, *60*, 60, *91*, 91
Begley, Ed 202, 228
Bel Geddes, Barbara 115
Bell, Marie 43
Bellamy, Madge 110
Belmondo, Jean-Paul 229
Belushi, John 150
Benedek, Lazslo 57, 236
Bennett, Compton 123
Bennett, Constance *225*, 225
Bennett, Joan 134
Benny, Jack *220*, 220
Benton, Robert 124
Berenger, Tom 29
Berenson, Marisa 41
Beresford, Bruce 37
Bergen, Candice 80
Berger, Helmut 53
Bergerac, Jacques 84
Bergman, Ingmar 70, 194, 199, 231, 238
Bergman, Ingrid 44, *44-45*, 61, *81*, 81, 84, 108, *204*, 204
Berkeley, Busby 23, 73, 74, 86
Berry, Jules 115, 231
Best, Edna 108, 139
Beymer, Richard *234*, 234
Bickford, Charles *115*, 115, 170
Bikel, Theodore 52, 58
Bisset, Jacqueline 39, 51
Bjornstrand, Gunner 70, 194, 199, 238
Blair, Betsy *140*, 140
Blair, Linda *69*, 69
Blanchar, Pierre 43, 212
Blondell, Joan 53, 73, 86, 177
Bloom, Claire 184
Blore, Eric 82, 125, 209, 212,

225
Blyth, Ann 144
Boardman, Eleanor 52
Bogarde, Dirk *36*, 36, 53, 54, *192*, 192, 213
Bogart, Humphrey *11*, 11, 18, 25, 30, 44, *44-45*, 54, 56, *100*, 100, *120*, 121, *137*, 137, *166*, 166, *226*, 226
Bogdanovitch, Peter 39, 127
Boland, Mary 172, 242
Boleslawski, Richard 81
Bolger, Ray 240, *240-241*
Bond, Ward 56, 178, *191*, 191
Bondarchuk, Sergei 233
Bondi, Beulah 110, 199, 204
Borgnine, Ernest 23, 78, *140*, 140
Bottoms, Timothy 127
Boulting, Roy 220
Bourvil 156
Bow, Clara 64, 239
Boyd, Stephen *27*, 27
Boyens, Phyllis 51
Boyer, Charles *81*, 81
Boyle, Peter 248
Bracken, Eddie 96, *144*, 144
Brady, Alice 149
Brambell, Wilfrid 96
Brando, Marlon 11, 84, *85*, 118, 148, *160*, 160 *208*, 208, 210 236, *237*
Brasseur, Pierre 69, 170
Brennan, Eileen 207
Brennan, Walter 23, 173
Brent, George 54, 74, *114*, 114
Bressart, Felix 153
Brest, Martin 28
Brett, Jeremy *148*, 148
Brialy, Jean-Claude 123
Brickman, Paul 186
Bridges, Beau 74, 153
Bridges, Jeff 127
Bridges, Lloyd 232
Broderick, Helen 212, 225
Bron, Eleanor 26
Bronson, Charles 92
Brook, Clive 195
Brooks, James L 215
Brooks, Louise *164*, 164
Brooks, Mel 220, 248
Brooks, Richard 46, 121
Brown, Bryan 37
Brown, Clarence 19, 108, 151
Brown, Eleanora 229
Brown, Joe E 201
Browning, Tod 64, 77
Bruce, Nigel 101, 126, 182, 191
Brynner, Yul *122*, 122
Bubbles, John W 42
Buchanan, Jack *25*, 25
Bucholtz, Horst 220
Bujold, Genevieve 123
Bull, Peter 157
Buñuel, Luis 47, 61, 158
Burke, Billie 225
Burke, Kathleen 134
Burr, Raymond 182
Burstyn, Ellen 69, 127
Burton, Richard 38, 69, *236*, 236, 251
Busch, Ernst 118
Busch, Mae 201
Butler, David 133
Byington, Spring 134, 248

Caan, James 79, 84
Cabot, Bruce 122
Cadel, Jean 235
Cagney, James 18, 73, 145, *177*, 177, *235*, 235, *246*, 247
Cagney, Jeanne 247
Caine, Michael *12*, 96, 244, *251*, 251
Calhern, Louis 22, *65*, 65, *118*, 118
Campbell, Glen *228*, 228
Camus, Marcel 34
Cantinflas 20
Capaldi, Peter *134*, 134
Capra, Frank 21, 110, 135, 145, 236, 248
Carey, Harry 145
Carey, Harry Jr 196
Carey, Joyce 38, 106
Carlisle, Kitty 152
Carmichael, Ian 52
Carné, Marcel 69, 115, 170, 231
Caron, Leslie *16-17*, 17, 84
Carradine, John 92, 101, *205*, 205
Carroll, Leo G 59, 101
Carroll, Madeleine 173, *219*, 219
Carson, Jack 144
Cary, Timothy 165
Casares, Maria *69*, 69, 163
Casilio, Maria Pio 230
Cassel, Jean-Pierre 61
Castelnuovo-Tedesco, Mario 17
Castle, John 132
Cavalcanti, Albert 57
Cazale, John *58*, 58, 84
Chakiris, George *234*, 234
Chamberlain, Richard 123, 127
Chandler, Helen *64*, 64
Chaney, Lon 102, *167*, 167
Chaney, Lon Jr *240*, 240
Chaplin, Charles 10, 50, *86*, 86, 92, 146, 189, 207
Chaplin, Geraldine 62
Chapman, Graham 147
Charisse, Cyd 25, 199
Charleson, Ian *46*, 46
Cherkasov, Nicolai *11*, 11, *111*, 111
Cherrill, Virginia 50
Chevalier, Maurice 84, 135
Christie, Julie 32, 54, *62*, 62
Christy, Dorothy 201
Chukrai, Grigori 24
Ciannelli, Eduardo *95*, 95, 140
Cilento, Diane 222
Cimino, Michael 58
Clair, René 10, 17, 83, 104, 135, 144, 204
Claire, Ina 153
Clark, Estelle 52
Clark, Mae 77, *177*, 177
Clayton, Jack 107
Cleese, John 147
Clement, René 113
Clements, John 74
Clift, Montgomery 78, 97
Clifton, Elmer 64
Cline, Edward 25, 149
Clive, Colin 37, 77
Close, Glenn *29*, 29
Clouzot, Henri-Georges 232
Clunes, Alec 184

Cobb, Lee J 160, 228
Coburn, Charles 125
Coburn, James 92
Cocteau, Jean 27, 163, 188, 190
Colbert, Claudette 20, *110*, 110, 164
Colman, Ronald 26, *135*, 135, *173*, 173, *213*, 213
Comingore, Dorothy *48*, 49
Connery, Sean 62
Connolly, Walter *155*, 155
Conte, Richard 232
Conway, Jack 213
Cook, Elisha Jr 30, 137
Cook, Peter *244*, 244
Cooper, Gary 26, *99*, 99, *134*, 134, *145*, 145, *147*, 147, *170*, 170, *173*, 173, *192*, 192, 239
Cooper, Gladys 155
Cooper, Jackie 46
Cooper, Melville 191
Cooper, Merian C 122
Coote, Robert 129
Coppola, Francis Ford 14, 84, 166
Corey, Wendall 182, 202
Cortese, Valentina 55
Costa-Gavras (Constantin) 250
Cotten, Joseph *49*, 49, 81, 136, 170, 195, 218
Coulouris, George 49
Courtenay, Tom 32, 62
Courtot, Marguerite 64
Cowan, Jerome *137*, 137
Coward, Noel 35, 38, *106*, 139, 219
Craig, Wendy 192
Crawford, Broderick *14*, 14, 26, 36
Crawford, Joan *91*, 91, 144, 242
Crawford, Michael 124
Cregar, Laird 97
Crichton, Charles 57, 128
Crisp, Donald 55, 101, 126, 183, 230
Cromwell, John 173
Cronyn, Hume 171
Crosby, Bing 83, 84, *186*, 186
Crosland, Alan 113
Cross, Ben 46
Cruise, Tom *186*, 186
Cruze, James 52
Cukor, George 10, 30, 36, 42, 54, 60, 81, 88, 100, 134, 148, 168, 205, 242
Cummings, Constance 35
Currie, Finlay 93
Curtis, Tony *58*, 58, *201*, 201, 210
Curtiz, Michael 10, 18, 42, 44, 144, 149, 247
Cybulski, Zbigniew *21*, 21

Da Costa, Morton 147
Dagover, Lil 42
Dahlbeck, Eva 199
Daltrey, Roger *243*, 243
Dane, Karl 30, *30-31*
D'Angelo, Beverly 51
Daniell, Henry 36, 92, 112
Daniels, Bebe 74, 137
Daniels, Jeff 215
Dantine, Helmut 146
Darby, Kim *228*, 228
D'Arcy, Alexander 173
Darrieux, Danielle 156, 188

Darrow, John 98
Darwell, Jane 92, 163
Dassin, Jules 22, 150, 184
Davalos, Dick *66*, 66
Davenport, Harry *88*, 88, 142
Davenport, Nigel *138*, 138
Davis, Bette *13*, 13, 36, *54*, 54, 114, *115*, *130*, 130, 137, *139*, 139, *155*, 155, *166*, 166
Davis, John Howard *157*, 157
Dawn, Marpessa 34
Day, Josette *27*, 27
Dead End Kids, The 18, 56
Dean, James *66*, 66
Dearden, Basil 36, 57, 129
De Broca, Phillipe 123
De Camp, Rosemary 247
Dee, Francis 134
de Havilland, Olivia 10, 42, *88*, 88, 97, 199
Dekker, Albert 26
Delannoy, Jean 212
Del Rio, Dolores 72
De Mille, Cecil B 170, 209, 231
Demarest, William 96, 115, 135, 164, 209
De Mornay, Rebecca *186*, 186
Demy, Jacques 165
Deneuve, Catherine 165
De Niro, Robert 38, *58*, 58, 84
Dennis, Sandy 236
Denny, Reginald 144, 182
de Oliviera, Lourdes 34
De Sica, Vittorio 29, *83*, 83, 197, 229, 230
de Wilde, Brandon *102*, 102, *194*, 194
Dexter, Brad *22*, 22
Dieterle, William 13, 102, 131, 170
Dietrich, Marlene *35*, 35, *59*, 59, 81, *147*, 147, *195*, 195, 239
Dieudonné, Albert *150*, 150
Digges, Dudley 148
Dillon, Melinda 51
Disney, Walt 24, 65, 70, 82, 169, 200
Donald, James *38*, 38
Donat, Robert 83, *90*, 90, 136, *219*, 219, *239*, 239
Donen, Stanley 26, 160, 193, 199
Donlevy, Brian 26, 231
Donnelly, Donal 124
Donner, Richard 210
Douglas, Kirk 23, *95*, 95, *165*, 165
Douglas, Melvyn 102, 144, 153
Dovzhenko, Alexander 66
Drake, Tom 142
Dressler, Marie 60
Dreyer, Carl 56
Dreyfuss, Richard 14, 51, 112
Dru, Joanne 196
Dumbrille, Douglass 55, 134
Dumont, Margaret *18*, 18, 55, 65, 152
Dunaway, Faye *34*, 34, 46, 47, 151
Dunne, Irene 122, 197
Dunnock, Mildred 57, 113
Duprez, June *74*, 74
Durante, Jimmy 139
Durning, Charles 207
Duryea, Dan 173
Duvall, Robert 39, 84, 140, 221, 228

Duvivier, Julien 43
Dymtryk, Edward 70

Earles, Harry 77
Edwards, Blake 56, 169
Eisenstein, Sergei 11, 108, 111, 172, 209
Ekberg, Anita *63*, 63
Ekerot, Bengt 70, *194*, 194
Ekman, Gosta 108
Elliott, Denholm 52
Enfield, Cy 251
Enright, Ray 53
Ericson, Leif 199, 202
Evans, Edith 106, 222
Ewell, Tom 10, 194
Eythe, William 101

Fabray, Nanette *25*, 25
Fairbanks, Douglas Jr *55*, 55, *95*, 95, 132, *173*, 173
Farley, Morgan *118*, 118
Farrar, David *34*, 34
Farrell, Glenda 132
Farrow, Mia 96
Faye, Alice 12
Feldman, Marty 26, 248
Fellini, Federico 63, 68, 161, 164, 207
Fernandel 43
Feyder, Jacques 119
Field, Betty 204
Field, Sally *153*, 153
Fields, W C 25, *54*, 54, *149*, 149
Finch, Peter 135, 151, 151
Finney, Albert *190*, 190, *222*, 222
Fisher, Carrie 96, 206
Fitzgerald, Barry 17, 84, 101, 150, 178
Fitzgerald, Geraldine *54*, 54, *245*, 245
Fitz-Gerald, Lewis 37
Flaherty, Robert 150
Fleming, Rhonda 95
Fleming, Victor 43, 88, 183, 240
Fletcher, Louise 161
Flynn, Errol 10, *42*, 42, 55
Fonda, Henry 92, 114, 115, 125, *145*, 145, *159*, 159, 228, 233
Fonda, Jane 116, *117*, *124*, 124, 159, 188
Fonda, Peter *68*, 68
Fontaine, Joan 95, 112, *182*, 182, 210, *211*, 242
Foran, Dick 166
Forbes, Bryan 129, 244
Ford, Glenn 75, 84
Ford, Harrison 14, 35, *180*, 181, 206
Ford, John 92, 101, 106, 110, 145, 178, 183, 191, 193, 196, 205
Forman, Milos 14, 161
Forster, Rudolph 64
Forsyth, Bill 134
Fosse, Bob 41, 123
Fossey, Brigitte *113*, 113
Fox, Edward 80
Fox, James 192
Foy, Eddie Jr 247
Francis, Kay 226
Franklin, Pamela *107*, 107
Freeland, Thornton 72
Frend, Charles 52
Fresnay, Pierre 92
Fridell, Ake 70

Friedkin, William 69, 77
Frye, Dwight 64, 77
Furness, Betty 212

Gabin, Jean 92, 115
Gable, Clark *88*, 88, *89*, *110*, 110, *148*, 148, 172, *183*, 183, *190*, 190
Galeen, Henrick 209
Gance, Abel 150
Garbo, Greta *19*, 19, 42, 91, 153, *178*, 178, 207
Gardiner, Reginald 139
Gardner, Ava 183, 197
Gardener, Joan 136, 191
Garfield, John *171*, 171
Garland, Judy *23*, 23, 68, *142*, 142, *205*, 205, 240, *240-241*
Garner, James 92
Garner, Peggy Ann 112
Garnett, Tay 171
Garr, Teri 223, 248
Garrett, Betty 160
Garson, Greer 90, *146*, 146, *172*, 172
Gaynor, Janet 205
Gazzo, Michael V 84
Genn, Leo 98, 199
Geray, Steve 84, 140
Germi, Pietro 61
Gibson, Mel 80, 136, 148, *247*, 247
Gielgud, John *118*, 118, 184
Gilbert, Bill 92
Gilbert, John 30, *30-31*, 178
Gilbert, Lewis 12
Gilliam, Terry 147
Gingold, Hermione 84
Gish, Dorothy *162*, 162
Gish, Lillian 33, *39*, 39, 108, *153*, 153, *162*, 162, 170, 233, *238*, 238
Goddard, Paulette, 44, 146, 242
Goldblum, Jeff 29
Goring, Marius 140, 184
Gould, Elliott 125, 140, *141*
Gould, Harold J 207
Goulding, Edmund 54, 55, 91
Gowland, Gibson 94
Grable, Betty 82
Grahame, Gloria 23
Granach, Alexander 118, 153
Granger, Farley *208*, 208
Granger, Stewart 123, 173
Grant, Cary *21*, 21, *39*, 39, 78, *95*, 95, 100, 105, 144, 148, *155*, 155, *168*, 168, 196, *210*, 210, *221*, 221, *225*, 225
Grapewin, Charley C 92, 166
Grayson, Kathryn *123*, 123, 197
Green, Alfred E 115
Green, Nigel 251
Greene, Richard 101
Greenstreet, Sydney 25, 44, 137, 140
Greenwood, Joan 106, 121, 138, 222, 235
Gregg, Everley 174
Grey, Joel *41*, 41
Grey, Virginia 242
Griem, Helmut 41
Griffies, Ethel 32
Griffith, D W 33, 39, 50, 64, 94, 108, 153, 162, 233
Griffith, Hugh 27, 222
Guinness, Alec *38*, 38, 62, 93, *121*, 121, 125, 128, *128*, 129, 138, 157, 206, 228

Gulpilil, David 127, 233
Guve, Bertil *70*, 70
Gwenn, Edmund 144

Hackman, Gene 36, 77, 210, 248
Hagen, Jean 22, 199
Hale, Alan 10, 52
Haley, Jack 12, 240, *240-241*
Hall, Alexander 99
Hall, Porter 108, 166
Hallatt, May *34*, 34
Halliday, John 108, 168
Hamer, Robert 57, 121
Hamill, Mark 206
Hamilton, Guy 52
Hamilton, Margaret 155, 240
Hamilton, Neil 55, 214
Hammond, Kay 35
Hancock, Tony 244
Hardwicke, Cedric 59, 123, 184, 216, 239
Harlan, Veit 114
Harlow, Jean *60*, 60, *98*, 98, 177, *183*, 183
Harris, Julie *66*, 66
Harrison, Rex 35, 122, *137*, 137, *148*, 148
Harvey, Anthony 132
Harvey, Lawrence 54
Hasegawa, Kazuo 81
Hasso, Signe 101
Hathaway, Henry 59, 101, 134, 228
Hauer, Rutger 35
Hawkins, Jack 27, 38, 52, 129, 251
Hawks, Howard 30, 39, 55, 104, 192, 229
Hay, Will 156
Hayakawa, Sessue 38
Hayden, Sterling *22*, 22, 84
Hayward, Susan 26, 54
Hayworth, Rita *84*, 84
Hedren, Tippi *32*, 32
Heerman, Victor 18
Heflin, Van 194
Helm, Brigitte *143*, 143
Helm, Levon 51
Helpmann, Robert *184*, 184
Henreid, Paul 44, *44-45*, *155*, 155
Hepburn, Audrey 128, *148*, 148, 188, 233
Hepburn, Katharine *10*, 10, *11*, 30, *39*, 39, 100, *132*, 132, 134, *159*, 159, *168*, 168, 228, *242*, 242
Herlie, Eileen 96
Hernandez, Juano 108
Herron, Robert 108
Hersholt, Jean 94
Herzog, Werner 155
Heston, Charlton *27*, 27, 118
Hill, George Roy 40, 207
Hiller, Wendy *137*, 137, *138*, 138, *177*, 177
Hirsch, Judd 162
Hitchcock, Alfred 32, 125, 139, 155, 175, 182, 204, 208, 210, 219, 221
Hobson, Valerie *93*, 93, 121
Hoffman, Dustin 14, *91*, 91, *124*, 124, *143*, 143, *223*, 223
Holden, William 36, 38, 151, 209
Holliday, Judy 10, 36
Holloway, Stanley 38, 96, 128,

148, 219
Holloway, Sterling 232
Holm, Celeste 13, 199
Holm, Ian 46
Holt, Jack *190*, 190
Holt, Tim *136*, 136 *226*, 226
Homolka, Oscar 194
Hope, Bob 44, 83, *186*, 186
Hopkins, Anthony 132, 148
Hopkins, Miriam 61, 97, 226
Hopper, Dennis *68*, 68
Hopper, Hedda 155, 209, 242
Horne, Lena 42
Horton, Edward Everett 82, 100, 135, 225, 226
Howard, Leslie *72*, 72, 73, *88*, 88, 108, *166*, 166, *176*, 177, 191
Howard, Ron 4
Howard, Trevor 38, 80, 148
Hudson, Hugh 46
Hudson, John *95*, 95
Hughes, Howard 98
Hulce, Tom *14*, 14, 150
Hull, Josephine *21*, 21, *96*, 97
Hunt, Linda *247*, 247
Hunt, Martita *93*, 93
Hurt, William *29*, 29
Hussey, Ruth *168*, 168, *230*, 230
Huston, John 11, 25, 47, 100, 114, 121, 137, 183, 226
Huston, Walter 13, 17, 33, *226*, 226, 247
Hutton, Betty *144*, 144
Hutton, Timothy *162*, 162
Hyde White, Wilfred 148, 239

Idle, Eric 147
Ince, Thomas 50
Inescourt *172*, 172
Ingram, Rex 75
Ireland, John *14*, 14, 95, 232
Ivashov, Vladimir *24*, 24
Ives, Burl *46*, 46

Jackson, Gordon 228, 235
Jacobson, Ulla 199
Jaffe, Sam *22*, 22, *95*, 95, 135
Jagger, Dean 23, 228
James, Sidney *128*, 128
Jannings, Emil 35, 127
Jarman, Claude Jr 108
Jeayes, Allen *57*, 57
Jeffries, Lionel 52
John, Rosamund *72*, 72
Johns, Glynis 73
Johnson, Ben 127
Johnson, Celia 38, 106, 219
Johnson, Katie 125
Jolson, Al *113*, 113, 115
Jones, Allan 152, *197*, 197
Jones, Jennifer 25, 170
Jones, Shirley 147
Jones, Terry 147
Jones, Tommy Lee 51
Josephson, Erland 70
Jourdan, Louis 84
Jouvet, Louis 43, 119
Julian, Rupert 167

Kahn, Madeline 248
Karloff, Boris 21, 36, *37*, 37, *76*, 77, 108
Kasdan, Lawrence 29
Kazan, Elia 66, 160, 208
Keaton, Buster *82*, 82, 189, 209
Keaton, Diane *19*, 19, 84

Keel, Howard *123*, 123, 193, 197
Keeler, Ruby 53, 73, *74*, 74, 86, 115
Keighley, William 10, 139
Kellaway, Cecil 108, 171
Kellerman, Sally 140
Kelly, DeForest *95*, 95
Kelly, Gene *16-17*, 17, 68, 107, 160, *198*, 199
Kelly, Grace 99, *182*, 182, 183, *221*, 221
Kennedy, Arthur 100, 129
Kerr, Deborah *34*, 34, *78*, 78, *107*, 107, *122*, 122, 123, 131, 137, 173
Kerrigan, J M *106*, 106
Kerrigan, J Warren 52
Keyes, Evelyn 115, 231
Kibbee, Guy 53, 86
Kidder, Margot 116, 210
Kilburn, Terry 90
King, Henry 12, 228
Kingsford, Walter *213*, 213
Kingsley, Ben *80*, 80
Kinskey, Leonid 44
Kinugasa, Teinosuke 81
Klein-Rogge, Rudolf *143*, 143
Kline, Kevin 29, 202, 202
Knight, Esmond 34, 98
Knowles, Patric 10
Korda, Alexander 174, 216
Korda, Zoltan 74
Koster, Henry 97
Kramer, Stanley 58, 107
Krauss, Werner *42*, 42
Kubrick, Stanley 60, 62, 165, 229
Kulle, Jarl 199
Kurosawa, Akira 181, 193, 219
Kyo, Machiko 81, *181*, 181

LaCava, Gregory 149
Ladd, Alan *194*, 194
Lahr, Bert 240, *240-241*
Lake, Veronica 104, 209
Lamour, Dorothy 83, *186*, 186
Lancaster, Burt *22*, 22, *78*, 78, *95*, 95, 134, 202, 210
Lanchester, Elsa *37*, 37, 54, 83, *174*, 174, 239
Landis, Jessie Royce 137
Landis, John 150
Lanfield, Sidney 101
Lang, Fritz 136, 143, 152, 215
Lang, Walter 122
Lange, Jessica 122, 171, 223
Langford, Frances 247
Lansbury, Angela 81, 151
Lassie, *126*, 126
Laughton, Charles 54, 102, *103*, *148*, 148, 153, *174*, 174, 239
Laurel, Stan and Hardy, Oliver 201
Lawford, Peter 68, 134
Lawrence, Gertrude 122
Lawson, Wilfred 177, 244
Lawton, Frank *54*, 54, 239
Leachman, Cloris 127, 248
Lean, David 35, 38, 62, 93, 106, 129, 157, 219
Leaud, Jean-Pierre *178*, 178
Leclerc, Ginette 70
Lee, Mark 80
Lee-Thompson, J 220
Lefevre, Rene *144*, 144
Leigh, Janet 134, 175
Leigh, Vivien *88*, 88, *89*, *208*,

208
Leighton, Margaret 239
Leisen, Mitchell 20
Lemmon, Jack *20*, 20, 56, 78, 110, *145*, 145, *201*, 201
Lenya, Lotte 64
Leonard, Robert Z 172
Le Roy, Mervyn 86, 104, 132, 145
Leslie, Joan 100, 247
Lester, Mark, *156*, 156
Lester, Richard 96, 124
Levant, Oscar 17, 25
Lewton, Val 23, 36
Liebman, Ron 153
Lindblom, Gunnel 194
Lindsay, Margaret 114
Lithgow, John 215
Litvak, Anatole 199, 202
Livesey, Roger 129, 131, 140
Lloyd, Frank 148
Lloyd, Harold 39, *189*, 189
Lockwood, Margaret *125*, 125, 206
Lom, Herbert 125
Lombard, Carole 149, *155*, 155, *220*, 220, 229
Loren, Sophia 38, *229*, 229
Lorre, Peter 21, 25, 44, *136*, 136, *139*, 139, 140
Losey, Joseph 192
Love, Montague 173
Loy, Myrna 28, 135, 144, 215
Lubitsch, Ernst 10, 97, 125, 135, 144, 153, 220, 226
Lucas, George 14, 181, 206
Lugosi, Bela 36, *64*, 155
Lukas, Paul 125, 134
Lumet, Sidney 151, 228
Lupino, Ida *100*, 100
Lyons, Ben *98*, 98

McAvoy, May 113
McCambridge, Mercedes *14*, 14, 69
McCarey, Leo 65, 84
McCarthy, Kevin 57, 108
McClory, Kevin 20
McCrea, Joel 56, 59, 164, 209, *231*, 231
McDaniel, Hattie 88, 155
MacDonald, Jeanette 135, *190*, 190
McDowall, Roddy 101, *126*, 126
McDowell, Malcolm *50*, 50, *105*, 105
Mack, Marion *82*, 82
McKay, Fulton 134
McKee, Raymond 64
Mackendrick, Alexander 125, 138, 210, 235
McKenna, Siobhan 62
McKern, Leo 138
McLaglen, Victor *95*, 95, *106*, 106, 178, 196
MacLaine, Shirley *20*, 20, *215*, 215
McLeod, Norman Z 100, 225
MacMahon, Aline 86
MacMurray, Fred 20, *63*, 63
McNally, Stephen 115
MacNaughton, Robert 66
MacNicol, Peter 202
McQueen, Steve 39, *92*, 92
Macready, George 59, 84
Maggiorani, Lamberto *29*, 29
Magnani, Anna 161
Main, Marjorie 56, 142, 242

Malden, Karl 160, 166, 208
Malle, Louis 22
Malleson, Miles 106, 121
Mamoulian, Rouben 10, 61, 135, 144, 178
Mankiewicz, Joseph L 13, 118
Mann, Delbert 140
Manners, David 64
Marais, Jean *27*, 27, 163
March, Frederic 28, 46, 57, *61*, 61, 104, 107, *155*, 155, 205
Marion, George F *19*, 19
Marlowe, Hugh 13
Marsh, Mae 33
Marshall, E G 228
Marshall, George 59
Marshall, Herbert 130, 226
Marshall, Marion 104
Marshall, Tully 52, 183
Marvin, Lee 23, 236
Marx Brothers *18*, 18, 55, *65*, 65, 100, 139, *152*, 152
Masina, Guilietta *207*, 207
Mason, James 59, 118, 155, 156, 205, 220
Massey, Raymond 21, 66, 73, 140, 173, 191, 216
Massine, Leonid *184*, 184
Mastroianni, Marcello 61, 63, 68
Matheson, Tim 150
Matthau, Walter 78
Mayo, Archie 166
Meek, Donald *205*, 205
Meeker, Ralph 165
Megna, John 221
Mejia, Alfonso *158*, 158
Mello, Breno 34
Mendes, Lothar 114
Menjou, Adolphe 30, 78, 165
Merchant, Vivien 12
Meredith, Burgess 186
Merkel, Una *59*, 59
Merman, Ethel 12
Merrill, Gary 13, 228
Mifune, Toshiro *181*, 181, 193, 219
Miles, Bernard 106
Miles, Sarah *192*, 192
Milestone, Lewis 13, 78, 232
Milland, Ray 20, 26, 135, *230*, 230
Miller, Ann 68, 123, 160, 248
Miller, George 136
Miller, Jason 69
Mills, Hayley 220
Mills, John 93, 219, 220, 228, 244
Milner, Martin 210
Minnelli, Liza *41*, 41
Minnelli, Vincente 17, 23, 25, 42, 84, 142
Mitchell, Thomas 135, 145, 205
Mitchum, Robert 30, 70, 153
Mix, Tom 59
Mizoguchi, Kenji 230
Monroe, Marilyn 22, 194, 201
Montand, Yves 170, *232*, 232, *250*, 250
Montgomery, Robert 99
Moody, Ron 156
Moore, Dudley *26*, 26, *244*, 244
Moore, Mary Tyler 162
Moorehead, Agnes 49, 112, 115, 136
Moreau, Jeanne *116*, 116
Moreno, Rita 234
Morgan, Frank 240

Morgan, Harry 163
Morgan, Helen 197
Morgan, Michele 212
Morley, Robert 25, 137
Mowbray, Alan 225
Mulligan, Robert 221
Muni, Paul *104*, 104, *131*, 131
Munshin, Jules 68, 160
Murnau, F W 127, 155
Murphy, Audie 59, 183
Murphy, Eddie *28*, 28
Murray, Bill *83*, 83, 223
Murray, James 52
Murray, Marie 94

Naish, J Carrol 26, 204
Napier, Alan *230*, 230
Natwick, Mildred 178, 196
Neal, Patricia 102
Neame, Ronald 228
Negulesco, Jean 115, 140
Nelson, Ralph 131
Newley, Anthony 157
Newman, Nanette 129, 244
Newman, Paul *40*, 40, *46*, 46, *102*, 102, 181, *207*, 207
Newmayer, Fred 189
Newton, Robert 98, *137*, 137, 157, 219
Nichols, Mike 91, 236
Nicholson, Jack *47*, 47, 68, *161*, 161, 171, *215*, 215
Niven, David *20*, 20, 55, *72*, 72, 125, 140, 149, *169*, 169, 173, 245
Nolan, Lloyd 96, 101
Nugent, Elliott 44

Oakie, Jack 92
Oberon, Merle 136, 174, 191, 245
O'Brien, Edmond 118
O'Brien, George 18, 110
O'Brien, Margaret 134, *142*, 142
O'Brien, Pat 78
O'Connor, Donald 26, 199
O'Donnell, Cathy 28
Ogier, Bulle 61
O'Hara, Maureen 30, 101, 102, *103*, 144, 178
Oland, Warner 113, 195
Oliver, Edna Mae 54, 134, 213
Olivier, Laurence 73, 96, *98*, 98, 113, *172*, 173, 182, 184, *185*, *245*, 245
Olivier, Paul 10, 144
Ophuls, Marcel 202
Ophuls, Max 188
Orsini, Umberto 53
O'Sullivan, Maureen 54, 96, *214*, 214
O'Toole, Peter 90, *129*, 129, 132
Ouspenskaya, Maria *240*, 240
Overmann, Lynn *231*, 231

Pabst, G W 64, 118, 164
Pacino, Al 84
Pagnol, Marcel 70
Pakula, Alan J 14, 124, 202
Palance, Jack 100, 194
Palin, Michael 147
Pallette, Eugene 10, 83, 125, 149
Pangborn, Franklin 25, 96, 164, 209
Parker, Cecil 125, 138, 206
Parker, Jean 83, 134

Parks, Larry 115
Parsons, Estelle 36
Pascal, Gabriel 137
Pasolini, Pier Paolo 90
Patterson, Elizabeth 108
Pawley, Martin *191*, 191
Peck, Gregory 188, *204*, 204, *221*, 221, 228
Penn, Arthur 36
Perkins, Anthony 174, *175*
Philbin, Mary 167
Philipe, Gerard 59, 188
Pickens, Slim 62
Pidgeon, Walter 91, 101, *146*, 146
Pitts, Zasu 53, 94
Place, Mary Kay 29
Platt, Louise *205*, 205
Plummer, Christopher 203
Poitier, Sidney *58*, 58, *131*, 131
Polanski, Roman *47*, 47, 124
Pollack, Sydney 223, 234
Pollard, Michael J 37
Porter, Edwin S 94
Portman, Eric 52, 73
Potter, H C 144
Poujouly, Georges *113*, 113
Powell, Dick 23, 53, 70, 73, 74
Powell, Jane 193
Powell, Michael 34, 73, 131, 140, 184
Powell, William *145*, 145, 149, 215
Power, Tyrone 12, 239
Prejean, Albert 64, 204
Preminger, Otto 127
Presle, Micheline 59
Pressburger, Emeric 34, 73, 131, 140
Preston, Robert 26, *147*, 147, 231
Price, Dennis 121, 228
Price, Vincent *127*, 127, 149
Prohorenko, Shanna *24*, 24
Prowse, David *206*, 206

Quinn, Anthony 163, 170, *207*, 207, 231

Radford, Basil *125*, 125, 235
Raft, George 201
Raimu 43, 70
Rains, Claude 10, 44, *44-45*, 99, *108*, 108, 145, 155, 240
Ramis, Harold *83*, 83, 150
Rampling, Charlotte 53
Rapper, Irving 155
Rathbone, Basil 10, 42, 54, 55, 101
Ratoff, Gregory 105, 108
Ray, Satyajit 19, 165, 244
Raymond, Gene 72, 183
Redford, Robert 14, *40*, 40, 162, *207*, 207, 234
Redgrave, Michael *57*, 57, 106, *125*, 125, 206, 220
Redgrave, Vanessa 116
Redmond, Joyce 222
Reed, Carol 156, 206, 218, 226
Reed, Donna 78, *110*, 110
Reed, Oliver 156
Reeve, Christopher *210*, 210
Reggiani, Serge 44, 170
Reid, Kate 22
Reinhold, Judge 28
Reisz, Karel 190
Reitman, Ivan 83
Remick, Lee 56, 130

Renoir, Jean 92, 204
Revere, Anne 151
Rey, Fernando 61, 77
Reynolds, Debbie 199
Rhodes, Erik, 82, 225
Richardson, Ralph 62, *74*, 74, 97, 184, 216, 244
Richardson, Tony 222
Richter, Paul *152*, 152
Ried, Wallace 33
Riefenstahl, Leni 158, 226
Riegert, Peter *134*, 134, 150
Rilla, Walter 191
Ritt, Martin 102, 153
Ritter, Thelma 13, 182
Roach, Bert 52
Robards, Jason 14, 116, 118
Roberts, Rachel *168*, 168, *190*, 190
Robertson Justice, James 235
Robeson, Paul 123, 197
Robinson, Bill 'Bojangles' *133*, 133
Robinson, Edward G 63, 121, *132*, 132
Robson, Flora 34, 245
Rocca, Daniela 61
Roeg, Nicolas 233
Rogers, Charles 'Buddy' 239
Rogers, Ginger *72*, 72, *74*, 74, 82, 91, *212*, 212, 225
Rooney, Mickey *23*, 23, 43, *151*, 151
Rosay, Françoise 43, *119*, 119
Ross, Katharine *40*, 40, 91
Rossellini, Roberto 83, 161, 164
Rossen, Robert 14
Rossington, Norman 96
Ruggles, Charles 135, 226
Ruggles, Wesley 105
Ruman, Sig 55, 153, 155, 220
Russell, Gail 230
Russell, Harold 28
Russell, Rosalind 78, 242
Rutherford, Ann 172
Rutherford, Margaret 35, 106
Ryan, Robert 23
Rydell, Mark 159

Sagan, Leontine 136
Saint, Eva Marie 155, 160
Sakall, S Z 'Cuddles' 44
Sanders, George 13, 182
Sandrelli, Stefania 61
Sandrich, Mark 82, 225
Sarandon, Susan *22*, 22
Savage, John *58*, 58
Savalyeva, Ludmila 233
Sayles, John 29
Schaffner, Franklin J 166
Scheider, Roy 77, 112, *124*, 124
Schertzinger, Victor 186
Schildkraut, Joseph 131, 162
Schlesinger, John 32, 54, 143
Schoedsack, Ernest B 122
Schreck, Max *155*, 155
Schwannecke, Ellen 136
Scofield, Paul *138*, 138
Scott, George C 62, 112, 166
Scott, Zachary 140, 144, 204
Seaton, George 144
Secombe, Harry *156*, 156
Segal, George 236
Seiter, William A 201
Sellers, Peter *62*, 62, 125, 169, 173, 244
Selznick, David O 60, 108, 170,

173, 210
Serre, Henri *116*, 116
Seyrig, Delphine 61
Sharif, Omar *62*, 62, 79, 129
Sharpsteen, Ben 65, 70, 169
Shaw, Robert 112, *138*, 138, *207*, 207
Shearer, Moira *184*, 184
Shearer, Norma 24
Shepherd, Cybill 125, 127
Sheridan, Ann 18, 104, 130, *139*, 139
Sherman, Lowell 196
Shire, Talia 84, 186
Sidney, George 123
Sidney, Silvia 56
Siegel, Don 108
Signoret, Simone 44, *188*, 188
Simmons, Jean 34, 93, 96
Simon, Simone 188
Sinatra, Frank 78, 160
Sinden, Donald 52
Sjostrom (Seastrom), Victor 238
Skala, Lilia *131*, 131
Skerritt, Tom *140*, 141
Skinner, Cornelia Otis *230*, 230
Smith, C Aubrey 17, *74*, 74, 134, 135, 173, 182, 214, 226
Soderbaum, Kristina 114
Sondergaard, Gale 44, 131
Spacek, Sissy *51*, 51
Spencer, Kenneth *42*, 42
Spielberg, Steven 51, 66, 112, 181
Spinetti, Victor *96*, 96
Staiola, Enzo *29*, 29
Stallone, Sylvester 186, *187*, 191
Stanley, Kim 208
Stanwyck, Barbara *63*, 63, 125, 202, *231*, 231
Steiger, Rod 62, 160
Stephens, Martin 107
Stevens, George 95, 194, 212, 242
Stevenson, Robert 112, 123
Stewart, Anita *73*, 73
Stewart, James 59, *97*, 97, *110*, 110, 139, 145, *168*, 168, *182*, 182, *248*, 248
Stiller, Mauritz 207
Straight, Beatrice 151
Stander, Lionel *145*, 145
Strasberg, Lee 84
Streep, Meryl 38, *58*, 58, 116, *124*, 124, *202*, 202
Streisand, Barbra 39, *79*, 79, 205, 234
Sturges, John 23, 92, 95
Sturges, Preston 96, 125, 144,

164, 209
Sullivan, Barry 23
Sullivan, Francis L *157*, 157, *239*, 239
Sundberg, Clinton 68
Sutherland, Donald 108, 124, 140, *141*, 150, *162*, 162
Swanson, Gloria 36, *209*, 209
Sydney, Basil 96

Talmadge, Constance 108
Tamblyn, Russ *234*, 234
Tamiroff, Akim 72, 134, *231*, 231
Tandy, Jessica 59
Tati, Jacques 59, 146
Taylor, Don 150
Taylor, Elizabeth 20, *46*, 46, 112, 126, 134, *151*, 151, *236*, 236
Taylor, Libby *105*, 105
Taylor, Robert 42
Taylor, Rod *32*, 32
Taylor, Sam 189
Temple, Shirley *133*, 133
Terry, Nigel 132
Thesiger, Ernest 37, 138, 239
Thiele, Hertha 136
Thomas, Danny 113
Thomas, Henry 66
Thompson, Jack 37
Thulin, Ingrid 53, 70, 238
Tierney, Gene 97, *127*, 127
Tikhonov, Vyacheslav 233
Tilly, Meg 29
Tingwell, Charles 37
Tobin, Genevieve 166
Todd, Thelma 100
Tone, Franchot 72, 134, 148
Totter, Audrey 171
Tracy, Spencer *10*, 10, *23*, 23, *43*, 61, 190, *242*, 242
Travers, Henry 110, 146
Travis, Richard *139*, 139
Travolta, John 191
Trevor, Claire 56, 70, 121, *205*, 205
Trieste, Leopoldo 61
Trintignant, Jean-Louis 250
Truffaut, François *55*, 55, 116, 178
Turkel, Joseph 165
Turner, Lana 23, 91, *171*, 171
Tushingham, Rita 124

Valentino, Rudolph *75*, 75
Vallee, Rudy 164
Vallone, Raf 229
Van Dyke, W S 190, 214, 215
Van Eyck, Peter 232

Van Fleet, Jo 66, 95
Van Sloan, Edward 64, 77
Vanel, Charles 232
Varnel, Marcel 156
Vaughn, Robert 39
Veidt, Conrad *42*, 42, *114*, 114, 209
Vera-Ellen 160
Vidor, Charles 84
Vidor, King 30, 46, 52
Vigo, Jean 22, 250
Vilar, Jean 170
Visconti, Luchino 53
Voight, Jon 46, *143*, 143
Von Sternberg, Josef 35, 147, 195
Von Stroheim, Erich 72, *73*, 73, 92, 94, 96, 209
Von Sydow, Max *69*, 69, 70, *194*, 194, 231, 238

Wadleigh, Michael 243
Waggner, George 240
Wajda, Andrzej 21
Walbrook, Anton 73, 81, 131, 184, *188*, 188
Walken, Christopher *58*, 58
Walker, Robert *208*, 208
Wallace, Dee 66
Wallis, Shani 156
Walsh, Kay 157, 219, 228
Walsh, Raoul 100, 235
Walston, Ray 207
Walters, Jessica *161*, 161
Walters, Charles 68
Warden, Jack 228
Warner, H B *135*, 135, 209
Warner, Jack 36, 125
Warrick, Ruth 49
Washbourne, Mona 32
Waters, Ethel *42*, 42
Waterston, Sam 96
Wathall, Henry B *33*, 33
Wayne, David 10, 170
Wayne, John 178, *191*, 191, *196*, 196, *205*, 205, *228*, 228
Wayne, Naughton 125
Weathers, Carl 186
Weaver, Sigourney *19*, 19, 83, 247
Webb, Clifton *127*, 127
Wegener, Paul *87*, 87
Weidler, Virginia 242
Weir, Peter 80, 127, 168, 247
Weismuller, Johnny *214*, 214
Welles, Orson *49*, 49, 101, 112, 136, *218*, 218
Wellman, William 26, 155, 163, 177, 239
Werner, Oskar *116*, 116

West, Mae *105*, 105, *149*, 149, 196
Whale, James 13, 37, 77, 108, 197
Whitmore, James *22*, 22, *123*, 123
Whitty, May *125*, 125, 146
Wickes, Mary *139*, 139
Wieck, Dorothea 136
Wiene, Robert 42
Wiest, Dianne 96
Wifstrand, Naima 70, 199
Wilcox, Fred M 126
Wilder, Billy 20, 63, 72, 135, 153, 194, 201, 209, 239
Wilder, Gene *248*, 249
Wilding, Michael 106
William, Warren 86, 240
Williams, Cindy 14
Williams, Emlyn 39, 136, 137, 206
Williams, Jobeth 29
Wilson, Dooley 44
Wilson, Lois 52
Winger, Debra 215
Winninger, Charles 155, *197*, 197
Winters, Shelley 59, 100
Wise, Robert 36, 203, 234
Witherspoon, Cora 25, *54*, 54
Wolheim, Louis 13
Wood, Natalie 144, 191, 234
Wood, Sam 55, 88, 90, 152, 173
Woods, Donald *213*, 213
Woodward, Edward 37
Woolley, Monte *139*, 139, 155
Wray, Fay 74, 122, 149
Wright, Teresa 28, 146 173
Wyatt, Jane 135
Wycherley, Margaret 235
Wyler, William 27, 28, 56, 79, 97, 114, 130, 146, 188, 245
Wyman, Jane *115*, 115
Wynn, Keenan *123*, 123
Wynter, Dana 108

Yamagata, Isao 81
Yates, Peter 39
York, Michael 26, 41
York, Susannah *138*, 138, 210, *222*, 222, 228
Young, Harold 191
Young, Roland 17, *54*, 54, *225*, 225
Young, Terence 62
Yurka, Blanche 204, 213

Zinnemann, Fred 78, 99, 116, 138

Acknowledgements

The author and publisher would like to thank the following people who helped in the preparation of this book: Elizabeth Miles Montgomery, the editor; Design 23, the designer, and Jean Chiaramonte Martin, who carried out the picture research.

Picture credits

All pictures are from the *Bison Picture Library* except for the following:

Museum of Modern Art/Film Stills Archive: 13 (bottom), 23 (bottom), 25, 29 (top), 35, 37, 42 (top two), 50, 55 (top), 64, 72 (bottom), 74 (top), 77, 82, 86 (top), 91 (bottom), 95 (top), 99, 106 (both), 109, 110 (top), 133, 143 (top), 150 (top), 156, 163, 167, 170, 175, 184, 186 (bottom), 191, 196, 197, 212, 216, 217, 226, 231, 238, 240-1, 246-7.

National Film Archive, London: pages 32, 51 (top), 72 (top), 87, 94, 108, 112, 113 (top), 122 (bottom), 127 (top), 139 (bottom), 154, 180, 182 (both), 194 (bottom), 204, 205 (top), 206, 219, 228.

Phototeque: pages 11 (bottom), 12, 13 (top), 21 (bottom), 22 (bottom), 24 (both), 26, 27 (top), 28, 29 (bottom), 34 (both), 36 (top), 39 (bottom), 47 (both), 48, 52 (bottom), 53, 55 (bottom), 56, 57, 62 (top), 63 (both), 68, 69 (top), 70, 73, 83 (both), 86 (bottom), 93, 98 (bottom), 103, 105 (both), 107, 110 (bottom), 111, 113 (bottom), 114 (top), 116, 119, 121, 130, 132 (top), 134 (bottom), 136 (both), 137 (top), 144 (both), 152 (top), 157, 158 (both), 162 (bottom), 164, 165 (top), 168 (bottom), 169, 176, 178, 181, 185, 186 (top), 188, 190 (bottom), 193 (bottom), 194 (top), 199, 201, 202 (bottom), 232, 233, 239, 243, 244, 249, 250.